LOCAL GIRL
MAKES
HISTORY

To Jeff and Audrey —
" Fondly,"

BOOKS BY DANA FRANK

Purchasing Power: Consumer Organizing,
Gender, and the Seattle Labor Movement,
1919–1929

Buy American: The Untold Story of
Economic Nationalism

Bananeras: Women Transforming the
Banana Unions of Latin America

with Robin D. G. Kelley and Howard Zinn:
Three Strikes: Miners, Musicians, Salesgirls,
and the Fighting Spirit of Labor's Last Century

LOCAL GIRL MAKES HISTORY

EXPLORING NORTHERN CALIFORNIA'S
KITSCH MONUMENTS

DANA FRANK

CITY**LIGHTS**FOUNDATION
SAN FRANCISCO

Book design by Victor Mingovits
Cover design by em-dash productions

For a list of photo credits, see page 235.

Fragments of Bertolt Brecht's poem, "Questions from a Worker Who Reads," were translated by Michael Hamburger and originally printed in *Bertolt Brecht Poems: 1913–1956,* ©1976 by Eyre Methuen Ltd. (London).

Library of Congress Cataloging-in-Publication Data

Frank, Dana.
    Local girl makes history : exploring Northern California's kitsch monuments / Dana Frank.
       p. cm.
    Includes bibliographical references.
    ISBN-13: 978-1-931404-09-9
    ISBN-10: 1-931404-09-7
    1. California, Northern—History, Local. 2. California, Northern—Description and travel.
3. Kitsch—California, Northern. 4. Historic sites—California, Northern. 5. Frank, Dana—Travel-California, Northern. 6. Frank, Dana—Childhood and youth. I. Title.

F867.5.F725 2007
919.794—dc22

2007025537

Visit our website: www.citylights.com

City Lights Books are published at the City Lights Bookstore,
261 Columbus Avenue, San Francisco, CA 94133.

to Gerri, Steve, Becky, and Ramona
with a lifetime of gratitude

CONTENTS

ACKNOWLEDGMENTS

THIS BOOK WAS only possible because hundreds of folks, locally and far afield, helped me out with interviews, historical documents, research leads, and other support. I hope the stories I have constructed give back some measure of my gratitude for this collective investigative process.

For all kinds of help in learning about the history of Big Basin's log, my great thanks to Liz Burko, Jared Farmer, Werner Foss, Susan Grove, John Kalb, Bill Lewis, Steve Oka, Carol Pevey, Steve Radosevich, Debbie Shayne, Andy Urlie, Denzil Verardo, Roy Vickery, Richard Wilson, and the staff of Big Basin State Park. My special thanks to Kim Baker for helping me so enthusiastically and for opening the archives to me. At the California State Parks offices in Sacramento, thanks to Joe Engbeck, Robin Ettinger, Donna Pozzi, Kelly Turner, and Jim Woodward. Will Jorae, at the California State Parks Photographic Archives, was especially helpful with and enthusiastic about my project. My thanks as well to staff members at the London Museum of Natural History and the California Science Center. Thanks to Mia Monroe at Muir Woods for information and documents. And my special thanks to Willie Yaryan for sharing so much of his own work with me, and starting me on my way.

At the Boardwalk, Charles Canfield generously granted me an

interview and opened the Seaside Company's archives; Bonnie Minford generously unearthed historical documents as well as photographs; Carl Henn took time out to take me on my wonderful tour of the Cave Train itself. My thanks also to Ann Parker, Jan Bullwinkle-Smith, John Robinson, and all the operators and custodians who keep the Cave Train running.

My great thanks to Rick Bastrup and R & R Creative Design for sharing so much with me; to Ed and Elizabeth Morgan for their time; and to Karl and Jane Bacon. For help with the photographs, thanks to the Smith Novelty Company, Nancy Selfridge, and, especially, Richard Bucich, who was extremely generous with his time and images. Thanks to the Disney Corporation for allowing me to get in and out of Disneyland for a mere $17.00.

I am eternally indebted to the ever-cheerful Dave Iermini for sending me to Betsy Jones and the Autorama Diary. Thank you so much, Betsy, for trusting me with the Diary and for keeping such an amazing set of documents. Thanks to all the anonymous contributors to the Diary, as well.

For accompanying me on the Cave Train Ride and sharing an array of comments, my great thanks to Anne Callahan, Julia Callahan, Tanya Thomas, Sami Chen, and Becky McCabe. Thanks to Mike Rotkin for his memories of the reopening ceremony, and to Robin Finke for allowing me to quote her letter.

My thanks to Diane Gifford-Gonzales for scholarly help in understanding Cave People, and to George Lipsitz for help with the Flintstones.

I could never have investigated the story of The Cats without the great generosity of family members on both sides. I am especially grateful to the glorious Robert Balzer, who opened the door to his family and trusted me with his grandparents' story. My great thanks to Betty Ann Balzer Weltz for sharing her home, her memories, and her photographs; to May Armann not only for the interview but for twice rummaging so thoroughly to unearth photographs, and for the zucchini. Thanks, also, to Jeff Balzer. And, hey, thanks Robert and Jeff for my beautiful floors—I could never have written this without you.

From the other side, Kirk and Pat Smith were magnificently generous with their time, their memories, their private documents, and their enthusiasm for my project. I want to thank them most deeply for their trust and openness in embracing my efforts to figure out daily life at The Cats. I am still astonished at the films they allowed me to view, as well. My thanks also to Geoff Dunn for first clueing me in that Cynthia Matthews was a Wood descendant, and to Cynthia for passing me along to her parents.

Let me once again thank all those who work at the Huntington Library and Gardens, in every capacity, for all they have done to make this book possible. None of them is responsible for the views represented here. I am especially indebted to Peter Blodgett for guiding me through the collection with such skill and for impressive diligence in helping me obtain photographs. Thanks to Suzi Krasnow for her labors, and to those who fetched books, cleaned the floors, cooked and served my lunch, and guarded the collections. Thanks to "Guadalupe," "Queta Durazo," and "Eugenia" for their memories of exclusion at the Huntington. Thanks to Elliot Young for sharing with me his investigation into C. E. S. Wood and Chief Joseph.

Up north, I am deeply grateful to Peggy Conaway for so generously opening up the full resources of Los Gatos Public Library and her own research, and for so many leads. Thanks to the rest of the staff at Los Gatos Public Library, as well. Farther north still, my thanks to Daniel Pope for steering me to Robert Hamburger's work, and to Shawna Gandy at the Oregon Historical Society.

Thank you, Ken Christopher, for sending me to Sallie Johnson, and to Sallie herself for the memories and wonderful phrasing. My thanks to Diane Ogilvie for her delicious food and delicious memories alike at the Cats Restaurant. And thanks to Paul Buhle for tipping me off about the Los Gatos Italians, and to Jennifer Guglielmo for helping me understand them.

Thanks to all the people who shared their stories about the Pulgas Water Temple, led me to informants, or otherwise helped me along in collecting its stories and tracing them down: Cliff Brown, Cathy Buller, Andy Butler, Casey Carlson, Connie Croker, Bob Curry, Lynn Dougherty, Matt Farrell, Mike Koepf, Greg Herken, Dave Iermini, Cheryl Lesesne, Andrea Lowgren, Sandy Lydon, Beth Regardz, Jozseph Schultz, T. M. Scruggs, Judith Ann Shizuru, David Sweet, and the marvelous "Zamora." Thanks, especially, to Joe Naras for all the documents as well as the interview.

My special thanks to Carol Peterson at the San Mateo County Historical Society, who was tremendously helpful and generous with her time. Thanks also to Mrs. Alhadef at the Redwood City Public Library, Kathy Shields and the reference staff at the Palo Alto Public Library, and Jason at the San Francisco Room of the San Francisco Public Library. Thanks to Alma Gilbert for her permission to use "Daybreak." My great thanks to the staff at the San Francisco Public Utilities Commission for last-minute help with photographs, especially Katherine DuTiel, Michelle Liapes, and Paul Murillo.

At the UCSC library, my thanks to Ken Lyons, Frank Gravier, Debbie Murphy, and all the people in Interlibrary Loan who make my work possible.

Meg Lilienthal, Stephanie Bauman, Pat Saunders, John Thompson, and Candace Freiwald all helped me pull off my day job so I could squeeze out time for this book. My special thanks to Stephanie Hinkle for three years of work together—it's been a great pleasure. Tim Guichard made it fun and fixed my computer, too, as did Jay Olson and Paul Sosbee. My great thanks to my colleagues in the History Department at UCSC for welcoming me so warmly and for such ongoing collegiality.

I am grateful to the UC Santa Cruz Institute for Humanities Research for funds to help me obtain the photographs for this book, and to UCSC for the sabbatical time in which to write.

UCSC's members and activists of the American Federation of State, County, and Municipal Workers, the American Federation of Teachers, the Coalition of University Employees, the United Auto Workers, and the University Professional and Technical Employees made all my work possible, welcomed me warmly into their struggles, and brought joy to my heart.

I want to specifically thank the staff of Logos Books and Records, including Debbie Shayne and Pam McLellan, for their interest in my ongoing literary projects; I am especially grateful to Dave Iermini and Kenneth Scott Clements for their wit behind the counter, research leads, and help in Clan naming.

I am also grateful to Victor Schiffrin, photographer, who allowed me to drag him around two counties in order to reproduce Mary and Vincent Marengo's family photographs and to capture the Cave Guy in the Tree. Thank you, Victor, for your excellent work and for your excellent company.

Thanks to all my beloved friends who supported me while I was writing this and continue to fill my life with love, wisdom, and enthusiasm for my literary endeavors: Craig Alderson, Frank Bardacke, Cathy Buller, Anne Callahan, Nancy Chen, Sami Chen, Stephen Coats, Eleanor Engstrand, Miriam Frank, Marge Frantz, Toni Gilpin, Julie Greene, Lisbeth Haas, Desma Holcomb, Anne Kingsolver, John Logan, Wendy Mink, Amy Newell, Iris Munguía, Priscilla Murolo, Paul Ortiz, Sheila Payne, Mary Beth Pudup, Greta Schiller, Karin Stallard, Vanessa Tait, Andrea Weiss, and Alice Yang Murray. Thank you, Kent Hughes and Steve Murray—both still smiling in my heart.

Many generous friends and colleagues took time out of their lives to read chapters, give me advice and tips, and help me rein in the jokes. My great thanks to Frank Bardacke, Anne Callahan, Breck Caloss, Dario Caloss, Beth Haas, Charles Hedrick, Hamsa Heinrich, Anne Kingsolver, Amy Newell, Gayatri Padniak, Karin Stallard, Vanessa Tait, and Mark Traugott.

This book stayed fun, interesting, and anything but lonely because of all the people I've just named and a few others whose faith in me as a writer and advice at every turn made it possible for me to take this creative leap and not fall into the cracks. In addition to reading chapters, Cheri Brooks shared with me the world of creative nonfiction and cheered me on for years; Nelson Lichtenstein sustained me with his astonishing and seemingly boundless enthusiasm for everything I write. Next door, Hamsa Heinrich saw my everyday unromantic life as a writer and brought great joy, wisdom, and support to it—and even got the jokes in *The Unstrung Harp*. Carter Wilson and Thomas Pistole cheered on my research for years and years and outflanked me in their enthusiasm for the quirky and fun in everyday life; I am deeply indebted to Carter for reading every word of the book and making it better at every turn, as well as for teaching me to unleash a metaphor.

I love them all despite the fact that not a one of them believes me when I swear I'll never write another book.

I am tremendously honored to be published by City Lights Books and to be a part of its tradition of independent, radical thinking. Thanks to everyone on the staff, including Chanté Mouton and Bob Sharrard. Elaine Katzenberger not only understood the book's concept from day one, but has been a terrific editor down to the last semicolon. They don't come any better. Fifteen years ago it was my pleasure to have Stacey Lewis, City Lights' marketing director, as my student; now it's an even greater pleasure to work with her on this book, and I am deeply grateful for her ongoing labors on my behalf.

Gerri Dayharsh, Stephen McCabe, Ramona McCabe, and Becky

McCabe, to whom this book is dedicated, have been central to my life for a total of 101 years as we have together explored the California landscape and its mysteries, and tried to figure out how to live meaningful lives, despite rocks in the road both quotidian and hefty. They have been there for me at every turn and brought me more love and joy than they'll ever know. This book was always meant for them, in hopes that I could begin to give back even a tiny, tiny piece of what they've given to me.

Finally, this book is about my family and how we explored creeks, kelp beds, historical markers, and obscure berry-laden campgrounds together as I was growing up. My parents took me to all the places I write about here, got me interested in their history, and opened up the world to me; my sister shared her own joys all along the way. My thanks to Laura for her memories, her enthusiasm, and for understanding what this book was all about. My deepest thanks to my mom, Carolyn, who has always stayed loving and positive, stayed down to earth, and taught me what I could find there. And my wonderful father, Joseph Frank—so wise, so funny, so loving—is still with us, I hope, in these pages as in our hearts.

PREFACE

FOR THOSE WHO grow up elsewhere, California beckons like
some kind of mythological paradise or seductive dystopia. But if you
grow up here, as I did, it's just where you live, and you are left to
your own devices to inscribe myth and mystery onto the landscape.
This book is about four places from that inventive landscape of my
childhood and what happened when I came back to them as an
adult and set out to explore their history. It's about how we make
and think about history; about the interface between my skills and
knowledge as a radical historian and the quirky monuments of my
private memories; and about the unexpected ways in which larger
historical politics are embedded in the landscapes of everyday life.

I grew up in Los Altos, where the San Francisco Peninsula
meets the Santa Clara Valley, in the years before "Silicon Valley"
had been invented and when suburban neighborhoods were still
patchworked with fruit orchards (from which we routinely stole).
Our address was actually Mountain View until our unincorporated
pocket got absorbed into Los Altos in the late 1970s; in my later
years I haven't quite known what to answer when people ask me
where I am from—especially since "Los Altos" means something
quite different today. When I was growing up, the neighborhood
was mostly white working-class families crossing over into the

middle class during the postwar boom. My parents were the only ones on the street who'd gone to college—a far cry from Los Altos today where the M.B.A.'s and M.D.'s and Ph.D.'s are about ten thousand per square mile.

Like other families, we took day trips on the weekends, following glittering little creeks into the Santa Cruz Mountains, poking around cold beaches up near Half Moon Bay, or dropping down Soquel-San José Road to stop at Maddock's bakery in Soquel and then go on to explore Santa Cruz. As a kid I mapped that landscape with my favorite places—some with obvious but very specific appeal, like the Silver Spur hamburger joint where you could stockpile an unlimited supply of pickles, or the plaster dinosaurs that loomed up over Highway 17 in Scotts Valley. Others had a more obscure, private appeal, a kind of magic aura you couldn't quite put your finger on.

I carried those places with me into adulthood, as I went to college in Santa Cruz and then spent ten years getting my own Ph.D. and then teaching in the East and Midwest. Eventually I settled in as a professional historian, and over the next two decades wrote academic and popular books about U.S. labor history, trade politics, women's history, and, most recently, banana workers in Central America.

When I came home to teach at the University of California, Santa Cruz, in 1991, the landscape of my childhood began to tug at my imagination once again. I started thinking about looking at some of my favorite childhood landmarks with a new lens, as an adult but also as an intellectual with an understanding of the cultural and political context out of which they had emerged. While diligently occupied with more official academic research projects, I started imagining little essays in which my political, historian self went back to try to trace the larger meaning of some of the landmarks of my childhood. Finally, I decided to see what would happen if I actually investigated a few of my places and wrote about what happened in the process. Hence, this book.

A friend calls these sites of mine "kitsch monuments"—although I think they're a bit more dignified than that (with the prominent exception of the exceedingly hokey Cave Train Ride). All of them are within day-trip range of where I grew up. With each, I chose a theme, and then followed wherever it took me in my research. I started with the slice of a 2,000-year-old redwood tree on display at Big Basin Redwoods State Park, and traced the narrative of imperialism inscribed on its rings. Then I took multiple trips on the Cave Train Ride at the Santa Cruz Boardwalk amusement park, and tried to figure out who its "Cave People" might be—and their gender and race politics. For my third investigation I took up the two stone cats by Highway 17 in Los Gatos. This time I wanted to know about the bohemian poets who erected them in the 1920s, and their complex relationships with the Italian immigrant couple who spent twenty-five years as their live-in servants. My last round was more playful: I delved into the Pulgas Water Temple, up the San Francisco Peninsula by Highway 280 on Crystal Springs Reservoir. In high school, I had heard all sorts of urban myths about the temple and its relationship to the legendary Hetch Hetchy water system. So I traced those stories down, along with the temple's connection to the culture of the 1960s. With each chapter, I never really knew where my investigation would end. Part of the fun was relaxing and watching where the story—and history—would take me.

I considered many other sites, and offer apologies to those who are disappointed that I didn't take up their favorites. If there had been a fifth chapter, it would have been about the mummy at the Rosicrucian Egyptian Museum in San José. I also considered Santa's Village in Scotts Valley, Hidden Villa Ranch in Los Altos Hills, Brookdale Lodge in Boulder Creek, and those baffling, round stone towers on the road from Watsonville to Sunset Beach. Many people wanted me to write about the Mystery Spot, but it was a little too obvious, and Santa Cruz weekly magazines had already done a good job of exploring it in various articles over the years; besides, I never got to go there as a kid (my sister did, and I was always jealous).

This is not your usual local history book, then. I've written it in the first person, and mixed in bits of memoir: not only my memories of trips as a kid, but also little ways in which the histories of my family, the people I grew up around, and my loved ones today are woven into these landscapes and their politics—often in ways I didn't expect when I started my research.

My research methods involved a sometimes comic mishmash of hearsay, assiduous door knocking, the skills of a professional historian, and a lot of ingenuity. My most productive approach was completely unscientific: for years, people I ran into, knowing I wrote books, would ask me what I was working on, and I'd tell them. They'd turn out to have a great little story of their own about one of my places, or to have grown up next door to the guy whose sister married the guy who originally built it. Gradually, I filled a drawer with scribbled slips of paper, and as I took up each investigation, I called those people back, sometimes years later.

As I spun each story out, I was repeatedly surprised at how my obscure little places weren't so obscure, after all. I'd thought of these places as markers of my private history, places I loved, remembered, and wondered about but never discussed with anyone else. But they all turned out to be very public: the joke was on me. After all, I'd only noticed them in the first place because they were out in public space where my private imagination could fasten onto them. Tens of thousands of other people who'd grown up in or visited the Santa Cruz area and the San Francisco Peninsula remembered and wondered about my monuments, too.

As I followed my landmarks out into their broader context, I was equally surprised by how they loomed larger and larger in the landscape of American cultural history and beyond. Redwood slices just like mine are on display in New York and London, I discovered.

During the 1920s, tourists from Paris and New York bought postcards of my two stone cats while visiting Los Gatos. Once, while I was paying my bill at the Tabard Inn, a cozy little hotel where I sometimes stay in Washington, D.C., the usually taciturn desk clerk saw my credit card with Santa Cruz on it and exclaimed, "Oh, that's where the Boardwalk is. I always loved the Cave Train Ride." My monuments also showed up as bit players in Hollywood movies from *Vertigo* to *The Doors*.

My places turned out to be part of the grander historical narrative of California and the West, at the point where California history becomes national history, and the mythological character of the state shapes the big story of U.S. culture. Redwood trees, most obviously, stand tall in the national imagination as magic and untouchable, lending dignity and a proud ancientness to a country that's only 230 years old. Similarly, the story of San Francisco's Hetch Hetchy water supply, with its heroes-and-villains narrative of urban elites destroying a beloved national park, took me into a tale of Nature versus Nation, in which my private Pulgas Water Temple turned out to be a strategic piece of propaganda. Charles Erskine Scott Wood, who erected my stone cats, turned out to have transcribed Chief Joseph's famous "I will fight no more forever" speech.

But the full significance of my monuments was even larger than that, and ultimately more disturbing. As I pieced together their larger meanings, they pulled me deep into reflections about the sobering politics of imperial ambition, racial projection, and subtle hierarchies of class and gender in the United States—embedded deftly and thoroughly in the innocent landmarks of my childhood, and hence my own passage into adulthood as a Californian and as a citizen of the United States.

In the end, my playful little book turned into a series of serious reflections on the politics of history and how historical politics are projected onto landscapes of everyday life. In order to understand my monuments I had to figure out how a codified history of Western Civilization, with the United States at the imperial center, could get inscribed in little date tags on part of an innocent, dead redwood tree; or how, exactly, prehistoric "Cave People" came to hang out under the Boardwalk, down by the sea. I landed in the middle of the thick, and ultimately very personal politics of who gets passed down in history as "famous" and therefore historically important, and who vanishes from the historical record without a trace. By the last chapter my head was swimming in a baffling swamp of urban myths, rumor, and the "truth," as it became less and less clear what counted as reliable historical evidence in the first place.

To my surprise, in the process of my research I thus changed history, first in the sense that I unearthed all sorts of new information and meanings that will change the way readers understand each of these places. In so doing I changed our collective memory, our local history, and our public history. Second, as a local girl I made my own history in another sense as well, in that I transformed my personal understanding of the place where I grew up, and transformed myself along the way.

Of course I am conscious that many of my readers remember these places, too, and have their own stories to tell. Whether they grew up in Santa Cruz, the Bay Area, or beyond, or are just passing through, I like to think that readers will send me another round of their own stories about these places, or bits of history I never uncovered—especially since I never solved all my mysteries by any means.

When I started this project I was a little afraid that, in investigating my places, I would somehow kill the mysterious aura that had attracted me to them in the first place. I leave it to the reader to decide if I did or didn't—and to use these stories to understand their own private mysteries, and the larger puzzle that is the historical culture of the United States.

The redwood slice at Big Basin Redwoods State Park, in an affirmative action photograph recruiting park rangers, 1987.

CHAPTER I

REDWOOD EMPIRES

WHEN I WAS a little girl growing up in Los Altos in the late '50s and early '60s, there were three attractions at Big Basin Redwoods State Park, an hour and a half away up in the Santa Cruz Mountains. The first was the store, a cornucopia of overpriced groceries, plastic toys, and small tourist gifts made of redwood. My sister and I rarely got to go inside, but if we were really lucky and begged really hard we might get to buy a Popsicle—a very particular long cylindrical kind we preferred, known as a "missile," that was impressive in its combination of pink, blue, and yellow ice, but always vaguely disappointing in its silky blandness.

The second, far greater attraction was the deer. In those days the park headquarters area was almost swarming with them. For over thirty years the rangers had performed a ritual they called the "Calling of the Deer," in which they would fill big troughs with oats, and summon the deer for the tourists every day at 4:30 p.m. By the late 1960s, newer rangers had halted the ritual, concerned that this dietary dependency might not be so good for the animals. But in my time, a vestige still remained: the store sold little paper bags of oats that visitors could buy to feed the deer. I remember vividly the thrill of pouring those oats into my hand and sticking it out, tentatively, for the deer, and how their cold noses nuzzled against my palm like moist, inquisitive velvet.

The third and most puzzling attraction was a huge slice of an ancient redwood tree that stood on display to the right of the headquarters building. On it were placed little metal markers by the tree's growth rings, indicating the dates of various world events that had taken place during the life of the tree. They were designed to impress upon visitors quite how old the tree was; older than "1513 Balboa Discovers the Pacific Ocean"; older than "1066 William the Conqueror Invades England"; even older than "500 Maya Civilization—Mexico." If your dad held you up, you could even reach out and touch the place where "Birth of Christ" stood almost at the tree's center.

After I hit my twenties I didn't visit Big Basin for a long time, although I was in and out of Santa Cruz. Finally, in 1990, after I moved back to town for good, I made a deliberate pilgrimage up to the park.

Much to my relief, the store was almost exactly the same, its brown log sides and porches just as I'd romantically remembered them. On the way inside I passed a little four-year-old girl with Day-Glo orange hair eating a long, multicolored Popsicle that wasn't quite the one I remembered, but close enough.

The deer, alas, were nowhere to be seen. The rangers had finally triumphed over the concessionaires as a new environmental consciousness swept the park in the 1970s, and the lucrative oat-selling trade was no more.

But the ancient redwood slice was right there where I'd left it, next to the log-style headquarters building constructed by the Civilian Conservation Corps in the 1930s. The slice was a lot smaller than I remembered, and somehow diminished in its glory, but still solidly there, complete with its little date markers and tiny rivets that highlighted the sequence of rings and their corresponding historical events. The rivet-to-date-marker ratio was a bit high, suggesting that a few of the tags had fallen or been picked off by errant youths. But Balboa still discovered, William still conquered, and the Mayans were still civilized.

I myself, though, was someone else now, a professional historian. As I stood in front of my beloved redwood slice, I got more and more intrigued by its history. Why those particular dates, with all their references to conquests, invasions, and civilizations? What concepts of time were embedded on that tree, and in my memories? Why was it all about imperialism—and why, for that matter, is the northwest coast of California known as the Redwood Empire? I decided I wanted to investigate the history of that tree slice someday.

When I finally took up that story ten years later, I got drawn into the ancient redwood's circles deeper and deeper. My log became less and less innocent as my fascination with it grew—and I discovered that my own private redwood tree might be part of something much larger, and more unsettling, than endearing childhood memories.

The author in Opal Creek, Big Basin Redwoods State Park, 1957-58.
PHOTOGRAPH BY JOSEPH L. FRANK.

Adventures in Rangerland

MY FIRST STEP was to call a friend, Willie Yaryan, who had written on the history of the coast redwoods and was researching a Ph.D. dissertation on Big Basin. Silver-haired, with wire-rimmed glasses, Willie looks sort of like a tree sprite recently escaped from the forest. He lent me a pile of books about the redwood parks. The next day I went to the university library and ordered everything else I could find on the history of Big Basin, redwood trees, and their preservation. I started calling the park rangers whose names Willie gave me, too.

Quickly, from the rangers, I began to gather bits of information—mostly about other rangers who would be, presumably, more well-informed about the park's history than whomever I was speaking to at the time. No one could tell me about the origins of the log slice, although I learned that they called it the "redwood round." I zeroed in on Kim Baker, a ranger at Big Basin, who controlled the all-important access to the archives at the park itself. But she was on vacation. Finally, after two weeks, I got an appointment to meet her at the park on a Sunday in October.

I drove from Santa Cruz up Highway 9 on one of those luscious California autumn days when the leaves are falling against the car and you can feel a new cold edge in the shadows. I slipped past the schmaltzy shops selling redwood burl items; past the purveyors of chainsaw art with giant horses' heads made of redwood; past the cabins for rent at Jaye's Timberlane Lodge. When I got to Boulder Creek I passed the little cut-out man with the neon chainsaw atop the Scarborough Lumber building and turned off onto Route 236 into the park. It was all a bit more developed than it used to be, but basically the same. I could still relive trips from my childhood along that same route—although sometimes we had driven in from the other side, winding slowly up Highway 9 from Saratoga in our 1956 green Chevrolet wagon with my sister and I in the back seat trying very hard not to throw up.

Kim Baker was in her thirties, enthusiastic and helpful, with medium-brown hair and wearing one of those tan park-service uniforms over a bulletproof vest. In her hand she carried an off-white L.L. Bean bag with "Ranger Kim" stitched onto it in navy blue, and on her waist a Smith & Wesson 4006 semi-automatic pistol, pepper spray, ammunition, a flashlight, handcuffs, a mask for CPR, rubber gloves, keys, and a new collapsible baton she demonstrated for me. Popping it out, she stuck it in front of my nose to sniff. It smelled like smoke. "It's great for putting out campfires," she grinned. All this hardware was arrayed along a "Sam Brown" belt especially designed for women, with a bit more of a curve.

Kim unlocked a room in back of the Nature Center, behind the displays with the stuffed bobcats and the embalmed snakes in clear plastic tubes. The back room was cramped and dim, and full of wall-to-wall gray metal cabinets, some unlocked, some tantalizingly locked, full of the park's archives. I spent two contented days there, poring over old photographs, the rangers' log entries, obscure correspondence, and a mishmash of promotional literature, maps, and even daily menus from when the Civilian Conservation Corps encamped there during the 1930s. I found nothing, though, on my tree slice—only a few historic photographs of the park headquarters building, in some of which the log made an appearance and in others of which it was mysteriously missing.

Frustrated, I decided to make a pilgrimage to Sacramento, to the general offices of the California State Parks. I set out over Highway 17 this time and immediately got stuck behind a Big Creek Lumber truck carrying boards of the purest redwood heartwood, a shining pile of deep pink four by fours, sixteen or twenty feet long.

Once in Sacramento I was adopted by a whole new set of park officials—landscape architects, geologists, archivists—such as Kelly

Turner, official California State Parks archaeologist, who pulled out drawers and drawers of materials for me on Big Basin.

Neither Kelly nor the keepers of the state's historical files in Central Records, though, could produce much on the history of the log, although I was learning more and more about the history of the park. I did meet Jim Woodward, who'd catalogued historic resources in Big Basin for the park's General Plan in the mid-1990s. He told me he'd made the tree slice entry Number 1 of 452 entries because it had seemed simple and easy to begin with. But he, too, had been stumped by the log's history.

The state records didn't contain correspondence about the history of the tree slice, about who exactly put up those markers, or why he or she picked those particular dates. It became clear that there was only one other way to track the log's history. I'd have to piece it together painstakingly from the photographic record.

My last day in the capital I crossed back west over the Sacramento River, driving through an obscure warehouse district to the State Park Photographic Archives. There, amid hundreds of shots of Big Basin, I finally found dozens of old photographs of the tree slice and the headquarters building. A few of them even captured the little date markers at different points in time. I couldn't read the fine print, though. Will Jorae, the curator, whose eyes proved better than mine, held the negatives up to the light and meticulously read the date tags to me one by one.

As far as I can reconstruct the log's history from the photographs, documents, and interviews, the original tree was cut down in 1934, forty miles south of Eureka in Humboldt County, in the area of northwest California now known as the "Avenue of the Giants." Someone up there then cut off this slice, which arrived in Big Basin in 1934 or 1935. A 1935 photograph shows it sitting on the ground horizontally, unmarked, lying flat on a few boards. Around this time the Civilian Conservation Corps (CCC) built the park headquarters building, and most rangers I talked with think the log, too, must have been propped up on vertical display by CCC members in 1936 or so.

The slice shows up in more or less its current location for the first time in a cartoon of the park that Petey Weaver, the park's first female ranger, drew sometime in the 1940s. I can't spot it, though, in any of the photographs of the headquarters building from the late 1930s or '40s. (I think it might have originally been placed farther back, to the side, nearer the George Washington Tree, and thus out of camera range.) But in a 1952 photograph there it is, clearly, for the first time, with a big plaque reading "OLDEST COAST REDWOOD. Cross Section from oldest coast Redwood tree on which there is authentic age data. Nearly 2200 years old when felled in 1934."

At some point between that 1952 shot and another in June 1954, someone added the little date markers on the rings and their corresponding rivets, plus a small plaque above them reading: "Some of the historical events that have taken place within the lifetime of this tree are indicated below." The original date markers read:

1934	*This Tree Felled*
1901	*Marconi Wireless*
1863	*Lincoln's Gettysburg Address*
1776	*Declaration of Independence*
1620	*Landing of the Pilgrims*

Then there's an empty space,
as if a marker had already fallen off.

1513	*Balboa Discovers Pacific*
1492	*Columbus Discovers America*

A bigger space—are
two or three markers gone?

1300	*Aztec Civilization Mexico*
1277	*Marco Polo*
1215	*Signing of Magna Carta*
1147	*Crusaders*
1066	*William the Conqueror*
878	*King Alfred*
800	*Coronation of Charlemagne*
630	*Mohammed*
530	*Justinian Age*
500	*Maya Civilization—Mexico*
4 A.D.	*Origin Japanese Empire*
—	*Birth of Christ*

In 1969, there's a new shot of the log. This time, the date tags have been switched. Marconi is at the bottom left, horizontal, by himself. The tags indicating "Tree Felled" through "Balboa" march along from rim to center tipped at a 45 degree angle to their left; thereafter "Columbus" through "Christ" suddenly tip rightward, almost vertical. It's getting a bit messy, what with the two general plaques, two different series of little markers, and an overall increase in markerless rivets. The Aztecs are gone; so are the Crusaders and King Alfred of the Anglo Saxons. A big chunk of the tree has fallen out of the crack in the center, too. Finally, in 1987, someone has cleaned it all up: the small plaque indicating "some of the historic events . . ." is gone, the date markers now march in uniform horizontal order flat along the rings, and order is restored to history, if not the unfortunate Aztecs, Crusaders, or King Alfred.

Empires Come, Empires Go

WHAT ABOUT THOSE dates, then? In one way or another, they're almost all about empire, conquest, invasions, or expansion—not just the obvious ones, like Columbus, Balboa, the Crusades, or William the Conquerer, but also more subtle references: "Justinian Age"—that marks the end of the Roman Empire and the birth of the Byzantine; "Marco Polo"—European expansion to the East in search of goods and markets. Three markers do venture out of this central tale of European expansion, only to bow to other, alternate "civilizations" and empires: the Aztecs, the Mayas, and "Origin Japanese Empire."

Inscribed on the log, then, is a particular version of human history that recounts—and celebrates—a Eurocentric narrative of upward progress through European and U.S. imperialism. How did those dates end up on the log? Without their original creator to ask, I realized I had to work backwards and sideways instead, delving into the literature on the history of redwood trees and their preservation, but also into the version of history that redwood enthusiasts echoed and expanded upon. Americans of European descent who wove stories about the history of redwood trees in late nineteenth- and early twentieth-century California, I came to see, brought a very particular concept of time, and their place in it, to their understanding of the trees, in the process weaving a tale of conquest, of domination by outsiders, and, ultimately, of racial supremacy.

The indigenous peoples who already lived on California's northwest coast when Europeans first arrived, by contrast, had very different concepts of themselves, their place, and the redwood trees. Roland Raymond and Walter Lara, Sr., a Yurok elder whose people come from what is now Humboldt County, explained in 1996, for example: "Since time immemorial the Yurok people have occupied 300,000 acres of land" in the area. "Our people were 3,000-plus members and were able to sustain ourselves for perpetuity." Walter Lara, Sr. continues: "In the beginning, the Creator permitted the spirits to decide what it is they wanted to be on earth. Some chose to be redwood trees." He goes on to describe how some trees came to be "guardians," others—which had already fallen down from storms or other natural causes—were used by the Yuroks to make canoes, huts, or tools.

Note the Yurok's sense of time: both people and trees had inhabited the area "since time immemorial." There's no story here of discovery, conquest, or empire; nor of historical "progress" upward or outward.

White Americans' first reaction to the coast redwood trees in the mid- to late nineteenth century, by contrast, was to cut them down, as many and as fast as possible. Coast redwoods (*Sequoia sempervirens*) have special rare and valuable properties as lumber. They're a bit smaller than their cousins in the Sierra Nevada (*Sequoia gigantea*) but their wood is easy to work with, lightweight, shrink-proof, and, most famously, resistant to fire and rot. Demand was high; by the 1870s, lumber mills proliferated from the Oregon border south to Big Sur, and by the 1890s the big trees were fast disappearing.

Enter the preservationists. At the turn of the twentieth century, a group of middle-class white men and women in the San Francisco Bay Area started to worry about the disappearance of the redwoods, particularly the big, grand, first-growth redwoods that stood over 250 feet high and were 30 feet around. They fell in love with what they called the "noble" redwoods, and wanted to save them. As Willie Yaryan's research into the preservationists' business relationships shows, they also, not coincidentally, wanted to save the watersheds, tourism, and nearby concessions on which their own wealth in many cases depended.

In order to build public support for the trees' protection in parks and to get tourists flocking to see them, the redwood preservationists launched a lyrical public dialogue about these trees, suddenly magical and precious. Out of that campaign emerged a codified narrative of the redwoods and their history, which is told and retold in the parks today—and which includes the date markers on my tree.

In trying to capture the redwoods' meaning, preservationists sought to convey two essential attributes they ascribed to the trees; first, their size, and second, their age. Size was relatively easy to communicate. Trees could be measured in feet or meters, and assigned statistics as to their height and circumference. Other assessments stressed the number of board-feet a given tree would produce if logged, often illustrated with a photograph of a big Victorian house in Humboldt County allegedly built entirely from the wood of a single tree. To indicate height many writers utilized a diagram showing a redwood tree lined up next to the Statue of Liberty, the U.S. Capitol, or, in some cases the campanile at U.C. Berkeley, all of whose heights the tree exceeded.

Once in the presence of an actual living tree, however, tourists had none of these comparisons; they could only crane their necks very, very far back and look up. Or, to measure circumference, they could take pictures of themselves standing in front of a tree, holding hands around it, or, my personal favorite, driving through one. "Where is the tree we can drive through?" was the most popular question visitors to Mariposa Grove, in the Sierra, asked in 1937. To this day it's the most frequently asked question at Big Basin. (The answer: the tree is over to the left of the headquarters building, but you could only ever drive halfway into it, not all the way through it, and now you're not allowed to get a car anywhere near it.)

The trees' age, though, was much more difficult to convey. These creatures were extremely old. As Howard E. Davenport wrote in a 1949 book, *A Story of California Big Trees, Largest Living Things on Earth*, "Ever since facts concerning the Giant Sequoias have become known, the great age of these trees has impressed itself upon people's minds fully as much as their huge size." Early commentators weren't exactly sure how old the trees were, so they often simply deployed "timeless," begging the exact age question. More commonly, they crossed over into an almost spiritual depiction of the redwoods as immortal—and here the European Americans weren't so different from the Yurok people. "These trees are the nearest material thing we know to Life Eternal," Davenport rhapsodized. In 1945, Donald Culross Peattie similarly entitled an article in *Frontiers* magazine: "Redwoods—America's Immortals." These descriptions echoed the trees' botanical name, "Sequoia *sempervirens*," or ever-living.

Originally, European-American observers thought the trees were perhaps 3,000 or 4,000 years old. But by the 1920s they had developed the wonderfully named science of "dendrochronology," or dating a tree's age. This is what made my tree's date markers possible. Archaeologists figured out that each year a redwood tree produced a new growth ring, hence by counting its rings the age of any given tree could be determined. Events in the tree's life such as a fire or a bit of rot could be identified, too. Emmanuel Fritz, a Berkeley professor of Forestry, explained this nicely in 1934 with pictures and arrows in a popular pamphlet on the redwoods that's available in the park today in exact reprint form as "Story Told by a Fallen Redwood."

There was one catch, of course: the tree had to be dead to be dated. Cartoonist Gary Larson, in his "Far Side" series, cleverly figured this out. In a 1986 cartoon, he shows two loggers with a big saw next to them on the ground, in front of a giant tree they've just felled. "And see this ring right here, Jimmy?" one of the men points out to his fellow logger. "That's another time when the old fellow miraculously survived some big forest fire."

Once they had a handle on exactly how old the trees were, journalists, preservationists, pamphleteers and other writers moved on from vague references to immortality to stating the actual age of each tree. The oldest trees turned out to be about 2,000 years old—neatly coinciding with the birth of Christ. Then, to explain the dates, they developed a standard story of parallel historical events, which they told over and over again—and which was in place well before anyone got the idea of placing date markers on tree rings. It shows up as early as 1899, at the dawn of the preservationist era, when *Sunset* magazine exuded: "The ides of March that saw the death of Caesar may have looked upon the spring of their maturity [i.e., the redwoods]. . . . Age was, perhaps, telling on them slightly when King John was granting the Magna Charta [*sic*] and Genghis Khan entering Pekin [*sic*] in triumph; and when Columbus set foot on Salvador a few may have begun to lose their pristine vigor." In another early version of this codified narrative, Theodore M. Knappen, writing on "The Undying Redwood Tree of Our Western Coast" in 1923, spoke of "individual trees that were aged when Attila was scourging Europe, and were as old as the Christian era when Columbus landed on San Salvador."

Writers often described individual trees as "witnesses" to this history. "In the passing centuries it has witnessed, if not the birth of man, at least man's development from the lowest estate," gushed J. D. Grant, chairman of the board of directors of the Save-the-Redwoods League, in a 1922 address. Or take James Clifford Shirley, a former ranger at Yosemite and professor of botany in Enid, Oklahoma, who opened his 1937 book, *The Redwoods of Coast and Sierra*:

> In far Cathay an empire grew and ancient civilization developed . . . . Saul, David, and Solomon established a Kingdom and developed a nation out of which came Christianity. Babylon, Greece, and Rome ruled the world and lost their sway. Europe and America developed a modern civilization. Throughout the long periods of time in which these events have taken place, the Redwoods of California have continued to live and grow.

Some writers went on for pages, listing empires and civilizations rising and falling as was their wont, while the trees slowly matured. Others, such as *National Geographic* in 1939, went for a boilerplate, quickie version: "The fallen giant was a sapling when Julius Caesar set foot on the British Isles; it had reached maturity when William the Conqueror arrived; and . . . was a graybeard when Columbus discovered a new hemisphere."

These stories of empires and conquest in the redwood forest are still alive and well and live on in books, pamphlets, and tourist literature in our own time. Richard A. Rasp, in his 1989 book *Redwood: The Story Behind the Scenery*, for example, on sale at Henry Cowell State Park, just down the road from Big Basin, writes: "The Tall Tree . . . had already lived on a century when Columbus arrived in the New World. . . . It was a seedling when Roman legions occupied what is now Great Britain."

Even kids have their own, updated version, *The Ever-Living Tree: The Life and Times of a Coast Redwood*, written in 1994 by Linda Vieira, with gorgeous illustrations by Christopher Canyon. It follows a growing redwood tree through the life of Alexander the Great, the Great Wall of China, the birth of Christ, the "kingdom of Kanem" in North Africa, then Marco Polo, Columbus, the Gold Rush, and finally astronauts and cosmonauts. Space, the final frontier.

Part and parcel of history as a succession of empires, projected onto these innocent trees, was the notion of human history as the rise and fall of civilizations. Richard Baker, for example, in a 1943 book called simply *The Redwood* (with the endearing subtitle "Famous Trees Library No. 1"), inserted in his standard tale of a redwood tree's purview: "By the time of the decline of Greece . . . it could look out with serenity on the rise and fall of civilizations." Each empire represented a new "civilization." Even rival, conquered, or brown-skinned peoples could qualify if they successfully constructed a hierarchical, geographically-dominant "civilization"—e.g. the Mayans, Aztecs, or Chinese.

Overall, civilization was presumed to be advancing at the hands of the Europeans and then North Americans, who were gradually taming the uncivilized "savages" of the world, and advancing human society in redwood tree narratives and in the version of history taught in every school in the country. As the nineteenth and early twentieth centuries progressed, many in the United States came to identify with previous "civilizations," while puffing themselves up with the notion that they were next in line, raising the civilizational standard.

When some anonymous Big Basin ranger chose those date markers in 1952, '53, or '54, I came to see, he or she was drawing on an already well-established story of empire, told and retold not only in books and pamphlets on the redwoods, but drilled into every high school kid and Western Civilization course in the country for decades. It almost didn't matter who the individual ranger was. Everyone knew that the redwood trees had spent their youth hanging out with Caesar, Attila, and Columbus.

Virility and Virginity

MY HEAD SPINNING from all the books, suddenly I was seeing empires everywhere in the park, not just on the date markers, and wondering if I were somehow exaggerating. "1901—Marconi Wireless" or "1863—Lincoln's Gettysburg Address," after all, didn't seem to be about imperialism.

But then, peering at an old, glossy, black-and-white photograph of the Big Basin store in 1962, right around the time I would have lusted after my Popsicle, I noticed a big advertisement for the *San Francisco Chronicle* at the top of a magazine rack in the store: "ROMULUS READ IT IN THE CHRONICLE," its big letters announced, with a drawing of the head of a Roman Legion soldier-type underneath. What was Romulus, the mythical cofounder of Rome and thence the Roman Empire, doing in the Big Basin store in 1962? That *Chronicle* advertisement must have appeared all over the Bay Area, where potential buyers were presumed to know who Romulus was and be willing to follow his advice as to which newspaper to read.

Or take the Girl Scouts. I remember visits to Big Basin with the Girl Scouts in the 1960s, once camping overnight with my troop when I was nine or ten. We slept in old-fashioned canvas tents and it rained so hard that in my memory our sodden sleeping bags literally floated inside the tent. We peeked outside with flashlights to find hordes of raccoons menacing us with bright yellow eyes. I remember another trip when I must have been twelve or thirteen, some kind of regional Girl Scout event during which we engaged in what I can only call "competitive camping": we raced as groups of four to see who could put up a tent, light a fire from scratch, or tie elaborate knots the fastest.

My innocent Girl Scout trips were in part about imperialism. Michael Rosenthal, in his 1984 study *The Character Factory: Baden-Powell and the Origins of the Boy Scout Movement* showed how the Boy Scouts originated at the turn of the twentieth century as an "institution intended to produce efficient recruits for the empire in generations to come." Baden-Powell, the Scouts' founder, was a career military hero who'd served in South Africa, India, and Afghanistan.

Girl Scouts practicing with their weapons, Big Basin Redwoods State Park, 1936. COPYRIGHT 1936, CALIFORNIA STATE PARKS.

In Baden-Powell's model, the Boy Scouts—and later we girls—would learn self-discipline, obedience, and hardiness, banded together in smart uniforms. As I competed in tent-raising and fire-starting in 1969, in other words, I was inadvertently echoing the discipline and fervor necessary to British imperialism—if in a vestigial, female rendition. Was I somehow being groomed to police the empire?

Markers of imperialism remain today throughout Big Basin. My first day researching in the park's archives, I followed a tour that Kim Baker regularly led on the park's history. At the very beginning of the tour she pointed out a broken-off tree with a rough top, perhaps thirty feet high, called the "Ruined Column." The name of this tree dates back at least to 1924, when it shows up on a tourist map of the park along with other named trees such as the George Washington Tree, the Santa Clara Tree, and the Father of the Forest.

The image of a ruined column comes straight out of Thomas Cole's famous 1836 series of paintings, *The Course of Empire*, now on display at the New-York Historical Society. Cole's dreamy, almost surreal paintings depicted the rise and fall of a mythical empire, implicitly Rome. Immensely popular in the mid-nineteenth century, they symbolized both nineteenth-century Americans' obsession with preceding empires and their presumption that while Europe's empires had collapsed from corruption, a superior civilization was rising in the West in the form of the United States. This was the time of the Monroe Doctrine, of Manifest Destiny, of the notion that the United States was destined to control the Western Hemisphere.

Cole's most enduring image was that of ruined columns, the detritus of a degenerated empire fallen to dust. In the final painting in the series, entitled *Desolation*, a huge vine-entwined column dominates the scene, surviving along with a few vaguely Greco-Roman arches in front of a swampy sunset. Ruined columns popped up in landscape paintings throughout the rest of the nineteenth century, a commonly understood code for fallen empires.

Once I realized that the redwood-imperialism trail led far back into the nineteenth century, I remembered Walt Whitman's poem "Song of the Redwood Tree," first published in 1874. Whitman himself never actually saw a redwood tree (he never made it farther west than Colorado), but nonetheless waxed rhapsodic on the trees' imperial portent in the New World, using redwoods to symbolize the rise of an American empire.

> Not wan from Asia's fetiches
> Not red from Europe's old dynastic slaughter-house, . . .
> But come from Nature's long and harmless throes, peacefully
>   builded thence,
> These virgin lands of the Western shore,
> To the new culminating man, to you, the empire new,
> You promis'd long, we pledge, we dedicate.

By the poem's last stanzas Whitman had warmed up to celebrate:

> The new society at last, proportionate to Nature,
> In man of you, more than your mountain peaks or stalwart
>   trees imperial, . . .
> I see the genius of the modern, child of the real and ideal,
> Clearing the ground for broad humanity, the true America,
>   heir of the past so grand,
> To build a grander future.

Whitman's imagination was at full throttle: Here was empire, "trees imperial," grandeur, a new world, a new man, and a new race, flourishing in the West free of the alleged "fetiches" of Asia and murderous infighting of Europe, all in one poem, and all embodied in a redwood tree, which he'd never seen.

For so many of these poets, painters, and park propagandists, the idea of an American empire, symbolized by the redwood tree, was deeply racial. In "Song of the Redwood Tree," Whitman, for example, refers to the trees as "a superber race . . . . / For them we abdicate . . . / To be in them absorb'd, assimilated. / Then to a loftier strain." In the poem's end he envisions a superior American people "arriving, assuming, taking possession, / A swarming and busy race settling and organizing everywhere."

Whitman's racial imperialism echoes throughout the twentieth-century redwood literature. Listen to Rodney Ellsworth, in *The Giant Sequoia* (1924), for example, writing about a particular tree known as the Grizzly Giant:

> The great white race which dominates the world today had made its entrance on the stage of history when the Grizzly Giant began its existence. And within the lifetime of this tree, this race, known as Indo-European, has made vast and noble contributions to the culture of man. Indeed, most of the triumphs of truth and genius over prejudice and tradition in

Thomas Cole, *The Course of Empire: Desolation*, 1836. COLLECTION OF THE NEW-YORK HISTORICAL SOCIETY, ACCESSION #1858.5.

every decade since have been the triumph of these gifts of the Indo-European people.

Ellsworth followed with a standard narrative of the rise and fall of empires and civilizations that his tree had witnessed.

Most redwood commentators were not quite this explicit in their celebration of global white supremacy, although they repeatedly referred to "the first white men" who had "discovered" the redwood trees. But they were comfortable with big racial concepts and hierarchies. In 1900, Carrie Stevens Walter, one of the founders of the Sempervirens Club, a key preservationist group, in an article for the *San Francisco Chronicle*, casually noted, for example: "It might be said that what the heart of Central Asia was to the Aryan race, this Big Basin region is to the water suppliers of the most populous part of California."

The men and women who saved the redwood trees eventually included a number of pioneering eugenicists, most notably Madison Grant, one of the founders of the Save-the-Redwoods League. Turn-of-the-century eugenicists subscribed to the notion of "race suicide," which warned the nation that proper Americans of white, Anglo-Saxon stock weren't having enough babies and would soon be overcome by hordes of Southern and Eastern European immigrants and African Americans who were allegedly reproducing at a more rapid rate. By the 1920s they supported selective breeding, through which superior Aryans would gradually weed out inferior strains. Susan Schrepfer, who has studied the Save-the-Redwoods League, found that "at least eleven of the leading men in the league subscribed to this science. Four were well-known, published eugenicists active in the late 1910s and 1920s." Women conservationists could be equally enthusiastic, Gray Brechin, author of *Imperial San Francisco*, has found, such as Mrs. Matthew T. Scott, President-General of the Daughters of the American Revolution (DAR), speaking at the Second Conservation

Congress in 1911: "We, the mothers of this generation—ancestresses of future generations—have a right to insist upon the conserving not only of soil, forest, birds, minerals, fishes, waterways, in the interest of our future home-makers, but also upon the conservation of the supremacy of the Caucasian race in our land."

The redwood literature is shot through with the idea of the trees themselves as a virile, manly race, symbolizing vigorous American men triumphing in the hemisphere and beyond. A 1940s "Guide to Big Basin Redwoods State Park," for example, issued by the State of California Division of Beaches and Parks, refers to the "ever-virile character" of the sequoias. Carrie Stevens Walter, this time in *Overland Monthly* in 1902, reinterpreted the trees' name, sempervirens, meaning always-living or always-green, to insist that "true to its scientific name 'sempervirens'—(always virile)" the sequoia "never ceases to reproduce itself." The redwood trees were, after all, big, tall, and phallic.

An even more enticing concept than virility was virginity. These were "virgin trees," "virgin timber," "virgin groves." To this day environmentalists are trying to save "virgin stands" of old-growth redwoods. The chaste trees grew, in turn, on the even-more-popular "virgin lands," the subject of a classic 1950 text by Henry Nash Smith, *Virgin Land: The American West as Symbol and Myth*. In all this imagery, redwood trees symbolized a triumphant race building a noble empire in the West. Whitman, the eugenicists, and Romulus all had the right stuff, and we could, too.

Cigar Store Indians

BEHIND ALL THIS imperial rhetoric lay a real conquest, of course, a real empire. Beginning in the eighteenth century, Europeans invaded, then nearly vanquished the native peoples of California, including the Yuroks of Humboldt County with their sense of "time immemorial."

By 1902, when Big Basin became a state park, the United States had not only taken what is now the western United States away from Mexico at the point of a gun, but had seized Alaska, Hawai'i, Puerto Rico and the Philippines. Ironically, the redwood trees themselves followed the path of that same empire. Felled by loggers, they were shipped in the nineteenth century to Hawai'i, Tahiti, Chile, Peru, and Shanghai.

On May 12, 1903, President Theodore Roosevelt, the hero of these overseas aggressions, visited Big Tree Grove at what is now Henry Cowell State Park in Felton. I dug up his speech to see what he had to say. Peering at an old copy of the *Santa Cruz Sentinel* in the university library's microfilm room, I was astounded by how directly his words fused imperialism and redwood preservation. Roosevelt was a big conservationist, and his brief speech focused on two themes: one, saving the redwood trees, and two, increased funding for the navy, to expand and protect U.S. overseas power. He congratulated the preservationists on their endeavors, then insisted: "We must have a first class navy. A nation like ours with the unique position of fronting at once on the Atlantic and Pacific must play a great and mighty part. . . . We must have the ships. We must see that . . . our war vessels be the best in the world."

After Roosevelt's speech, according to the *Santa Cruz Sentinel*, "a luncheon . . . was served under the shade of the gigantic trees." The visitors ate "broiled steaks, Spanish beans, strawberries, and coffee cake," washed down with "Ben Lomond wine." During the lunch, "It was whispered to the President by Fred W. Swanton that the woman who had prepared the Spanish beans is the mother of thirty-four children." Roosevelt laughed heartily. Then, the *Sentinel* tells us cryptically, Santa Cruz mayor Clark "told the President a story to illustrate the fact that the race-suicide theory does not apply to Santa Cruz." Race suicide? There it is, right there in Henry Cowell Redwood State Park. Mayor Clark is presumably joking that the fecund mother is either of northern European descent and thus doing her bit to keep up white supremacy by having lots of babies, or dark-skinned and dangerously undermining it.

The next day in a speech at Stanford University forty miles away, Roosevelt went further, fusing redwood preservation with imperial conquest of virgins: "I feel most emphatically that we should not turn into shingles a tree which was old when the first Egyptian conqueror penetrated the valley of Euphrates." By choosing "penetration" as his metaphor, Roosevelt could subtly evoke the metaphor of virile imperial expansion, whether in the Middle East or the American West's "virgin lands."

"Turn into shingles": Here was the final conquest in the empire story. The trees needed to be preserved as early as 1903 precisely because they were mostly dead and conquered already. Fifty years of logging had by Roosevelt's time destroyed most of the old-growth redwoods in California. They could symbolize imperial invaders endlessly, but they themselves had been conquered.

As Gary Larson figured out in his cartoon, you couldn't indicate time on the growth rings of a tree if it wasn't already cut down. Once dead, it could be mounted on a plaque or wall. My log slice was like a pelt, a trophy animal on display, sort of like the big game animals Teddy Roosevelt was so famous for shooting. Or like a cigar store Indian: a caricature of a culture that has come to be revered as noble, long after its people have been conquered and corralled by the government into reservations.

My beloved tree was not just dead, but forced after its death to symbolize, even celebrate the very conquest that felled it. I'd finally gotten to the core of my log's history, and, like the little date markers, it stood for empire, conquest, and domination just as thoroughly as Roosevelt's Great White Fleet and his big stick. I could even buy a stuffed Teddy Roosevelt bear at the Henry Cowell Redwoods State Park gift shop, complete with Rough Rider uniform and a red scarf to keep the dust off his neck while riding to power in the colonies.

Switched at Birth?

I WAS WRONG, though. I wasn't at the core of my tree's history. In fact the slice I was reflecting on in 2001 wasn't the same slice I had seen as a kid at all.

Talking to Steve Radosevich, a district curator for California State Parks, I suddenly found out that the log I was looking at in 2001, on display right next to the park headquarters building for supposed decades, had been removed in the late nineties and replaced by a new, improved slice. The old log was now at rest in Henry Cowell State Park, down the road in Felton.

I sped up the San Lorenzo Valley once again to compare the two, starting with what I now called Log #1, the original slice, in Henry Cowell Park. It was indeed old-looking, I realized, missing all its bark, with a huge crack running at an angle across it and held together only by a thick cable wrapped around its circumference. Christ was still at the center, though, and the date markers were roughly the same as in 1954.

Log #2, by contrast, in the place of honor at Big Basin, was newer-looking, shinier, with its bark intact. Since it was a bit smaller, it was also younger, and it had four new dates at the center: "960 Sung Dynasty in China," "600 The Height of the Mayan Civilization," "570 The Prophet Mohammed is Born," and "544 Tree Sprouted. Byzantine Empire (Emperor Justinian)."

Suddenly back where I had started, I launched a new venture to find out the history of the second log and figure out how the old one had ended up in Henry Cowell Park.

Steve Radosevich told me that another local ranger, Steve Oka, had helped found Log #2 and set it up in Big Basin. Steve Oka turned out to be retired. But he agreed to meet me in Henry Cowell, by Log #1. He was slender with trim black hair, wearing khaki shorts and a royal blue t-shirt and looking nowhere near old enough to be retired. He was not only friendly and helpful, like all the rangers (I now realized this was their job) but told me about a folder of documents on the new log, in the ranger headquarters building at Big Basin.

He said Susan Grove, who now worked at Castle Crags State Park in Northern California near Mount Shasta, had been the one who'd found the log. Over the phone she told me that in early 1992, while working at Big Basin, she'd gotten wind of an old diorama on display in the Los Angeles Museum of Science and Industry (now the California Science Center). It was going to be thrown out as part of the demolition of a whole wing, so she went down to check it out. Once there she also saw Log #2, slated for destruction, too, and obtained both the diorama and the slice for Big Basin.

The trick was getting both diorama and slice up to the park. The log was too big to get out any of the museum's doors, so the Big Basin people had to wait until its whole wing of the museum was demolished and then pay the contractor to ship it up. In 1994 they finally installed the diorama in the headquarters building, and put the new log up next to it outside in Log #1's site. This new log, Log #2, got a nice new shelter, a new plaque in front, and date markers to match those on the old log, more or less. Steve Oka told me that he had talked with another ranger, a historian, and that she had suggested the four new dates.

Log #2 turns out to have its own imperial story. Along with the diorama, it came from a longtime redwood-parks exhibit in the Los Angeles Museum of Science and Industry. Constructed in 1946, the exhibit featured a giant, floor-to-ceiling, fake redwood tree, ostensibly growing up through the room, and numerous instructional dioramas, one with a waterwheel, another with a little electric train, and a third the shape of a full-sized redwood log lying sideways, through which visitors could peer to see "typical park settings." Around the corner, mounted vertically on the wall—with no date markers at all—was the tree slice. The exhibit was called the Redwood Empire Room.

(One day, in the middle of investigating these various logs, I mentioned to my friend Debbie Shayne, manager at Logos Books and Records in Santa Cruz, that I was writing about a slice of a redwood tree. Before I could mention Big Basin, she exclaimed "I loved that tree slice!" She meant the one in the museum in L.A. As a kid growing up in Pasadena she used to visit the Redwood Empire Room regularly with her mom. She was especially intrigued by the date-marking scheme. "I asked my mom if I could slice off the end of my finger to see if it had rings inside.")

The Redwood Empire Room, in turn, was sponsored by the Redwood Empire Association, a tourist-promotion agency representing the area of Northwestern California, from San Francisco to the Oregon border, known as the Redwood Empire. The association's 1958 letterhead called it an "Official Non-Profit Governmental Instrumentality Operated by Nine Counties Since 1926," with offices in San Francisco. In the 1940s the Redwood Empire Association supported a $19,000 appropriation by the state legislature to pay for the exhibit. Throughout the 1940s and '50s it supplied pamphlets, movies, and other promotional materials to the room, all the while lobbying the state legislature for new appropriations. It continues to operate today as a tourist agency promoting the northwest California coast, and has a web site at Redwoodempire.com.

Empires everywhere. The idea of the north coast as the Redwood Empire seems to have originated with promoters in the 1920s; not just the Redwood Empire Association but the Southern Pacific Railroad as well, which beginning in 1928 offered a "Redwood Empire Tour" by train and bus from Grants Pass, Oregon, through Eureka, California, to San Francisco.

Today you can still find a 1966 glossy picture book by Stuart Nixon, *The Redwood Empire*, in used book stores. At Big Basin and at tourist outlets all the way up the coast to Oregon you can buy a postcard sending "Greetings from THE REDWOOD EMPIRE," featuring eleven shots of drive-through redwood trees, tree houses, and a monumental Paul Bunyan and his blue ox, Babe. Hundreds of businesses, community groups, and government agencies use the name, including the Redwood Empire Bonsai Society, the Redwood Empire Swing Dance Club, and the Redwood Empire Sheep Dog Association. There's even a logging company called Redwood Empire that still fells trees in the Santa Cruz Mountains.

In this final, "Redwood Empire" strand of the imperialism-in-the-redwood forest story, the trees themselves become the emperors. D. R. Lane, writing in *Motorland,* for example, entitled his article "Empire of Giants, the Redwood Parks." When the trees aren't emperors, they are often merely "aristocrats" or "monarchs," ruling over "the redwood's realm." In Big Basin, over by Opal Creek, along the road to Boulder Creek, there's a tree called the "Fallen Monarch."

Postcard, Humboldt County, 2004.
PHOTOGRAPHS BY BOB VON NORMANN.

(Ruined, again, like the Ruined Column.) The *Good Times*, a weekly Santa Cruz entertainment paper, headlined its cover story on the anniversary of Big Basin "Lord of the Rings."

No less than John Muir called the redwoods "kings of the forest, the noblest of a noble race," putting monarchy together with racial hierarchy once again. As recently as 1988 the state parks system's official magazine, *California Parklands*, picked up the phrase directly from Muir to entitle a story "Redwood Parks: The Noblest of a Noble Race," evidently oblivious to the implications of white supremacy embedded in the phrase.

I wasn't so wrong, after all. Just as swiftly and inexorably as my first slice, Log #2 had circled me right back to redwood imperialism.

Guerrilla Docents

WHAT ABOUT THE fate of Log #1? Ranger Steve Oka helped me here, too, since he'd helped facilitate its move to Cowell Park. In general, Steve was pretty low-key in answering my questions, but when I asked him about what it had been like to be a ranger discussing the log slice with visitors, he was suddenly poetic and talkative. "We usually started our guided walks there." It was a good way to gauge the tour group, he said. "You either got no reaction—they didn't fathom it—*or* it really hits, and they'll put their hand up there in awe and wonder, as if that would help them grasp it."

Steve's affection for the original log was nothing compared to that of Bill Lewis, whose name Steve gave me. When I tracked Bill down over the phone, he told me the whole story of how the old slice had been rescued, restored, and reinstalled by a group I like to call the Guerrilla Docents. For ten years Bill Lewis was a docent—a volunteer aide and tour guide—at Big Basin and Henry Cowell parks. After the Big Basin rangers put up the new slice, Bill was upset that the old redwood round was just dumped, unprotected, on the ground in a parking lot at Big Basin for a year; people even picnicked on it. The park's officials had no plans for it. So Bill and a group of other docents simply appropriated it. They got a maintenance worker to move it somewhat surreptitiously down Highway 9 to Henry Cowell in a park truck.

At Henry Cowell Park the Guerrilla Docents took the slice behind the Nature Center, put it up on planks, and covered it with plastic. The log was sodden with rain, so on dry days they were careful to take off the plastic to let it dry out. They took off all the date signage, then spent several weeks sanding the front side lovingly with electric sanders and heavy gauge sandpaper, circling around and around until the original rings were visible—maybe an 1/8" down. "We tried shellacs, lacquers, nothing looked good," testing them on the back side to be safe, Bill recounted. Ultimately they decided to "leave it natural." Meanwhile, they found money out of a special independent docents' fund and paid the parks district to build a permanent shelter for the log's display. Steve Oka found an extra set of the original date markers in a locker at Big Basin, and they screwed them in next to new rivets in the old holes. "It was like a religious experience to work on it," sighed Bill.

In 1998, when the log was all restored, the docents had a dedication ceremony. Thirty or forty people attended, almost all docents plus a few visitors who happened to be there. One or two rangers showed up. "We all spoke, said whatever was on their minds," says Bill. "We knew how fortunate it was that this round had been saved."

These docents had developed their love for the round through years of guiding tours through the park, which they began at the log, just as Steve Oka had. "It had always been a focal point to the park, because you could talk about it," Bill explained. As a docent, he recalled, "you could just weave a hundred different stories about it," whether about history or biology. There was also "just the marvel of the thing." It had some magic quality. "People were mostly awed with the round. They just wanted to touch it."

My own nostalgia for the log, then, wasn't so special at all. Bill Lewis shared it; Steve Oka shared it; the docents shared it. "If there was one thing in all of Big Basin that people came back to see, to revisit, that's it," says Steve. "Some people love the new one. Other people are almost angry that the old one's not there. They want to know where it went." Bill Lewis tells of a woman who came up to him after a campfire program he led at Big Basin in the 1990s. She was in her sixties, very aristocratic, "New England-looking," "obviously a very reserved person," according to Lewis. She confessed to him that when she was sixteen, she got her "first real kiss" in front of the round.

Nostalgia for Big Basin in fact has its own long history. In the early sixties, just as I was developing my own Kodak moments, a writer for *News and Views*, the park rangers' internal magazine, was discussing contemporary visitors' nostalgia for the still-earlier days of Big Basin in the thirties and forties, when people camped out for a month, played tennis, danced on a log platform on the far side of Opal Creek, and paddled in a big swimming pool in the meadow by the Redwood Loop.

What was all our nostalgia exactly for? For a long-gone innocent childhood? For one's first kiss? For visits like Debbie Shayne's, with Mom to a museum that itself evoked nostalgia for earlier camping trips in the actual redwood forest? For a magic moment when you could touch the center of a tree and somehow hope to connect with two thousand years of history—and two thousand years of empire?

Log Revisionism

BY NOW, CONFIRMED by the trail of Log #2 down to Los Angeles and up the North Coast, I was looking for, and finding, redwood tree imperialism all over the state. References to other redwood slices on display with dates on them proliferated, popping up in tourist literature, old diagrams, and rangers' tips.

Two particular logs with date markers showed up frequently in materials from the 1930s, one at Richardson Grove, in Humboldt County, and the other at Mariposa Grove, in Yosemite. I began to suspect that they were the original models for my Big Basin friend and that its dates had merely been copied from one or both, since the dates were very similar. When I finally made it up to Richardson Grove, though, I found the log abandoned by a minor trail off the beaten track, moss-covered, with a huge crack up and down its middle and no date markers at all. I did find a postcard featuring a log slice from the nearby Avenue of the Giants, with a quickie set of markers printed onto the card: "1148 A.D.; 1215 Magna Carta Signed; 1341 Significant Fire Scarred the Tree; 1492 Columbus Discovers America; 1579 Drake Lands in California; 1620 Pilgrims Land at Plymouth Rock; 1776 Declaration of Independence Signed; 1843 Humboldt Bay Discovered By Land; 1919 Save the Redwoods League Founded."

I never made it to the Mariposa Grove, but at the visitors' center by the General Grant Grove in Sequoia National Park I could read that redwood preservationists were "Giants Among Men" and that "when the wooden horse was wheeled through the gates of Troy over 3,000 years ago, some of the still living giant sequoias had probably just begun to grow."

Closer to home, acting on a tip, I made a pilgrimage to Portola State Park, off Skyline Boulevard on the San Francisco Peninsula. There I found a little, somewhat forlorn slice sitting right by the entrance road between a storage shed and a stop sign. It was maybe six feet high, with "Voyage of Columbus" at its center.

A generous ranger at McArthur-Burney Falls State Park northeast of Redding sent me Polaroid photographs of a slice of a ponderosa pine on display there, sort of a redwood tree wannabe. A mere 300 years old, the log makes up for its youth by boasting a total of eighty-three white date tags. Spiraling up and around one side, a first set indicates the U.S. presidents from Washington through Reagan, while a second set names miscellaneous inventions, forts, wars, and invasions, plus natural events such as the eruption of nearby Mt. Shasta.

In the basement atrium of the Hoover Institution for War, Revolution, and Peace, at Stanford University, by contrast, there's a slice of a redwood tree with significant events in the life of Herbert Hoover gracing the rings.

I even heard of a redwood slice in London, at the Museum of Natural History. All I could extract by e-mail from its guardians was that it had "597 St. Columba Founds Mission at Iona" marked on its center ring, "1892 Panama Canal started" on its outermost.

The prize for the biggest and most creatively decorated log, though, goes to the New York Museum of National History, whose enormous log boasts a dizzyingly diverse array of tags chosen with an amusing fealty to the place of elite colleges in history. Its century-by-century world-shaking events include "800 Irish Explorers Reach Iceland," "900 Vikings Discover Iceland," "1000 Citadel at Zimbabwe Begun; Chinese Perfected Gunpowder," "1200 Cambridge University founded in England," "1500 Columbus discovered Orinoco River in South America," "1700 Yale College Founded," and "1800 Napoleon Seizes Power in France."

I found redwood slices in films, too, such as *The Big Trees* (1952), which Willie lent me. A spectacularly cocky Kirk Douglas stars in it as an aspiring lumber baron who arrives in California from Wisconsin, bent on mowing down the redwoods. He gets a speech from a pseudo-Quaker elder, who expounds on the sacred nature of the redwood trees. Leaning over a stump, the elder points to different rings and explains with eery familiarity: "It was a living sapling when the Norman Conquest invaded England. It was about this size when Columbus discovered America. . . . "

The most famous redwood round of all appears in Alfred Hitchcock's classic 1958 film, *Vertigo*. The film's plot is fabulously complex. In the first half, Jimmy Stewart, the protagonist, tails Kim Novak, whose character is pretending to be Madeleine, the wife of a San Francisco shipbuilding magnate. Madeleine, in turn, is supposedly possessed by Carlotta Valdes, her great-grandmother. At one point, Kim Novak lures an increasingly obsessed Jimmy Stewart to Muir Woods National Monument, where she gradually goes into a fake trance, channeling Carlotta. As they wander about the forest, the two arrive at a redwood round, complete with our now-familiar "Battle of Hastings," "Magna Carta," and "Discovery of America" date tags. In what critic Terence Rafferty, writing in the *New Yorker*, calls "the film's key image," Hitchcock's camera zeros in on the tags one by one, then onto Madeleine's black-gloved hand, pointed at the rings. "Somewhere in here I was born," she drawls. "And there I died."

In the film's second half Kim Novak is living in the "Empire Hotel."

My own fascination with redwood rounds has grown and grown. The *Oakland Tribune* headlined a 1958 story, "Big Basin Still Casts Its Spell," and I was definitely taken. "You've fallen in love with your subject," teased my friend Willie, the dissertation writer. "And it's a piece of wood." (I retorted that he himself had just spent seven years researching Big Basin.) Like the Guerrilla Docents and Jimmy Stewart, I had spiraled further and further in, not out. Was it just a coincidence, I started to wonder, that I was born in Sequoia Hospital, in Redwood City, or that I had grown up in Los Altos, home of the Sempervirens Fund?

As I spiralled into the deepest point in my obsession, though, Mia Monroe, a ranger at Muir Woods National Monument, pointed the way out. I called the park to confirm that the scene in *Vertigo* had in fact been filmed there; it had. Monroe was brisk, efficient, and professional on the phone; all business. And she knew mine better than I did. As I described my interest in the date markers and their problematic historical content, she told me that Muir Woods' staff had changed their own log's date markers fifteen years ago. The original version, she said, "represents a kind of history we don't talk about anymore." By the 1980s, a lot of people had begun to complain about the markers—that they were "Eurocentric," or that "No one knows these dates, knows those kinds of things any more." Monroe and her colleagues surveyed all the redwood parks in the state, and found perhaps twenty rounds. All had roughly the same dates. She and the staff at the park debated what to choose instead, an especially difficult task because on their particular log the original dates had been etched deeply into the corresponding rings, all the way around the circles of the tree; so they were stuck with coming up with new markers for the same dates. They put up new markers reading:

909 A.D.	*A Tree is Born*
1100	*Building of Cliff Dwellings*
1325	*Aztecs Begin Construction of*
	Tenochtitlan, Mexico
1492	*Columbus Sails to America*
1607	*Jamestown, Virginia,*
	Founded by English Colonists
1776	*Declaration of Independence Signed*
1849	*California Gold Rush*
1908	*Muir Woods Established*
1930	*Tree Falls*

There's a lot less conquering and invading going on here, finally. Columbus doesn't "discover" America, he just sails there. But three of nine markers still tell of invasion and conquest: Columbus, Jamestown, and the Gold Rush. Monroe told me, moreover, that in choosing the signs, "We tried to honor civilizations rather than individuals." Civilizations, again.

For another nearby sign that explains the growth-ring system of age dating, though, the Muir Woods rangers came up with a radically different concept. The sign reads: "While we may observe Halley's comet once in a lifetime, this tree, cut in 1930 at 1,021 years of age, endured through the return of the comet thirteen times." Here's an entirely different understanding of human history and the passage of time, not tied to civilizations, invasions, or empires in any way.

Since Muir Woods changed its markers, other parks have inquired about the new dates, although Monroe didn't think any of them had changed theirs yet. Visitors to Muir Woods do notice the markers are different, she said. And the rangers make their reconceptualization of history an integral part of their tour now. There's even a poster of the round that shows both series of markers, with "Muir Woods Through the Ages" as its caption—deliberately highlighting the park's own debate over history.

Along the way I did pick up other hints that the date markers' version of history had been contested. In the State Parks' Central Records, I unearthed a 1968 letter from A. Hewlett Mason, a "Consulting Engineer" in Arlington, Virginia, to then-California Governor Ronald Reagan. Mason complained that the Big Basin tree section was marked with 1620, when settlers first arrived in Massachusetts. "I understand that 1607, the date of founding of Virginia and the Nation, is lacking," he charged. Mason suggested an eighteen-word quotation honoring Jamestown be added "to mark the representative ring properly." On Reagan's behalf, William Penn Mott, Jr., director of the state parks, replied: "You may be assured, Mr. Mason, that no affront to our Virginia friends was intended."

According to the *Santa Cruz Sentinel*, a visitor to Big Basin named Mike Carter objected in June 2003 that the "Birth of Christ" at the center of the park's tree slice got a bigger, brighter tag than the log's other entries, and inappropriately mentioned one religion but not others—thus blurring the line between church and state. "You walk in there, and there's Christ right in your face. . . . It's kind of like, 'Oh boy, this is a Christian park now.' I wish I didn't have to deal with this, it shouldn't have to be an issue."

During the 1970s, critics brought feminism to the tree. Donna Pozzi, now Chief of Interpretation and Education for the California State Parks, tells of being a newly hired "seasonal" at the parks in 1974, just out of college at U.C. Davis. Encountering one of the rounds, probably the one at Richardson Grove, she thought the date markers were sexist, "an old way of doing things." She pestered her superiors: Why Columbus and not Queen Isabella, his patron? Why Christ and not Buddha? And, for that matter, why not Mary, the mother of Christ?" Her supervisors were not impressed.

Mia Monroe sent me a cartoon from the "Charlie" series, evidently from the 1987 *Oakland Tribune*. It shows three visitors standing in front of a big redwood round. Signs along the side, with arrows leading to the tree's rings, read: "Joan of Arc Martyred. Marie Antoinette Born. Florence Nightingale Born. Queen Victoria Reigns. Madame Curie Born. Betty Friedan Publishes The Feminine Mystique. Geraldine Ferraro Nominated for V. Pres." Next to the tree stands a lipsticked lady ranger in a skirt, hands behind her back.

The cartoon's humor rested, of course, on readers' familiarity with the original dates on these logs, and with the logs themselves, as did Gary Larson's cartoon. Redwood rounds weren't just some private memory, or even a local thing, but ubiquitous; unwilling missionaries all over the state, the nation, and even the world, of redwood imperialism.

Muir Woods, though, taught me that the trees' meaning could change. I myself, talking with dozens of rangers about my interest in the tags, had both initiated and become part of that process of rethinking their history. In the middle of writing this essay, I got a phone message: "Hi Dana, This is Kim Baker calling from Big Basin. You'll be happy to know that the redwood round has new tags on it, and we're going to put a new coat of deck seal on, which I never realized needed to be done until you came along and I read the memos." She hadn't changed the dates or legends, but she had replaced the broken plastic ones, including "The Prophet Mohammed Was Born."

The challenge, in the end, is whether we can separate our "wonder and awe" at the sheer ancientness of these trees, from our narratives of imperialist conquest. No question: there's a glorious dignity about the trees and their ability to speak to us across two thousand years of history; what Bill Lewis calls "the marvel of the thing." That's why there's an oily spot on my original tree slice in Henry Cowell State Park today, where children (and grownups) for over sixty-five years have wanted to touch the tree and somehow grasp the sheer passage and meaning of historic time and our place in it. I was only one of tens of thousands of those kids, burnishing the tree's lessons into my deepest memories alongside rainbow Popsicles and velvet-mouthed deer. Today, I still want to hang on to that memory, and hold other kids up to the log so they can touch it, too.

But the other memory marked on the tree, the glorification of conquest, still lures us in, too. Will the circle be unbroken? We can't change the history itself. But we can change the stories we tell about it. In the end, though, the real question is whether we can imagine a future for the United States without ourselves at the imperial center.

Cave people playing cards inside the original Cave Train Ride, 1991.
PHOTOGRAPH BY NANCY SELFRIDGE.

CHAPTER 2

CLAN OF THE
CAVE TRAIN RIDE

I WAS INITIATED INTO the Clan of the Cave Train Ride on June 20, 1992. It was a hot, sunny Saturday. I had unsuspectingly offered to help escort a group of girls on a trip to the Santa Cruz Beach Boardwalk to celebrate the sixth birthday of a girl I call my "niece," Becky McCabe. At the merry-go-round entrance I met up with her parents, Gerri and Steve, her little sister Mona, six girls, and another mom who was along with her daughter. We bubbled along in a happy pod past the Giant Dipper, the spinning cups, and the Fun House, down toward the far eastern end of the Boardwalk by the river, where the little-kid rides cluster on a lower plaza.

As we trotted down the wide, curving, concrete steps to the plaza, Mona, who was just a toddler, tripped and cut her lip, just a tiny bit. All attention turned to Mona; out of nowhere youthful Boardwalk officials suddenly appeared to whisk Mona and her parents off to the nursing station at the other end of the Boardwalk. Suddenly I was responsible for the six little girls, and the extra mom—who had never been officially helping out—evaporated with a thin smile. Mona's dad thrust a wad of Boardwalk tickets into my hand and suggested the Cave Train Ride.

I herded the girls onto the ride's little choo-choo train and took a deep breath, relieved that I had at least achieved the semblance of successful parenting.

And then suddenly I was in the world of the Cave Train Ride. Thumping music pounded as we entered a tunnel, rounded a curve, and passed through a spinning tube designed to simulate lava. Weird little DayGlo creatures in black light glared out of alcoves. A big, tacky, DayGlo dinosaur charged at us on a track. Soon we chugged past bizarre humanoids in little groupings. They had leering orange faces and skin, wide mouths, big ears, and narrow pointy foreheads, and wore an array of stylish leopard-skin togas and matching choker necklaces. In one scene, three sinister-looking Cave Men cheated at cards while a Cave Woman looked on. In another, a Cave Woman holding a club had just knocked out a man lying in a wheelbarrow, which she was pushing with a sicko grin into a "Wedding Chapel." In the best scene, which we slowly curved around as the train started back toward the entrance, Cave People cavorted in a bar with hip jazz music on the loudspeakers, while Cave Waitresses popping out of low-cut lime green togas waited on their menfolk. In between, alternating with passages of passive darkness, we got to see bats, a two-dimensional pterodactyl, a Cave Man pushing a broken-down car, a Cave People laundromat, a sleeping Cave Fisherman, and a spectacular Busby Berkeley-style array of three terraced fountains shooting multicolored water up and down, up and down. Just before we chugged out of the tunnel, a big fake explosion went off, as two unwitting Cave Men set off a box of Cave Dynamite.

Then we were outside again, blinking in the sunlight, the girls giggling and laughing and grabbing each others' popcorn.

What was *that*? I asked myself, in shock, as I gracefully suggested the next ride, a track with little automobiles that kids got to pretend to drive. I went into parenting mode and concentrated on the kids until Mona, Gerri, and Steve reappeared, all happy smiles with a yellow Donald Duck bandaid on Mona's upper lip.

But the Cave Train Ride stuck with me. What was that tacky,

bizarre, outdated, and incredibly sexist thing, lurking underground beneath the seemingly innocent concrete plaza? What was it doing in Santa Cruz, my town full of feminists, artists, intellectuals, and sunlight? It seemed the opposite of everything the town was about, its secret underground nemesis. What, moreover, were Becky and the other little girls learning from that visit? They didn't seem to be irrevocably warped by the experience; they just seemed to be having fun.

I decided to write about the Cave Trade Ride. I thought I'd contrast the town and the ride and startle readers with the difference. But the minute I started mentioning the ride to various friends and strangers, I found out that I was dead wrong. Far from the opposite of Santa Cruz culture, nor even secret, the Cave Train Ride turns out to be deeply beloved, with an enormous cult following. Aptos High School students, for example, decorated the entrance to their 2006 Boardwalk-themed graduation party to look like the entrance to the Cave Train Ride, complete with Cave People clad in leopard skins wielding clubs. Somewhat puzzled, the *Santa Cruz Sentinel* reported in May 2000 that the people of Santa Cruz "have a strange, protective love for the cave train."

Why such love? What is it about the Cave Train that inspires such loyalty? And what exactly is going on in there, anyway? The Cave Train Ride always seemed to be stuck in some bizarre time warp—but what time, exactly, wasn't clear; sort of half paleolithic, half late 1950s.

Answering all that turned out to be a lot harder than I expected, even after I tromped all over the state tracking down its builders, designers, fans, and even found a secret diary kept by its operators. To really put my finger on the Cave Train's appeal, I'd have to figure out who Cave People were, in the first place, and how they keep popping up in American popular culture. I'd have figure out the genealogy of those bizarre, sexist humanoids under the Boardwalk—

and how gender and race politics have been projected onto their relatives for centuries.

The catch was, the more I investigated the Cave Train Ride, the more I talked with its managers and fans, and the more I took the ride, the more I became a member of its cult.

The Big, the Exciting, the Authentic Cave Train Ride

I STARTED BY making various tentative phone calls to Boardwalk officials, usually public-relations people, explaining politely that I was a historian looking for archival materials on the Cave Train Ride. I got nowhere: it was August, the height of summer, the absolutely worst time to try to get the attention of a Boardwalk PR person, and while they were very nice about talking with me, they clearly didn't have time to sniff around in the archives.

So I decided, instead, to start at the very top and try to interview Charles Canfield, the famous owner of the Santa Cruz Seaside Company, which includes the Boardwalk, the Coconut Grove, the Surf Bowl, and two motels. It was startlingly easy. All I had to do was call his secretary, explain my project, and he called me back right away. The secretary helped fit me into his schedule between golf games and lunch.

I dressed up in my best friendly professional outfit, put on my good black shoes, and drove the ten blocks or so from my house to the Boardwalk. It was a kick to give my name to the young man in the booth at the parking lot and have him wave me through for free.

Of course I was familiar with the Boardwalk. When I was growing up in Los Altos, over the hill on the San Francisco Peninsula, we'd come to the Santa Cruz area regularly on the weekends during the 1960s. My parents never took us to sandy beaches to bask on towels like normal families, though. Instead we went to places like Año Nuevo, up the coast—which had just been bought as state park land—where we'd dig clams, tiptoe around smelly, dead elephant seals covered with kelp, and hang out, vaguely bored, while my dad dove for abalone out toward the island.

Sometimes, on the way back, we'd go to the Boardwalk. Usually we just strolled around; sometimes we rode the Merry-Go-Round or just stood, riveted, happily watching its automated orchestra. No matter how much we begged our parents to let us go on the other rides, mostly we just got to play Skee-Ball, where you rolled round wooden balls up a ramp and tried to land them in plastic circles. If you did well, yellow tickets would pop out from a slot near where you put your dime in, and you could exchange them for all sorts of exciting, small, useless plastic items, or for those red-and-white straw snakes you stuck your fingers into at each end, and then couldn't pull them out. Only very rarely did we go on the "real" rides. When we did, it was the tame, mid-range ones like the Haunted House or the Ferris Wheel. It was a major rite of passage when I was finally old enough to go with my big sister onto the Bumper Cars.

After the Boardwalk, we'd walk out to the end of the wharf and back. When I was little, that part always scared me. In those days, the wharf was made of wooden slats, and I was always afraid I'd slip through, down into the water underneath. But I loved having dinner afterward at the Ideal Fish Restaurant at the entrance to the wharf, with its dark, cove-like atmosphere; round, red, glass candle holders with white plastic fishnet wrapped around them; and a giant sea turtle with glass eyes on display by the front desk.

My mom grew up in Merced, in the San Joaquin Valley, and when she was a kid they'd go on vacation trips to the Boardwalk, too. She swam in the Plunge, the indoor swimming pool filled with seawater, that now houses Neptune's Kingdom. She danced with beaus in the original Coconut Grove, still intact today with its mirror ball, spectacular ocean view, and thin balconies overlooking the dance floor. According to my grandmother, the family would arrive at the Mir-a-Mar Motel in the afternoon, the kids would get sent down to the beach to play, and my grandparents "would have time to knock off a quick piece" (i.e., make love).

For all my familiarity with the Boardwalk, though, meeting its owner was something else altogether. Following directions, I easily found the "Administrative Offices," which I realized I'd never noticed before, in an entryway to the left of Neptune's Kingdom. I was early, so I wandered out to the main deck. It was a weekday morning in September, after Labor Day; the rides were shut down, there were no tourists to be seen, and it was eerily quiet, with only a few seagulls cawing and some whirring construction noises in the distance. A gray corrugated metal door had been pulled down over the entrance to the Fun House. I sat on a bench and watched a little gray kitten play in the sand below while I listened to two janitors discuss their supervisor.

At 10:00 I walked back to the entrance, opened the door, introduced myself to the gray-mustached receptionist, Dave, and entered the inner world of the Boardwalk. Suddenly I was inside a parallel universe. Outside, however quiet the day, the colors were bright, loud, shouted at you. Overstimulation was the name of the game and there was an overabundance of things to buy, play, eat, react to. Inside all was cool, dark, and calm, with tasteful yellow walls and blue and green Victorian trim, just a hint of the splashy scene outside. I followed a series of twisting staircases and windowless halls up toward Canfield's office. As I came around a corner I would suddenly bump into a stuffed monkey in a box offering to tell my fortune, or other antique carnival paraphernalia—a sort of discreet, parallel version of the Fun House. Mostly it was lovely, the walls hung with old sepia photographs of the Boardwalk.

I was scared, I'll admit, to meet Charles Canfield. He's a legendary figure in Santa Cruz, the powerful, wealthy heir to the Seaside Company and Boardwalk. I'd heard, though, that he was a nice person, and it turned out to be absolutely true. When he met me at his office door, trim and fit in a light-green polo shirt and slacks, I was surprised by how young and boyish-looking he was, although he had to have been in his mid-sixties. He was incredibly friendly and helpful. We sat down at a big wooden table in his corner office with a stunning view of the Boardwalk and Monterey Bay, and in a slow, almost folksy, down-to-earth voice he told me how the original Cave Train Ride had been born.

In 1952, Charles Canfield's father, Lawrence, bought the Seaside Company—now including the Boardwalk, the Coconut Grove, two

The original Cave Train Ride's entryway, 1963. **PHOTOGRAPH COURTESY OF SANTA CRUZ SEASIDE COMPANY.**

motels and the Surf Bowl—after being on its board of directors for many years. The Boardwalk had been around since 1907, but Lawrence Canfield wanted to expand and rejuvenate it with a new area to the east toward the San Lorenzo River, where there'd been an old dilapidated boardwalk. He decided on a concrete structure that would open two levels for new rides. "That's when the idea of the Cave Train came up," Charles remembered. "It was such a big space, we started kicking things around. You had to have a conveyance to get people around. Most parks have a train. We could get a train *and* a dark ride in there."

Two of the three key conceptual elements of the Cave Train Ride were thus in place: First, a train. To this day one of the main attractions of the ride remains the train, with its charming nineteenth-century style, its coal car, its horn and bell that toot and ring, and its comforting plastic fake-wood cars you can slide your behind across as you file into the seats. Trains tap into some deep American collective memory and, as Lawrence Canfield knew, were a sure-bet part of any amusement-park design. Trains are also profitable. As an amusement-park-industry pamphlet I later dug up put it, "The fact that each patron is moved past the displays at a given speed produces very high capacities."

Canfield pulled me immediately into the business world of amusement parks. Suddenly I was trying to decode terms like "conveyance," "cams," or the "IAAPA"—the International Association of Amusement Parks and Attractions. I realized, reluctantly, that the Boardwalk existed not just to produce fun, but to produce profits. Those "high capacities" on the train meant that lots of paying visitors could get onto and off the ride quickly.

Second was the idea of a dark ride. "A Dark Ride is a display of animated effects illuminated by black light, past which patrons are conveyed continuously by a number of vehicles," explained the same industry pamphlet. First popular in the early twentieth century, when patrons would be moved past a series of brightly lit tableaux in the pre-black-light era, they were making a comeback in the 1950s and have stayed popular ever since. Today their fans even have a website, "Laff in the Dark, Official Website of the Dark Ride and Funhouse Historical Society." It lists sixty-one operating North American dark rides, most of them with haunted castle themes like the "Monster Plantation" at Six Flags over Georgia or the "Spook-A-Rama" at Coney Island, or with vaguely related themes like the "Den of Lost Thieves" in Monticello, Indiana (or, my personal favorite, the "Jersey Junk Yard" in Wildwood, New Jersey).

Lawrence Canfield measuring up to the Cave Train Ride's bear, 1963.
PHOTOGRAPH COURTESY OF THE SANTA CRUZ SEASIDE COMPANY.

For all the slick, new dark rides out there today on all sorts of themes, though, there's only one *Cave* Train Ride in the world, evidently, the one in Santa Cruz.

That was the third element: to put cave people inside. As so many of us have guessed, the idea came straight from *The Flintstones*, which was hot on TV in 1960. "We needed a story line," Charles said. "*The Flintstones* was working at the time. It was a theme to take off on." The Boardwalk couldn't use the actual "Flintstones" name for copyright reasons. But they could take the theme and run with it all they wanted.

Next, Charles and Lawrence Canfield gathered together various Boardwalk mechanics and a few artists, and started brainstorming interior scenes and gags. "We were just kicking things around. We just went through it, a bunch of people sitting around, and we'd figure out some sets." Gradually they worked up a sequence of cave scenes. "A lot of these things just evolved," Charles Canfield told me. "We had quite a few dark spots we started filling in."

A man and a woman out of Los Angeles made a set of fifty or so cave people to put in the ride, he said. "They were all the same when they arrived. Then we'd cut them up, bend their knees, et cetera. It was a kick." His father got hold of a stuffed grizzly bear and they stuck it in front of a cave man, who poked a spear at it. The actual train and several of the original gags were built by the Arrow Development Company in Mountain View. Canfield mentioned that its owners were Ed Morgan and Karl Bacon. Karl *Bacon?* I knew Karl Bacon! He and his wife, Jane, and their daughters Susie and Nancy, lived around the corner from me when I was growing up. Back then my sister and I thought it was way cool that Karl Bacon had built the Flying Saucer Ride at Disneyland. This was about as cool as you could get in 1963.

At that time Disneyland loomed like the Matterhorn over the whole amusement park industry. Before it opened in 1955, the industry had been on the decline. Other than world's fairs, amusement parks had become associated with seedy carnivals and rundown beach resorts. "Disneyland brought a whole new level of sophistication to the industry," Canfield said. "A lot of the old amusement park people never thought it would fly; that they'd never get their money back out of it." Instead, Disneyland reinvigorated the whole industry.

The Boardwalk's builders could never afford Disney's level of design, though, as they put together the Cave Train. "We tried to keep it real simple. Disney animatronics are real expensive. All our movements are real simple."

After I talked with Canfield, I tried to beat a fast track to Karl Bacon, to hear about how he'd built the Cave Train. But at 93, after several strokes, he wasn't quite up to talking with me, and he sent me to his partner, Ed Morgan, in Scotts Valley, up in the Santa Cruz Mountains.

On an extremely dark and stormy November afternoon I wound up Bean Creek Road, my own private dark ride all too real. I prayed the trees wouldn't fall, the hillsides wouldn't slide, and crept toward Ed's beautiful exposed-beam house looking out on twenty-seven redwood acres along the creek. Wearing a blue-and-red plaid Pendleton shirt, with a gray crew cut, Ed sat in a pool of light in a Naugahyde armchair and told me great stories about the history of Arrow Development and the technical nuances of flume ride engineering.

Alas, he didn't remember much about the Cave Train Ride. His company had built a lot of rides for Canfield, he remembered; first a little-kid boat ride, then a rehab of the Giant Dipper, and over the years many others. But as he talked I meekly realized that my obscure Cave Train was nothing in comparison to the six hundred carousels Ed and Karl had built all over the world, or, most glamorously, the Disney rides: the cool Flying Saucers, but also the Alice in Wonderland ride, Mr. Toad's Wild Ride, the Tea Party, and even the biggies—the classic Matterhorn (except the mountain itself), It's a Small, Small, World (except the excruciating song), and the greatest dark ride of them all, Pirates of the Caribbean. Disney's "Imagineers" designed the concepts and the gags for those rides, but Ed Morgan and Karl Bacon actually built them, and many others for Disney. At the time they built my humble Cave Train Ride in 1961, Arrow Development was the technological gold standard of the world's amusement-park industry.

Before the Cave Train Ride opened, Canfield and company added two clever exterior touches. First, with Arrow Development's help, they built a pond in back of the cave entrance and in it put a Brontosaurus-type dinosaur that was green and skinny and literally all neck, about ten feet of it, with a tiny head. Mostly he hid in the pool, but at five-minute intervals he would suddenly loom up. "Part of the intent of that," said Canfield, "was to hold people longer, waiting to see it come up again. The whole key is to keep people in the park as long as possible. The longer they stay, the more money they spend—they get hungry, and spend money on food." In high capacities.

Finally, they needed to lure people down toward the cave entrance in the lower plaza in the first place. So they constructed three plaster Cave People that looked just like the regular ones but had more tasteful togas and shiny weatherproof complexions, and placed them outside to remind people of the ride. Two, a male and a female, ride the gondolas to this day, over and over again, endlessly surveying the beach with their idiotic grins, rain or shine. (Canfield told me that after the Loma Prieta Earthquake in 1989, someone called the Boardwalk in a panic, insisting that two riders were stranded up on the gondolas.) You can spot one of these riders briefly in the opening sequence of *The Lost Boys*, a vicious vampire pic shot at the Boardwalk in 1987.

A third sits in a tree outside the cave entrance, eating an ice cream cone, at eye level with the main Boardwalk. He used to talk; he was sort of a Cave Man carny, hawking the ride to passersby:

Cave man snacking in his tree outside the Cave Train Ride, 2007.
PHOTOGRAPH BY VICTOR SCHIFFRIN.

Yoo hoo! Yes, I'm talking you—no don't look over there—
I'm up here in the tree. You're wondering what to do next,
aren't you? Well, I suggest that you—c'mon, hey! You girls
and boys walking by—I'm talking to you, too! Yes, right
now, as I was saying, for unequaled excitement, laughs, and
dozens of silly happenings, step down a few stairs and climb
on the cave train ride. Jog along through the mysterious
underground where there's a surprise around every turn.
There's a cave train leaving in just a moment. Go right down
these stairs to my left for the *big*, the *exciting*, the *authentic*
CAVE TRAIN RIDE!

In June, 1961, the original Cave Train Ride opened at the Boardwalk. Seventy-five thousand people rode it in its first month alone.

Clubbishness

I HAD TRACKED the ride's origins; but I still hadn't begun to figure
out exactly what was going on inside that cave, let alone what it
all meant. To do that, first I had to try to reconstruct its original
"vignettes." Canfield sent me to Bonnie Minford, the Boardwalk's
archivist. After an extended search she produced a series of gorgeous
eight-by-ten, black-and-white glossy photographs of the original
Cave Train Ride during the 1960s. They only showed the exterior,
though, with the exception of one enigmatic dinosaur photo from
inside the tunnel. Mostly I got to see the original train, an original
conductor, the dino pond without the dino, and Lawrence Canfield
in a suit pointing a measuring tape up at a grizzly bear. Surprisingly,
the Seaside Company didn't have any photographs of the original
ride's various interior scenes.

I had only one slim lead left to follow for additional photos: a postcard I bought at Long Drugs showing three vivid shots of the ride's interior. So I played detective with it. A Boardwalk official gave me the number of the Smith Novelty Company in San Francisco that had printed the postcard. I called them up, but they didn't have the pictures anymore. Try Nancy Selfridge, in Monterey, they said; she had the originals. I called Nancy; she looked for the photographs but couldn't find them. She said to try her ex-boyfriend, Richard Bucich, with whom who she had taken the pictures. The two of them, professional photographers, had been hired by the Boardwalk to take some promotional shots in 1991.

Yes, he still had those slides, Richard said when I called. We arranged to meet at the elementary school in Pacific Grove where he was a fifth-grade teacher. I wove up through the Naval Postgraduate School housing compound to find his school at the top. Bingo! In

Cave people at the bar inside the original Cave Train Ride, 1991.
PHOTOGRAPH BY RICHARD BUCICH.

his classroom, amid an impressive array of animal skulls and fossils (and a nice two-foot-wide redwood round) Richard pulled out the slides he and Nancy had taken. There it was, the inside of the original Cave Train Ride, suddenly alive and visible in all its lurid colors and loony charm. Or at least a few of its key scenes: the bar scene and dancers, the card game, a pterodactyl, a fisherman, "the world's first waterbed," and assorted dinosaurs.

Richard volunteered to lend me all the slides I wanted, and together we picked out twenty representative shots. I was stunned by how generous he was in lending his work to a complete stranger. Just sign this little form, he said. In the fine print it said that for each slide I didn't return, I would be liable for $500. He was a professional, of course, and had to protect his livelihood. All the hour-long drive home around a glistening Monterey Bay I thought about those slides in their clear plastic folder next to me on the seat, worth $10,000. This was my first warning sign that I might be getting a little too deep into the Cave Train Ride. How crazy could I get, risking ten thousand dollars just to write about a stupid Boardwalk ride? In a panic, I started listing all the things that could happen to the slides: I could get in a car accident; I could spill coffee; I could be held up. I took notes on the slides that night, called Richard the next morning, and got those babies back in three days.

Then I started trying to understand what the scenes inside the cave were all about, and who "cave people" are, anyway. We take for granted that there were cave people in the first place, but most of our visions of them turn out to be as much fiction as fact. To unravel the two, this time I followed a more academic (and economically safer) approach, and started reading and talking with anthropologists, art historians, and people who study popular culture.

The cave people in the tunnel aren't *real* cave people; we know that. They're some exaggerated creatures, larger than life. As my friend Sami Chen, age seven, pointed out after we took the ride together, "they look like they came from a cartoon." Large, lumpy, in bright colors, they look a lot like Barney, the purple dinosaur so popular in children's TV and videos. Or like the population of *Sesame Street*, with their wide smiles and lumpy, jolly bodies—some formula designed to charm and disarm kids.

The original Cave Train people were modeled on a very specific cartoon, *The Flintstones*, the first animated show on prime time pitched to adults, running from 1960 to 1966. *The Flintstones*, in turn, was explicitly modeled on *The Honeymooners*, a long-running TV situation comedy from the 1950s starring Jackie Gleason, in which two working-class white men complained about their crummy jobs while their wives assiduously henpecked them. Fred and Wilma Flintstone, with their best friends Barney and Betty Rubble, exactly matched the Ralph and Alice Kramden characters from *The Honeymooners*.

The difference was that the Flintstones lived in "prehistoric" time and they were animated, which gave their creators wide license to invent comic scenes and play fast and loose with historical "reality." The Flintstones wore togas and interacted with rocks a lot, but they also had cave-people versions of modern appliances and vehicles (albeit made with rocks). (They lived in Bedrock, after all.) The humor rested, in part, on the preposterous juxtaposition of the modern things they couldn't possibly have, and the primitive times they lived in. The series' opening theme song underscored this in introducing the Flintstones as "a modern Stone-Age family."

The Flintstones, in turn, worked because they drew on images and jokes using cave people that were solidly enmeshed in American popular culture by the 1950s. Vincent Hamlin's cartoon strip *Alley Oop*, for example, which began in 1934 and was eventually syndicated into 800 newspapers, featured a cave hero, Alley Oop, with giant chest and shoulders, skinny hips, and odd ankles that widened out into huge feet. He always had a gnarled club slung over his shoulder and wore the animal-skin toga that is is de rigueur in cave fashion. Alley Oop had a time-travel machine through which he flitted about in history and into the present to comment on events from a cave perspective. When I was growing up he still appeared, buried deep in the classified section of the *San Francisco Chronicle*. (Hamlin's successors still produce *Alley Oop* years after his death.) I could never figure out the strip's jokes or the appeal; I just thought it was weird, especially those ankles.

Cave people jokes are still a stock element in early twenty-first century American humor. Think of the comic strip *B.C.*, or all the *New Yorker* and Gary Larson cartoons involving cave people, or the ludicrous scenes at the beginning of Mel Brooks's *History of the World, Part I*. There's always a cave man with bad hair, leopard-skin toga over one shoulder, carrying a club and interacting with a) a wild beast, b) rocks, or c) other cave men. Sometimes he's dragging a cave woman into the cave by her hair (or, in the Mel Brooks movie, a cave

Charles Robert Knight, *Neanderthal Flintworkers*, 1920, at the American Museum of Natural History, New York, New York;
IMAGE #618B, AMERICAN MUSEUM OF NATURAL HISTORY LIBRARY.

man.) Sometimes he does a little painting on the cave wall. Usually there are a volcano and dinosaurs nearby—despite the fact that human beings and dinosaurs existed about twenty bazillion years apart. ("I think there should be cartoon confessionals," Gary Larson quips, "where we could go and say things like, 'Father, I have sinned—I have drawn dinosaurs and hominids together in the same cartoon.'")

These comic scenes, in turn, draw on "serious" visual depictions of cave people enshrined in "official" dioramas, most famously in the Museum of Natural History in New York City. As my colleague at the University of California, Santa Cruz, archeologist Diane Gifford-Gonzales, has pointed out, such dioramas rest partly on serious scholarly research—they include placards around the edges explaining carbon dating, for example, and sometimes real artifacts like flints from actual caves, that have been worked into the scenes. But they are still "science fictions," as she calls them, made from near-whole cloth by the artists.

This mix of fact and fiction captured popular imaginations more recently in Jean Auel's 1980 best-selling novel, *Clan of the Cave Bear*, and its mammoth sequels, which speculate about the hypothetical meeting of ascendant Cro-Magnon people with the doomed Neanderthals. A less successful film version (with a screenplay by John Sayles, of all people) starred Darryl Hannah as the Cro-Magnon heroine who introduces abstract thinking, a superior throwing arm, and better hair to the bewildered Neanderthals.

In *Ancestral Images: The Iconography of Human Origins*, art historian Stephanie Moser has traced the origins of visual images of cave people all the way back to Greco-Roman myths. She found that symbolic pictures of earliest human life were deeply established in western art "long before prehistory ever became a discipline," and dominated visual representations long after anthropologists developed archaeological understandings of prehistoric humans. Even up to the present, she writes, "it has been almost impossible for the scientific approach to dismantle some of the traditions of representation." Moser found a series of stock scenes codified by the late nineteenth century: cave men hunt, cave people eat, cave men make tools, cave man starts fire, cave man combats wild beast (usually a cave bear), and cave man makes art. And of course, cave man carries club. "Have we ever found a wooden club, especially a particularly gnarled one that any design-conscious Neanderthal simply must carry as an accessory?" asks anthropologist Clive Gamble in his introduction to Moser's book. "The answer is no."

Cave people rose in popularity in the late nineteenth century, in part to explain the theory of human evolution. But they were also increasingly popular in that period, Moser and others argue, because they heightened the distinction between "modern," "civilized" people, the carriers of "progress" (i.e., Us), from "uncivilized," bestial "savages" (i.e., Them), precisely as Europeans and Americans conquered and colonized non-Europeans all over the world. If European-descent people were civilized, the others weren't, and thus needed imperial tutelage. In precisely the same historical period that the United States invaded the Philippines and Puerto Rico, and when celebratory versions of imperial history were projected onto redwood trees, cave dioramas and imagined cave scenes popped up for the first time at world's fairs and museums in the United States, next to supposedly reconstructed, "authentic" scenes of the savages of Borneo or of newly conquered peoples indigenous to North America.

The backwardness of cave people thus served to highlight smug, late-nineteenth-century notions of progress. In 1960, when the Flintstones were born, they still served a similar function. The Flintstones' sheer, stupid technological backwardness reinforced viewers' contentedness with mid-twentieth-century technological advancement. As Tina Stockman has written, "In *The Flintstones*, the inadequacy of primitive man is highlighted by providing him with items he couldn't possibly have—but a typical WASP family would."

The Flintstones were soon paired on prime-time TV with the Jetsons, a sleek family of the future that zipped around in private saucers and pushed a few buttons to produce dinner. By pairing the Cave Train Ride with the "futuristic" Autorama, Lawrence and Charles Canfield built the same deliberate contrast into their 1961 extension to the Boardwalk. The *Santa Cruz Sentinel*, in an editorial greeting the new rides, similarly observed that with the Cave Train and the "modernistic Autorama," the Boardwalk combined "the past with the present in an elaborate new setting."

In related ways, the historic cave-people scenes were also about race. The cave people were always brown-skinned, with dark hair, sloping foreheads, wide lips, and bulging eyes: not "us," the Europeans, but "them," especially Africans. Cave dioramas appeared at the same time that U.S. and European scientists were constructing evolutionary trees that always coincidentally had northern Europeans at the top, Asians on lower branches, and African peoples down by the trunk. Only in *Clan of the Cave Bear* does the Cro-Magnon cave heroine get to be a superblonde instead of the usual dark-skinned, dark-haired cave dweller, but that's only to highlight her superior evolutionary status in contrast to the stooped, dark Neanderthals her people will supersede.

Cave people's racial politics surfaced most recently in a series of television advertisements (which are being launched as a television sit-com as I write). The ads start out with an easily identified cave man— with wide face, a protruding brow, messy dark hair, and deliberately light skin—who takes offense at an advertisement promising "so easy, a cave man can do it." In a sequence of spots building on each other, the cave man works through his feelings first in a bar, then with his therapist, about being misperceived and discriminated against. The humor rests on the viewer's presumed knowledge that this cave man is, in fact, stupid and inferior; therefore he is wrong to be objecting to stereotypes. Cave people once again serve as an easily accessible coded stand-in for African Americans and other people of color, as the ads explore themes of discrimination and stereotyping—while subtly implying that black people are wrong to be protesting against discrimination when in fact they are, indeed, not as smart as whites.

The Cave Train Ride's original inhabitants all had short, sloping foreheads, wide mouths, round faces, and bulging eyes. They usually, but not always, had dark hair. Their skin was a lurid, deep orange. They weren't obviously "dark" in their skin color, but neither were they painted literally white or the pale tannish pink color of northern Europeans. Certainly their facial features sent a symbolic message more powerful than the ambiguous crayon orange of their skin.

The original Cave Train was thick with gender commentary, too. In the card-game scene, for example, the men are having all the fun and the woman is just watching, standing by to serve the men while bursting out of the top of her low-cut toga. In the bar scene all the musicians are men and the waitresses women, wearing even lower-cut togas. Most glaring is the wedding chapel scene with its club-wielding female dragging her unconscious man inside to be married against his will.

Diane Gifford-Gonzales, my anthropologist colleague, studied gender in 136 contemporary visual representations of Cro-Magnon people in popular books, postcards, and textbook illustrations. Eighty-four percent of the scenes showed men, but less than half had women in them. Of the 136 scenes only three showed just women, but scenes containing solely men were widespread. Of all the figures 49 pecent were men, but only 22 percent women (the rest were children and old people). Throughout the images, she found men portrayed as active, women as passive—and often stooping. Frequently women appeared on their knees, scraping a hide, in a standard scene she calls "Drudge-on-a-Hide." Men, by contrast, dominated the rest of the scenes, which she calls "Deer-on-a-Stick," "Man the Toolmaker," "Man the Hunter," and "Guy-with-a-Rock"—confronting a wild beast. These scenes, she writes, are "enticingly real" but reflect contemporary assumptions far more than archaeological evidence. "If [women] had been as abject as the Drudge, we would never had made it out of the Stone Age."

The original Cave Train vignettes fit right in with Gifford-Gonzales's patterns: lots more men than women. Active men, passive women. Man-confronting-cave-bear with a spear. Plenty of clubs. On the Cave Train Ride, as in dioramas and thousands of other popular representations, cave people serve as a blank slate onto which to project contemporary concepts of appropriate gender roles—despite clear archaeological evidence to the contrary. Even anthropological "findings" themselves can serve as a blank slate for debating women's proper place. The popular magazine *Archaeology*, for example, reported as late as 2007 that "it may have been gender equality" that led to the Neanderthals' evolutionary doom. "The ability of female modern humans to stay at home, collecting berries and sewing weather-resistant clothing with bone needles" meant that humans could live in higher population densities and thus prosper. (I guess that means I should drop my job, whip out my sewing machine and start making raincoats, or we're all doomed.)

The Cave Train's wedding chapel scene, though, has something else going on. Yes, the cave woman is wearing a toga; yes, a cave denizen is dragging the other along, as in classic cave people vignettes. But this time it's a woman doing the dragging. ("At least it's not the other way around," commented a friend who counsels victims of domestic violence.)

The wedding chapel scene comes from a different, but related source, Al Capp's immensely popular comic strip *Li'l Abner*, which started in 1934 and ran until 1977, at its peak appearing in over 900 daily newspapers in 28 countries. The series featured Li'l Abner Yokum, a stereotyped white Appalachian "hillbilly," his perennial girlfriend and eventual wife, Daisy Mae, and the residents of Dogpatch, an imaginary community. Its humor rested in part on the contrast between Abner's innocent moral rectitude and the sleazy, lying city slickers he ran into. But more deeply, its jokes, like dioramas of Neanderthals or of "primitive" natives, drew on the supposed backwardness of poor, rural people, in contrast to the civilized, savvy readers of the strip. If it seems farfetched to say Li'l Abner's "hillbillies" were viewed like Neanderthals or indigenous peoples, Capp himself referred to Dogpatch as "an average Stone-Age community"—deliberately echoing *The Flintstones* theme song's "modern Stone-Age family."

In San Luis Obispo, California, on the central coast, there's a garish pink hotel called the Madonna Inn (named after the Alex Madonna family, not the rock star). It has rooms decorated with various themes, one of them the "Cave Man Room," featuring walls, ceiling, and an actual waterfall made of rocks, and leopard-skin bedspreads. A old postcard of the room promises that "the room connects with the Daisy Mae Room" next door, "for the convenience of traveling couples and their families." A later card linked the two again as it chirped (rather suggestively): "Hope you will enjoy her company in this predominately rock room."

Al Capp's Dogpatch had two basic kinds of women: superstacked babes like Daisy Mae, bursting out of hot pants and scanty tops; and ugly, strong, matriarchal types. In 1956, Capp introduced the story of Dogpatch's "Sadie Hawkins Day," in which the town's "spinsters" chased its available men around town at gunpoint. By the 1960s Sadie Hawkins Day spread out into U.S. popular culture as if it were an actual "tradition". When I started my high school in 1970, its officials had just phased out an annual Sadie Hawkins Day that culminated in a dance to which girls, just once a year, got to ask boys.

During the late fifties and sixties, *Li'l Abner* was full of jokes mocking women who aggressively pursued potential marriage partners. The Cave Train's wedding-chapel scene—conceptualized in 1961—with its dumb, aggressive, overly-strong female (with a club) was straight out of Dogpatch. At a historical moment at which women's roles were defined in perhaps their narrowest and most repressive in all U.S. history, the Cave Train Ride confirmed that we "modern" humans weren't like the backward cave people or Appalachians—we, by contrast, kept women in their place. We laughed at scenes of women asserting themselves; we pitied their poor menfolk, who, as in *The Flintstones* and *The Honeymooners*, were always henpecked.

Cave people images, in other words, draw on an element of scientific, scholarly research about prehistoric human beings, but are really about imagination. They're projections of contemporary cultural and social concerns onto another time, another place, long, long ago. When Charles and Lawrence Canfield sat down at the table to brainstorm scenes for their cave ride, like it or not they were channelling their own time and place—through *The Flintstones*, *The Honeymooners*, *Alley Oop*, *Li'l Abner*, and all those "authentic" dioramas—straight into their Santa Cruz cave.

The Keeper of the Autorama Diary

EVENTUALLY, AFTER MONTHS of research, I started wondering why exactly I was spending so much time on the Cave Train. Christmas arrived and I started running into people out shopping, people I didn't know so well. If they asked what I was working on these days, I'd say the Cave Train Ride at the Boardwalk. Why? they'd ask. In about three minutes I would go from proud to sheepish to confused to feeling really stupid. I could, after all, be writing about something useful like world peace or Central America.

Then I went to a Christmas party and mentioned the Cave Train in a mumble to two nice, hip women in their forties. "Oh, that's the thing that Serena's obsessed with," they replied. I liked those two ladies right away—*they* had a friend who was a fellow member of my cult, and I knew it was all okay. Maybe I should start a Cave Train Cultists Anonymous club, I thought, and we could privately share our obsession and exchange secret smiles at holiday parties and put up cult symbols like the tiny trumpets painted on underpasses in Thomas Pynchon's *The Crying of Lot 49*. So what if Richard Bucich, the photographer, didn't grasp why I was so excited that he held the only remaining extant photographs of the original Cave Train Ride. I am the Keeper of the Flame.

Then I met the Keeper of the Autorama Diary, who was way ahead of me. All along, I'd been thinking that if I were fully going to understand the ride, I needed to find someone who had actually worked on the Cave Train Ride and see what their point of view was. After all, someone had to take our tickets, herd us into the seats, drive the trains, and keep us from fondling or trashing the exhibits, depending on our proclivities. I kept asking around town if anyone knew anyone who'd worked the ride. I tried approaching current operators, but they were too busy and I didn't want to harass them. Then my friend Dave Iermini, who had operated the Giant Dipper twenty years ago, gave me the phone number of his friend Betsy Jones who, he thought, had worked on the Cave Train back then.

It was another one of those dark and stormy afternoons when I visited Betsy in her cottage in Santa Cruz, near the San Lorenzo River. Sitting at her kitchen table, she told me that between 1978 and 1981, after working at the Boardwalk for a year, she had been promoted to Head Operator in the Pit, the section of rides in the lower plaza at the river end of the Boardwalk that included the Cave Train Ride, the Autorama, and the Rock-O-Plane—a defunct ride in which people in individual baskets were turned upside down while riding a ferris wheel. As a dutiful employee, she decided to start a log book of daily events on her three rides. "It was originally supposed to be modeled after the 'Dipper Diary,'" Betsy recalled, an official Boardwalk log book at the Giant Dipper, the big, classic roller coaster. The Dipper Diary, she said, "was very formal and dignified, recording the number of rides and written in the passive voice." The Autorama Diary, though, "just immediately degenerated into ride operator venting and humor," although its multiple, mostly anonymous authors kept the mock-serious third-person voice.

Betsy passed the diaries across the table, nine volumes in all, in 3 x 5" spiral-bound school notebooks. She also handed me two handwritten, folded notes, originally passed from one Cave Train operator to another around 1980. She had minutes from Boardwalk employee council meetings, too, and a list she'd kept of mistaken names she'd heard patrons use for the rides—e.g. the "Giant Diaper," or the "Tit-o-Wheel." She also had a little piece of paper where she'd written down the speech the cave man in the tree gives. She'd not only kept all these documents, but had typed up the Autorama Diary's handwritten entries, photocopied them, and distributed the copies among former co-workers. No question, I'd been outflanked on the Cave Train history front—and uncovered a whole new branch of its cult.

What the diary reveals, above all, is the work culture of alienated young Boardwalk employees and the stupid jokes they worked up to keep themselves entertained. "The Boardwalk was kind of like the best of high school," said Betsy. "People could kind of run amok and get away with it." The diary is also the product of deep boredom—that's why employees called it the "Boredwalk." On June 17, 1980, someone wrote: "A new committee has been formed! The B.S. Committee. Bored Society Committee." Its motto was "We save our sanity by being Crazee."

Much of the humor centered on the true dark underside of the Boardwalk: the frequent injuries suffered by Autorama ride operators and, sometimes, patrons, as the aging gas-operated cars slid out of control, bumped into each other, slammed into operators trying to stop them, and ran over their feet. (It was taken out a year or two later.) The Cave Train was much safer. But its operators complained that the sound level inside was dangerously high. Betsy's notes from the Employee Council for September 5, 1980, include: *"EARPHONES ON CT*—Management doesn't think it's necessary to provide earphones because the cave train isn't loud enough to cause *real ear* problems. If the noise bothers you, feel free to use cotton or ear plugs. Thank you."

Otherwise, the main problems were that the Cave smelled really bad and, along with the Autorama, was full of rats. "It got to the point were they were getting run over on the track," recalls Betsy. On August 17, 1980, an operator entered in the Diary: "This is a true Cave Train Rat! It must be fed daily. Those of us who frequent the Cave Train have observed that this particular species feeds primarily on any customer foolish enough to get in reach. So please be kind and take it for a walk through the line twice a day." September 3, 1980: "It's sooo slooow that the rats are sunbathing on the walk."

In all that boredom, any aberrations were big events for the operators. On February 23, 1980, someone inscribed: "Excitement in the cave—as the train goes by the Stoned Room it is squirted by a fire extinguisher in the hands of a demented tourist who has jumped off the train. Security, mechanics and supervisor are summoned to deal with the situation." On February 24: "Another demented tourist is discovered walking around inside the cave."

The operators themselves were quite capable of playing around in the cave, too, Betsy pointed out—sneaking in on their breaks, smoking pot, etc., especially in the bar scene officially called the "Stoned Room." June 24, 1980: "Two new dummies were added to the Cave Train's stoned room scene. However they were not permanent fixtures. One ride operator was spotted drinking stones, while another was said to be making advances to a lonely cave man. Andrea & Cindy [two operators] were quite shocked."

Most popular of all were vomit jokes. It seems that vomit control was a large part of the daily life of Boardwalk ride operators, since visitors were constantly throwing up during and after taking the rides. The Cave Train ride was actually one of the mildest rides. But it had its share. April 13, 1980: "Also today on Cave Train a little old lady got so upset during the explosion scene that she threw up. . . . People all day were stepping in it, we couldn't get people not to, so we charged two more tickets to walk thru it," he or she complained.

In a goodbye note to the diary on October 5, 1980, someone captured the overall Cave Train operator experience in the beautiful language of ordinary people: "This is my last day. And I want to say that working here would have been even more unbearable and gross than it is. If it weren't for the great people who work here. *Thanks everybody.*"

With Betsy's Autorama Diary, then, I'd unearthed an entirely new branch of the Cave Train Ride's cult. These people were affectionate for the ride, too, but from a somewhat less wholesome perspective: their beloved ride included garbage, rats, boredom, and all that regurgitated candy. The ride's operators also reminded me that thousands of people in Santa Cruz County remember the Cave Train not just as a favorite kiddie experience, but as their first dead-end job, from which they were very, very happy to emerge.

L.A. Makeover

BY THE LATE 1990S the original Cave Train was about to ride off into the sunset for good. Charles Canfield snatched it back just in time, but the ride's near-demise and resurrection brought the cult of the Cave Train Ride into the public light for the first time. When a redesigned ride rose again, transmogrified into something new, it wasn't clear, though, whether whether its fans would embrace the ride's new incarnation.

By the late 1980s the Cave Train Ride was admittedly getting a bit seedy. It wasn't just the rats and the icky smell and the constant breakdowns. The Cave People themselves were slipping from hip contemporary into merely tacky and dated. "World's First Waterbed" wasn't all that funny anymore. Then, in October 1989, the 7.1 Loma Prieta earthquake hit Santa Cruz. It didn't really hurt the Cave Train, but after the earthquake the Boardwalk's maintenance people inspected the whole park meticulously and discovered that cables running through the concrete that held up the entire lower plaza were slowly disintegrating and would need a retrofit. The bell tolled for the Cave Train Ride.

In 1997, Charles Canfield shut it down. "When we took it out, we weren't going to put it back," he told me. "We were going to put something else in." As word got out, though, dozens of fans of the Cave Train started sending in letters, e-mails, and cards, pleading with the Boardwalk to reopen the Cave Train. One kid wrote in pencil on blue-lined school paper that he had planned to take his little brother on the ride as soon as he was big enough, and now his brother would never get to see it. Fifteen people from Soquel, Aptos, and Santa Cruz signed a petition entitled "SAVE THE CAVE TRAIN RIDE. WE, THE PEOPLE, REQUEST CONTINUANCE OF THE CAVE TRAIN RIDE." In a cover letter, Robin Finke, who circulated the petition, lamented: "We loved the Cave Train and were dismayed it closed." She continued: "We just had to hear the song one more time. You know, that tune that was always played in the Stone Room as you rode by the Cave Man with the card stuck in his toes. . . . We weren't sure of the exact tune of that song so on my 31st birthday we went to the Boardwalk to check it out." Canfield told me that people called the office to demand the Cave Train reopen and mentioned the song so often that Ann Parker, who was head of Public Relations at the time, started singing it to them—"Bi Mir Bist Du Schoen," a jazz tune popular in the 1950s.

As the letters and calls kept flooding in, Canfield began to grasp the Cave Train's cult status. "We didn't realize that until after we closed it." So, rather than scrap the ride for something new and trendy, he decided to reopen the Cave Train but in a new, modernized form. He ultimately paid $1 million to have it redesigned.

Canfield generously gave me the phone number of R & R Creative Amusement Design, the firm down in Los Angeles that he contracted for the new design. When I reached Rick Bastrup, one of its partners, over the phone, though, I realized quickly that he was talking about visual materials and that I'd need to see whatever designs and photographs he might have. I held my nose and shelled out for a preposterous ticket to fly from San José to Orange County and back in the same day. On the plane the woman next to me was reading Jean Auel's *The Mammoth Hunters*, a sequel to *Clan of the Cave Bear*.

I picked up my rental car and drove from John Wayne Airport along four freeways to Rick's office in Anaheim. As I pulled up to the office I saw it was in his home, a classic 1960s California tract house—off-white, facing a four-lane boulevard, with a trim lawn and some impressive, almost cartoonish, giant cacti on either side of the front door. Rick welcomed me inside with a firm handshake. He was tan, fiftyish, with graying hair and a thick brown mustache, wearing a gold necklace with a tiny gold surfboard dangling from it. It was street-sweeping day, Rick said at the door, and I couldn't park anywhere on the street; so he called his parents around the corner and arranged for me to park in their driveway. I complimented his mom on her yard ornaments. "When you come back, I'll show you the bear grotto," she offered.

Rick's house was dark inside, with a sunken living room, an orange shag carpet on parquet floors, and leather and wood furniture. He led me through a passageway off the kitchen into a good-sized, brightly lit, windowless room, with piped-in music and a loud air conditioner blowing across it. In the middle was a work table; around the sides were flat filing cabinets, a drafting table, and a bookcase full of red plastic photo albums with photographs of all the rides his company had designed.

In that room, talking with Rick, I was deeper than ever inside the amusement park industry, this time on its conceptual side. Rick and his partner, Richard Ferrin, started their firm in 1981. When I met him they were well-established in the design scene, specializing in water parks and dark rides. Looking at the photographs and designs on the walls, I realized, again, that my Cave Train was small fry—these guys had designed rides for Six Flags Over Texas, MGM Grand, and Magic Mountain. There on the wall was a mock-up for a megaproject at Knott's Berry Farm.

Canfield had first hired Rick and Richard to design Neptune's Kingdom at the Boardwalk. When he later contacted them to think up the new Cave Train Ride, "we came up with a couple of different concepts," Rick remembered. He himself preferred an undersea world theme—playing off the "Under the Boardwalk" song. But Canfield said no; he wanted cave people.

Rick pulled out a binder and showed me the original storyboards his firm then developed for the ride. In the pen-and-ink drawings I could see the whole chain of scenes that now make up the ride: first the lava tube, then a series of paintings of volcanoes. Then the sequence of animated scenes beginning with beach scenes—a barbecue, the "Sharkosaurus," and various Boardwalk rides. Then comes the restored card-game scene and the rotating bar scene from the original, around which the tracks curve to send us back to the entrance. On the way out we get a set of jungle scenes and finally an ice cave with a red sea monster at the end.

In contrast to the original ride, which was basically a series of unrelated tableaux, each with its own humorous intent, the new Cave Train has a tightly developed "story line," a sequence of places and developments the rider moves through in some rough logical sequence. Often the humor depends on what Rick called "the setup and the payoff"—you see a man entering a cave, and he doesn't see the monster about to eat him—at which we knowing riders laugh as the train moves ahead past both. The ride has a recurring theme of two juvenile dinosaurs, rolling on their backs, laughing at the stupidity of the cave people. The core story line, Rick said, is about entering the cave people universe. "You find yourself in this lost world," he said.

Rick told me he and his partner deliberately tried to maintain the hokey feel of the original ride. "Everything's meant to be friendly, a little goofy. It's supposed to be silly and fun. It's an adventure." They kept many of the original cave people mannequins, but tried to tone down the sinister edge of their faces. For additional cave people they designed all-new faces and bodies. "We wanted to come up with new characters that looked like the old ones, but were nicer." They gave them simple, deliberately dorky animatronics with only two or three motions per character.

While in the original, most of the cave people had dark brown hair—although a few, later figures sported silver or yellow locks—the new cave, by contrast, is a sea of blondes. I wondered if this had been some deliberate attempt to tone down the potential racial politics of the new Cave Train, so I asked Rick, as tactfully as I could slip it in, why they were all blonde. His answer was technological: the new ride, unlike the old one, which used an array of lighting systems, is lit entirely in black light. Rick and Richard originally painted lots of the cave dwellers with brown or black hair, he said. But when they turned on the black light, all their hair disappeared. So they repainted the hair yellow.

After years of designing rides, Rick turned out to be well aware of the potential controversy regarding the racial politics of rides ("It's a minefield") and talked freely with me about his efforts to address the issue. Originally, he said, he and Richard had wanted to show an array of "different races," but had backed off that concept. "We gave them a flesh tone" at first, he said—meaning, presumably, the color of Europeans. "We experimented with some darker people, but it doesn't show up very well. We experimented with Black people." Finally, they decided to make the cave people look like they do now, with light skin and blonde hair but once again big wide mouths, big eyes, and short sloping foreheads. "They don't really have a nationality," Rick said. "It's just goofy people. They're their own race. You don't need an oriental cave man."

And they're mostly guys. Or of indeterminate gender. (Sometimes you have to look real close at the exact cut of the toga and what's under it to decide who's what.) Gone are the almost topless waitresses in the bar scene. That was deliberate: "It's a family ride," Rick said. "There was no place for that." Gone is the woman in the low-cut toga waiting on the men in the card-game scene, although it's otherwise exactly the same. Gone is the wedding-chapel scene and its wheelbarrow. But we still get the original figure of the club-carrying gal dragging along her man—this time onto the dance floor. She's the transition from the card-game scene into the bar. "I wanna play cards," he protests as we pass by. Mostly the women are just gone altogether. Of forty-nine adult figures in the new cave, thirteen are woman, thirty-six are men. We do get nine kids, all new; but except for the dance-hall scene, where women are evidently necessary as dance partners to avoid suggestions of homosexuality, almost all the action is once again done by men, for better or worse: men explore caves, men battle monsters, men buy hotdogs, men get eaten by dinosaurs, and, of course, men grill meat. No one washes cave dishes, and, in contrast to the original cave, there are almost no old people, except one old man who is dancing with a cave woman twice his size—a holdover from the original's ride's jests about overly powerful women.

I kept wondering what little girls and little boys were learning as they passed through the new ride, and what they were thinking, as well, about people with wide mouths and short foreheads.

I myself learned more from Rick in two hours than I ever imagined knowing about the redesigned Cave Train Ride. It was 1:30 when I emerged from his back room into the glary L.A. October light. My plane didn't leave until 7:00. I was trying to figure out what to do with the afternoon, and since I was in Anaheim, after all, I casually asked Rick where Disneyland was. He explained how I could easily drive past it on the way to the airport. I figured I'd just drive by, since Disneyland was after all central to my Cave Train story, always looming there.

I had absolutely no intention of paying the $43.00 I knew it cost to get in; I'll just drive by, I thought. But as soon as I saw the Matterhorn itself pop up on the other side of a hedge, something clicked in. I knew I was already in deep trouble when I chokingly paid $8.00 just to drive in and park, then took a near-empty shuttle to the actual ticket entrance, sitting next to a bored-looking journalist on his way to a promotion for the opening of "A Bug's World." As soon as that tram hit the entrance plaza I could feel some giant sucking magnet pull me in. Suddenly I was perking up, as super-friendly, super-familiar music came piping out of a hundred different loudspeakers across a plaza the size of thirteen football fields. Soon I was humming along with John Williams's theme from *Star Wars*, with the martial swelling strings, and trotting away, horrified by how easily the Disney Corporation had snared me.

I went right up to the information booth and explained that I was a professor doing research on the Cave Train Ride at the Boardwalk. Could I please get in for free just to see the two original classic dark rides, the Pirates of the Caribbean and It's a Small, Small World? (I slipped that "dark ride" lingo in there to show I was a pro.) She said no right off, but said there was something called a "shopping pass" that could admit you for one hour; I should try Member Services. I took off across the giant plaza again, marching in step to "Seventy-six Trombones," and tried my rap with the young woman at Member Services. This time I pulled out my manila folder with the promotional clips I'd gotten from R & R Design, and flashed my business card. No, she said, the shopping pass was only to go in and shop; you had to show your receipts afterwards, and you couldn't go on rides. Hadn't I written ahead for complementary tickets? I saw my opening. Now I knew free tickets existed. I explained how I was just there for the day doing research and hadn't planned on having time to visit Disneyland. She said try Member Relations. Back across to the opposite side of the plaza.

This time I pulled out all the stops. For a while I got nowhere; then I could see the nice young German-accented woman in a blazer hesitate. I knew I had her. She called up to the Pirates and the Small World and asked how long their lines were; they were ten and fifteen minutes, respectively. It was now 2:00. She said I could pay the $43.00 on my VISA card, and if I got back by 3:30, she'd cancel the charge. I begged for 4:00, just to be safe. She gave it to me. I had two hours, knowing if I didn't get back in time I'd turn into a pumpkin.

Needless to say I was elated that I'd talked my way into Disneyland for free (the perky music didn't hurt my mood, either). And here I was, suddenly, in Disneyland, on about half an hour's notice. I flashed my ticket at the gate, zipped up Main Street U.S.A., paid $2.50 for a pickle, $2.50 for a bottle of water, and $4.00 for a plastic container with six carrot sticks, seven pieces of celery, three cherry tomatoes and one broccoli flowerette, and wove through the line into the Pirates of the Caribbean.

As we pulled out in the ride's boat, I realized immediately how breathtaking the Pirates ride was, and how small indeed was my modest Cave Train. The sheer visual artistry of it blew me away. We plunged down a tunnel past swamp-tree roots to enter a vast underground world with high ceilings, giant pirate ships, and hundreds of jolly, laughing, singing animatronic pirates with thirty-five individual motions per character, wearing horizontal-striped t-shirts and wielding swords. I was entranced, thrilled almost to the ride's very end, when the leering swashbucklers finally got a bit tired. I emerged full of stunned admiration for this ride that was, after all, fifty years old and nearly untouched from its original form.

I quickly darted through Fantasyland and Cinderella's Castle to the line for It's a Small, Small World, dumbfounded by how incredibly precise my memories were of my only other visit to Disneyland, forty years earlier. Once I got to the line for the Small World, though, it was hot and way too bright, and they were piping out that horrible chirpy theme song ("It's a world of laughter, a world of tears . . . "). I figured I'd never be able to bear it for the whole ride. So I cut out and instead quickly hopped into a green caterpillar through the Alice in Wonderland ride. This one was much more like the Cave Train, in now-familiar black light with day-glo cutout figures. But it was really classy—crisp in its design, fast-paced, and lots of fun as we rode right up to doors that snapped open just as we were about to hit them.

I made it back to Member Relations with thirty minutes to spare, got my money back, and arrived at the airport by 4:30. I asked if I could get on the 6:05 flight. "We can put you on the 4:55," the clerk said, and I was at my front door in Santa Cruz by seven. That preposterous plane ticket had been worth every penny.

The Resurrection?

WHAT ABOUT MY humble old Cave Train Ride—did Rick and Richard's new version measure up to our modest, if somewhat crackpot expectations? "The Cave Train's Maw Yawns Wide Once Again," read the *Sentinel's* page-one headline on May 27, 2000, when the ride opened again. "The poor old cave train got its day in the sun Friday during a gala reopening, complete with cave cake and visitors pounding each other with inflatable clubs."

Mike Rotkin, who was on the city council at the time, got invited to the opening ceremony, and told me about it in detail. It was a warm, beautiful day, he said. The lower plaza in front of the ride was packed with a festive crowd, maybe 500–1,000 people. Boardwalk employees in leopard-skin togas wove through the crowd while guests traded stories about their favorite Boardwalk rides. Ann Parker, at the time the Boardwalk's head of public relations, hosted the event on a platform they'd erected in front of the Cave entrance. She introduced Rick and Richard of R & R Design, then the construction company, the head foreman on the job and his crew, and the head of security at the Boardwalk. "Finally they got to Charles Canfield," Mike recalled. The owner began to say how much this ride meant to him and everybody in Santa Cruz. "He related that people had said that this isn't the modern type of ride they're doing these days. But to him, this symbolized everything that was important about the Boardwalk, even though the marketing people told him that this isn't the kind of ride that was making money." "I can't imagine the Boardwalk without this ride," Canfield insisted, "So even though it cost us a great deal of money to construct this, for me there was never a question of not rebuilding and reopening this ride."

"At first he was all full of energy, happy and excited," Mike recalled. "As he's making these comments his eyes started to water up. He made some comment about his father and his family specifically. And how this brings back the glory days of the Boardwalk." Soon Canfield was sniffling; then he got all choked up and had to be led off the stage. "I have to say it was kind of moving," Mike said. "We think of big business owners as cold and corporate but here's this guy breaking down with emotion. Clearly this was very moving for him to reopen this ride."

During our interview I discreetly asked Canfield about the re-opening ceremony. "It was a pretty emotional thing," he said, clearly embarrassed. "I got a little choked. There was a lot of pressure to get it all ready. It was difficult to get all the trades together"—i.e., to coordinate all the carpenters and painters and electricians.

He was right to be worried. Ann Parker immediately ended the ceremony, and everybody who could fit filed onto the train to take the first ride. It chugged into the tunnel and then, in the middle of the ride, in the dark, full of all the dignitaries, the train suddenly stopped. An official explained that it was just a minor glitch and would be fixed momentarily. They all sat there in the dark. "People were making the jokes like when an elevator stops," Mike said, as if they'd be stuck there forever. "It'll be like watching Flintstones reruns till we die," someone moaned. After ten minutes, the train chugged forward, the dignitaries emerged from the tunnel, and the crowd cheered. The Cave Train Ride lived again.

But did the new Cave Train Ride measure up to its cult status? I felt that if I answered that question, I could finally put my finger on its appeal.

Canfield, the consummate professional, thought the new one was great. "It's more state of the art"—with "better sound, better graphics," he told me. "The scenes are so much better now. The rock work is all styrofoam. The old ones were plastic, harder to work."

Mike Rotkin loved it, too. "I was amazed. They had upgraded the ride, spiffed it up. But it still had the same charm, the same camp quality, that it had before the earthquake."

I decided to consult the true experts: teenaged fans of the original. I started with my niece Becky, now sixteen. We took the new ride together on a foggy Sunday and afterward I asked her if measured up. The dinosaur in front was gone, she noted, replaced by a new pop-eyed frog. She thought the new ride was shorter (which it is), but it was hard to tell. Generally, she was positive about the new one, in keeping with her impressively positive personality. "I really like the monster-cave area. It's fun. They didn't used to have that, I don't think." But she did have opinions: "The old one was a little bit more fun. It was a little bit more hokey." I asked her if she noticed anything about the men and the women in this one. "Well, there were a lot *more* men," she said. "There weren't very many notable female parts in this one. I think there might have actually been more women in the old one." On the other hand, she noticed, "There are some stupid guy scenes. The scenes where he doesn't realize he's about to be eaten by a monster, they're all men."

For the true test, I turned to a priestess of the Cave Train Ride, Julia Callahan, a first-year student at UCSC who grew up in Santa Cruz. In high school Julia memorized the entire original ride, even researching the music from the bar scene. All Julia's friends from high school loved it, too. Julia, her mom, and a high school friend named Tanya met me at the Merry-Go-Round on a cool fall day. It turned out neither of the young women had been on the redesigned ride yet. "We knew it had been opened and redesigned, like, I'd heard about it, and everybody was saying, oh, it's not the same." This would be their first time. "We're virgins," they announced.

Afterward these Vestal Virgins of the Cave Train sorted out their feelings. They had noticed immediately that the ride started on the opposite side of the entrance area. They missed the dinosaur in the pond. And Julia was sure: "The old one was *way* longer." Anne, her mom, didn't like the new name: "Cave Train Adventure. I can't get used to that 'Adventure.'" But she was generally appreciative of the new ride: "It amazes me that this is a remodel. Because it seems just as kitschy as the first one. The animation, and the little creatures; you'd think they would have gone a little more high-tech." Julia disagreed: "I think the new one is insufficiently tacky. It's just bad. I like the old one better. The old one was much more pink and green and faded."

Tunnel of Love

JULIA, TANYA, ANNE, BECKY, MIKE—they all were zeroing in on the essence of the new ride. But it wasn't until I went on my own last Cave Train adventure that I knew what my own opinion was—and finally grasped the heart of the ride.

I'd been trying for months to arrange an actual walk-through tour of the Cave Train itself. I knew this would be the ultimate intimate Cave Train experience. Finally I connected with Carl Henn, Director of Maintenance and Facilities at the Boardwalk. We got into his shiny white pickup truck with wide gray leather seats we both filled comfortably, and drove two blocks along the back of the Boardwalk.

Cave people dancing in the bar inside the original Cave Train Ride, 1991. PHOTOGRAPH BY RICHARD BUCICH.

After he parked, we walked down a ramp I'd never seen before that curved around the end of the Giant Dipper under the Boardwalk.

Suddenly I was in the Cave Train Ride's ultra-clean workshop area, with a decommissioned Cave Train in front of me, glossy and shining brown and gold with its fake plastic coal. Next to the train were about thirty glider cars from the gondola ride, squished together in tidy rows. We walked around them over to a wall by the trains, Carl pushed a button, and the corrugated metal wall rolled up. And there was the cave on the other side.

I stepped inside the cave, and it was magic. We were opposite the best part, the dance scene. I could actually touch the cave people right in front of me, the hip couples spinning together. Without their black light, though, they weren't dayglo colors, but drab green, with pinkish whitish yellowish skin and blonde hair. And they were *huge*. I got Carl to stand next to one; he said he was six foot two, and the cave guy was even taller.

I realized at that very moment, and much to my surprise, that I, too, loved the Cave Train Ride. Not just the old one, but the new one as well, the one that I didn't used to think was tacky or weird enough; the one that doesn't have enough active women characters and is all-blonde; the one that has all those stupid laughing dinosaurs and the woman dragging the guy into the bar. It's real; it's alive; it's dorky; it's bad at being dorky. There, in the bar, I wanted to hug those weird creatures and shout my love.

I didn't. I realized quickly that my time in the cave was limited, and that Carl was edging away from me down the tunnel. We walked off to the left, toward the exit, along the edge of the tracks. There I could see all kinds of things you can't see in the dark: walkways marked in white lines for the workers, a one-inch square black plastic box that's a trip sensor for the sound system, lots of plastic plants. With Carl along I viewed the whole thing from a maintenance point of view: those plants, he pointed out, had to be dusted. The fog has to spurt at the right angle. And riders are constantly dumping garbage and trashing the exhibits.

Partway back, along by the jungle scenes, Carl reached over and Pop! a door opened, just like in Disneyland's Alice ride, and we walked through into the beach scenes, facing a wall with a painted beach, a volcano, and an obligatory dinosaur. By now I was used to all the black paint on the other walls and what the black-light paint looked like in fluorescent overhead industrial lighting. I could also tell which were the original cave people and which were the new ones. The old ones have more horizontal eyes with heavy eyelids; the new ones have big round vertical eyes. The new ones have smoother skin, too. Eventually we reached the dance floor and slipped back out through the metal crank-up door, the train repair area, and the curving ramp into the daylight. I didn't look back.

Happy Cheesiness, Proprietary Nostalgia

THAT WAS IT. I would never get any closer to the original Cave Train Ride. In the end I couldn't even completely reconstruct its scenes, let alone hear its soundtrack, meet its inhabitants, or ride through it ever again. The original Boardwalk Cave Train Ride only exists in the imagination; mine, and about two million other people's.

The new one turns out to be almost as elusive. Just when I thought I had it, there with Carl in the tunnel, when I could touch it and walk through it slowly and nurse my quiet love, its magic slipped away. Without the black light, the colors were all wrong. I needed the music, the voices, the sound effects. To grasp the Cave Train Ride I could only begin at the beginning, pay my money to Mr. Canfield like everyone else, sit in the cars, and take the ride properly, for five and a half minutes; and ride it over and over again.

I was older now; I could never recapture what it was like when I was a kid. I had to rely on other kids or other former kids' memories. When I put all our different stories together, I could see our silly loyalty was in part about life cycles. The Cave Train Ride is basically designed for little kids—three, four, five, six years old. Parents or parental figures ride it with them, with maybe a protective arm around their shoulder. But then the kids start growing up. "When Julia was really small I would go on it with her," remembered her mom. "And then at some point the big deal was letting them go on by themselves, and waiting for them at the exit with all the other parents. And then they would go on it with *their* friends, when they got to be grade-school age—that was one of the rides where [they] could all just go together as little kids." Julia piped in: "And then we all started going to the Boardwalk by ourselves."

The biggest shift was when those older kids, in high school now, crossed over into themselves taking littler kids on the rides; or, more commonly, started remembering going on it when they themselves were small. "You'd just go on it for nostalgic purposes," Julia said, "and try to remember everything."

Becoming nostalgic for the Cave Train Ride was some kind of adulthood ritual, I realized. The Cave Train didn't exist as a single memory, but as a series of interlocked experiences that built on each other—like the kid who wrote in to Canfield and said he loved the ride, and wanted to take his little brother on it as soon as he was old enough. That's why people are so territorial about the Cave Train Ride—they have a kind of proprietary nostalgia. One man in an e-mail angrily insisted that Canfield had no right to shut down the Cave Train Ride because it belonged to the people, he said, not to the Seaside Company. He'd gone on it as a kid; his parents had gone on it when they were kids; his grandparents had gone on it in the 1940s, he insisted (ignoring the fact that the Cave Train Ride wasn't built until 1961).

But all that nostalgia still doesn't completely explain the cult of the

Cave Train. There has to be some basic experience we're nostalgic *for*. At rock bottom, the Cave Train Ride is also just plain fun, whatever that is—riding on a train, riding through a dark tunnel, laughing at the ridiculous cave antics.

We also love it because because it's hokey and inadequate. That's partly why we enjoy the ride even more when it breaks down. My niece Becky told me that once when she was little she was on the original ride with her dad and the train suddenly stopped partway through. The train operator "got out and started walking along the tracks. I said to my dad, 'What's going on?' " The passengers sat for about ten minutes in the dark. "And then the train started again." She loved every minute of it.

Almost everyone I talked with turned out to have a beloved breakdown story about the Cave Train Ride, old and new. I had my own semi-exciting experiences on the new one. Once we tore through the first part of the ride, and I heard the operator in back yell "Slow it down!" and then we crawled through the rest of it. Another time I arrived at the Cave Train to find it closed, and saw two confident men in dark blue coveralls enter a secret door behind the pond, reemerge, and then start the train back up. "It was only a toy some kid threw on the track," the operator explained. Even favorite Disneyland stories turn out to be about breakdowns. "We were on the Alice in Wonderland ride," Becky's mom, Gerri, told me, of a trip to Disneyland when she herself was little, "and suddenly stopped there in the dark for about ten minutes. Suddenly a man with a flashlight popped out of a toadstool and led us all outside. It was the best part of the whole trip."

What is it about the breakdown stories? Why do we love the breakdowns as much as the official ride? I think it's because the breakdown stories replicate the essence of the dark ride experience, only better, because they're *real*—sort of. We are thrilled by how the breakdown-rescue story approximates danger even better than the ride can. And at some level, we like the fact that the ride isn't perfectly constructed and can thus offer another layer of surprise in the dark. In the case of the Cave Train, the breakdowns add to our delight in the ride's absurd funkiness. That's why it was perfect that the redesigned Cave Train broke down on its maiden voyage with Mike Rotkin and the dignitaries aboard.

The Cave Train Ride, in other words, is kind of stupid. That's the key to why we loved the old Cave Train so much. Because it was an old, broken-down thing that didn't work half the time and smelled funny and wasn't the Pirates of the Caribbean by any stretch of the imagination. It was cheap; it was local; it was bad at being a ride. It was "cornier than Iowa," said the *Sentinel*, "a thrill ride without thrills." All the opinions about the new one revolve around its ability to measure up to that tackiness. The Cave Train Ride, in both renditions, is all about happy cheesiness: our joy in the fact that it doesn't quite measure up, that it's funky and weird, that this is Santa Cruz, and we like it that way. That's why I could learn to love the new one: although it's a bit too coherent and well-designed to be as bizarre as the old one, it's successfully bad at being good, and therefore good.

I learned, in the end, not to take the Cave Train Ride too seriously. I could do my whole academic analysis of cave people and what the ride was tapping into in our collective historical memory, but I'd only get so far. "It doesn't matter what's in there," said Carl Henn, bringing me up short. "People just love a dark ride."

Afterwards, when we come out of the tunnel of imaginary cave people, into the "real world," how do we emerge? Twenty-six hundred people took the Cave Train Ride on Saturday, September 1, 2002. Were they irreparably warped by the experience? I thought about those six little girls at Becky's birthday party ten years before and all the girls I'd taken the ride with since. They were all growing up into great women: strong, opinionated, savvy, self-possessed, with plenty to say about the Cave Train Ride. I'd spent an awful lot of time inside the cave myself, and I was doing okay, too. It was a small, small world in there, full of serious sexism and racism and you-name-it weird creatures. But it was also a lot of fun. We were all happy members of the cult, and none of us wanted to be deprogrammed.

Visiting the cats, 1963: left to right: Carey Couse, Laura Frank, the author. **PHOTOGRAPH BY JOSEPH L. FRANK.**

CHAPTER 3

UPSTAIRS, DOWNSTAIRS
AT THE CATS

BEFORE THEY BUILT the freeway in the 1960s, in order
to get to Santa Cruz from our house in Los Altos you had to wind
through surface streets to Saratoga, then turn left for a straight shot
to Los Gatos, and finally turn right onto Highway 17 to go over
the mountains. Highway 17 was pretty much the same terrifying
experience then that it is now, with the same sense of sudden death
potentially lurking around every corner. When I was around five or
six someone actually put up a series of giant billboards along 17 with
pictures of glowing skeletons and dead bodies rising out of coffins,
hoping, I guess, to terrify drivers into slowing down. I suspect now
that adult travelers must have found them preposterous. Mostly they
just weirded out us kids.

Highway 17 did have its pleasures, though. We always thought it
was exciting to see if the water level in Lexington Reservoir was high
enough to go over the spillway, and it was really cool if it was so high
that the live trees at its edges were part way underwater. (We were
never quite sure if that was good or bad for the trees.). My sister
and I also liked the restaurant at the top of the pass, known then as
Cloud 9. Our parents never let us stop there, but we still found it
exciting for reasons I now find unfathomable.

There was one really big moment on the car trip to the coast.
After the dull parts on the surface streets, just as we pulled right
onto 17, we'd pass two giant, white stone cats on the right hand side
of the road, tucked into a hillside. They were about twenty feet tall,

seated high and erect, sphinxlike, marking two sides of the entry to a mysterious road leading up into the oak forest. My sister and I loved those cats. They were the big event on the trip to Santa Cruz, and we always made sure we looked back at the exact right moment to catch them on the way out, then waved at them dutifully again on the way back home. Once, my parents actually stopped the car so we could see them up close, and I still have the picture: My cousin Carey, seven at the time, is on the left, then my sister and me, ten and seven, wearing matching stretch knit outfits with striped tops and knotted sailor ties across our chests. I'm seated against the cat on the right, which looms placidly above us as we both look out at the highway, me with an impish grin, the cat unfazed, as always.

As I grew up I always wondered who built those cats and what exactly was up the road they guarded. Then, one summer when I was in graduate school, living briefly in Palo Alto, I spent a week in the Hoover Institution Archives at Stanford, doing some research on the feminist movement in the 1920s for one of my professors. She had me reading the papers of a local progressive activist named Alice Park, who'd been active in the suffrage, peace, and labor movements in the early twentieth century. One day, inside a gray archival folder, I came across a small handwritten note on pristine, cream-colored paper. The letterhead at the top read:

SARA BARD FIELD

THE CATS

LOS GATOS

Above the letters sat a tiny line drawing exactly capturing my two stone cats.

I was thrilled. Not only did I suddenly know who had lived up the hill behind my cats, but it turned out that Sara Bard Field was a well-known suffrage activist and poet. She was married, I soon learned, to a bohemian fellow-poet, anarchist, and civil libertarian named Charles Erskine Scott Wood, and together they built The Cats, their estate in Los Gatos. I filed the discovery away in my head, hoping I'd write about them some day.

In the fall of 1999, well ensconced in my job and house in Santa Cruz, I was having some new linoleum put into my bathroom by a guy named Robert Balzer. While we were sitting around in my kitchen waiting for the glue to dry, I asked him where he'd grown up. "Los Gatos," he said. "Where?" "Do you know where the cats are?" "Yes," I said. "That's where Sara Bard Field and C. E. S. Wood lived." It turned out that his grandparents, Vincent and Mary Marengo, both Italian immigrants, had been Field and Wood's gardener/chauffeur and cook, respectively, during the 1920s, '30s and '40s. Robert and I both nearly fell out of our chairs. He said it was the first time in his entire life he'd ever met anyone who knew who the "crazy people" were that his grandparents had worked for. As a kid he'd wandered all over their estate, and he started telling me stories about arbors dripping with grapes, dogs with names like Brutus and Trotsky, and an upper gate shaped like a spider web. The labor historian in me was riveted by the story of these two Italian immigrants who had worked most of their lives as live-in servants to Wood and Field.

I kept thinking about Vincent and Mary Marengo and their lives in service to the two poets. I wanted to know what was going on up there at The Cats—not just who those two famous poets were and why they erected my roadside sphinxes, but how they had treated their servants and what their servants had thought of them. I knew there were two stories here; or, more precisely, one story of four intertwined lives. In this upstairs, downstairs story of masters and servants, moreover, did it matter that Wood was an anarchist, Field a feminist? How would the story of Wood and Field's bohemian dinner parties with famous authors and private-label wines change if Vincent and Mary Marengo, who cooked the dinners, washed the dishes, weeded the grapevines, and filled the bottles, were equally important?

I plunged into researching The Cats, confident of my ability to dig up the story behind them. But researching my four people turned out to be more difficult than I'd thought. I learned a lot, quickly, about Sara Bard Field and C. E. S. Wood. Vincent and Mary popped up fairly quickly, too. They were there, like quiet, efficient servants to my historical tale. But they weren't so easy to figure out. I had to piece together their story slowly, bit by bit, from a growing but not entirely satisfying pile of tiny, sometimes contradictory tidbits of information.

Researching The Cats' tale of masters and servants pulled me

The cats in their original incarnation [n.d.]. PHOTOGRAPH COURTESY OF THE HUNTINGTON LIBRARY.

into fundamental questions about the politics of local history, about who does or doesn't matter to official history, and why. I had to deploy my full range of skills as a professional historian as I plunged into archives, trolled through microfilm, and tracked down obscure documents in libraries. But at the same time, as I interviewed grandchildren of both couples and gradually pieced together their stories as best I could, I moved deeply into the very private world of family history, including, at times, my own. As more and more people shared their memories, photo albums, and opinions, the line between local history, "American history," and family memories got blurrier and blurrier, and it was easy to lose my way.

For all my training, as I tracked down my two implacable stone cats, their voluble masters, and their potentially inscrutable servants, it wasn't clear if I would ever figure out what was really going on up at The Cats. Nor was it clear whether I could, indeed, make the two couples who dwelled there equals in the eyes of history.

Zeus on the Mountaintop

IT WAS SURPRISINGLY easy to find out a lot about "Colonel" C. E. S. Wood, so much and so fast, in fact, that I even got a bit sick of him. In the UCSC Library I found a biography and memoir written by his son, and a mildly academic biography by a University of Oregon professor named Robert Hamburger. I found a published collection of Wood's writings containing additional biographical information, and I found a bibliography of everything he ever published. I could easily track down hundreds of his publications: poems, book reviews, rants, satires, letters to the editor, you name it.

Once I jumped into this sea of materials, though, it gradually became clear that Wood was not so much famous for what he wrote, as for who he was. He was what is known as a "colorful character";

and, a bit of a genius at self-promotion and successful posturing, he himself did most of the coloring. This man was never quick to underestimate himself.

Charles Erskine Scott Wood was born in 1852 and grew up in a rural area outside Baltimore, Maryland. When Wood was seventeen, his father, the first surgeon general of the U.S. Navy, packed him off to West Point. After five years of embarrassing grades, absenteeism, and general troublemaking, Wood eventually graduated in 1874 and joined the Army, which sent him west.

Wood spent the next ten years hunting down and often killing Native Americans, in Northern California, Oregon, and Washington, alternating with episodes of trying to befriend the exact same people whose lives he had been destroying. In 1877, Wood joined General O. O. Howard as a special aide in chasing the Nez Percé people across Oregon, Idaho, and Montana to the Canadian border. Wood is probably most well known for having transcribed Nez Percé Chief Joseph's famous surrender speech, in which Joseph vowed, "I will fight no more forever." Some historians even think Wood may have written the speech himself.

Putting his armed phase behind him, Wood convinced the army to let him go to law school at Columbia University in New York. By the time he graduated in 1883 he had developed a tight circle of rebellious artist friends in the city. In 1878 he married his childhood sweetheart, Nan Moale Smith, a high-society southern belle whose adolescence appears to have been one big dance card. In 1884, Wood quit the army, whisked her off to Portland, Oregon, and began a new life as a lawyer to the richest of the rich.

Here's where Wood came into his own and where his contradictions started to emerge, according to Hamburger. For a while, Wood simply played the role of elite attorney. He and Nan had six children and, with their eastern style and class pretensions, set themselves up at the top of a Portland high society eager to defer to presumably superior easterners. Wood's clients included the most elite of bankers and real estate interests; Nan, for her part, put on lavish dinner parties with just the right edge of snobbery. They built a big Victorian house, surrounded by porches and rose bushes. They hung out with all the "best people" of Portland. "He sent all us kids to the best private schools," remembers their son Erskine in his memoir. During these years Wood was appointed a lieutenant colonel in the Oregon State Militia. Although he'd only been a second lieutenant in the Army, he enjoyed letting the title "colonel" stick for the rest of his life.

Gradually, though, Colonel Wood began busting out of his role. Always a tall, handsome, dramatic figure with a wide face and an angular nose, he started wearing loose flowing shirts and European-seeming ties; he let his bushy hair grow out and sported an equally bushy beard. He crossed over from arranging public commissions for his East Coast artist friends to befriending local bohemian Left intellectuals like the famous John Reed. Gradually he started making in-your-face speeches at local meetings of the Democratic Party on topics like "philosophical anarchism." By 1905 he was openly supporting the radical Industrial Workers of the World (Wobblies) in their free-speech fights; and when the notorious anarchist Emma Goldman came to town in 1908 and was denied the right to rent a hall, Wood put her up at a girlfriend's house, found another venue, and gave a public speech introducing her. Throughout the next decade he lent his support to dozens of progressive causes.

But Wood was clearly careful to not quite chew off the business-elite hand that fed him. He continued to attract clients among Portland's richest bankers, landowners, and corporations, and appears to have been exceedingly clever at charming just about everyone into accepting, or at least ignoring, his politics. His biggest client was the French banking firm Lazard Frères, which he represented for dozens of years in trying to sell off a massive hunk of land in Southeastern

Oregon. Wood was so well-positioned in Portland that while he waited for the sale—and hence his enormous commission—he ran up debts to his banker friends of over $200,000. A lot of that money went to shoring up his position as cultural arbiter to the Portland elite. Wood was the one who knew which exact Chinese screen or European oil painting or Persian carpet to buy. Meanwhile, he started publishing poetry and prose in progressive literary magazines. It's not clear, though, whether they published him because he was good, because he was a regular donor or, in case of the *Pacific Monthly*, because he was a co-owner.

Wood was an expert at charming women, too. As he marched leftward, outward, and upward on the cultural and political fronts, he seems to have found his wife Nan too boring. During his Portland years Wood acquired several mistresses, whom he was skilled at stringing along with tales of anguished divided affections. His private secretary, Kitty Beck, twice tried marrying to get him out of her system, and eventually killed herself, as did another of his later lovers in California. No question, Wood was a potent charmer.

In 1910, his friend Clarence Darrow introduced him to Sara Bard Field. Unlike Wood's wife and previous girlfriends, Sara was more than his match on the literary front. She was beautiful; she was political; she was unhappily married. He was 58; she was 28. Wood was taken, but not so taken that he would leave his wife. For almost a decade he flung himself at Sara while simultaneously picking up other mistresses and putting off leaving Nan until the Lazard Frères land grant sale went through and presumably he'd finally be rich and independent. In 1918 the land sold at last and Wood got the full $750,000 that was his share—the equivalent of about $9.6 million today. He paid off his debts, told Nan it was over, set her up with a third of the money in a trust fund, gave another third to his kids in trust, and moved in with Sara down in San Francisco.

For years Wood had thought of himself as oppressed by marriage and social conventions. Deeply embedded in Left intellectual circles by this point and an active defender of civil liberties during World War I, at the age of 66 he was now free to live openly with Sara and devote himself to his writing. In 1919 he bought 34 acres in the hills above Los Gatos as a possible retreat. During the early 1920s the two would go down there on the train for sojourns, staying in a small house they called "the shack." In 1925, Wood and Field built a new, bigger house on the Los Gatos property and stayed there for good. Wood lived there until his death in 1944; Field stayed another eleven years and eventually died in 1974.

At The Cats, as they came to call the estate, Wood finally emerged as the bohemian cultural figure he'd been crafting for years. He and

Interior of the main house at The Cats, 1955, from a real estate flyer when the house was sold. **PHOTOGRAPH COURTESY OF THE HUNTINGTON LIBRARY.**

Sara regularly held court at their house and cultivated relationships with literary and artistic figures like Lincoln Steffens, Robinson Jeffers, Yehudi Menuhin (who lived nearby), and the composer Arthur Elkus. Wood himself had been published in small Left literary journals for years, but in 1927 he crossed over with an actual hit, *Heavenly Discourses*, a collection of pieces he'd written for Greenwich Village's famous magazine *The Masses*. In each essay Wood imagined humorous dialogues between God and various contemporary and historical figures such as Mark Twain, Madame Curie, Charles Darwin, or Thomas Paine. *Heavenly Discourses* sold 75,000 copies—not Stephen King territory, but still a strong number, even today. A 1937 sequel, *Earthly Discourses*, never did as well; nor did an anarchist tract, *Too Much Government* (1931), in which Wood railed against the institution of marriage and celebrated individual freedom. But he had claimed his place in the literary firmament.

As early as 1905, Wood declared: "I deify Rebellion. I glory in being a rebel and a fanatic." For the rest of his life Wood would indulge in this "tendency to cast himself in the heroic mold," in the words of his biographer Robert Hamburger. Even his use of "deify" and "glory" so early on presaged his later obsession with classical mythology and his own place in it—he was Pan, he was Prometheus, he was, especially, Zeus. Tracking down his books in the Special Collections archive at UC Santa Cruz, I found a copy of his collected poems, published by Sara in 1949, after his death. Someone had pasted into the frontispiece a giant signed black-and-white photograph of Wood—despite the presence of another full-page photograph of him on the following page. He's wearing some kind of silly pseudo-bohemian outfit, presumably in a vibrant color, with a loose tunic to his knees over matching harem pants, and an extra swath of fabric wrapped round his waist. And sandals, of course. He's standing with his legs far apart and his arms at his waist, elbows out, in a posture of triumphant artistic swagger. "All dimensions of his being were spacious," wrote a local paper when he died. "He was himself a kind of era and realm."

Even in his prime in the 1920s and '30s, though, Wood was most famous for being famous and for knowing famous people. "He and his wife . . . are widely known in literary circles and their guest book would disclose names of the great and the near great from many parts of the world," summarized a local paper upon his demise. Sara herself complained early on that Wood put way too much of his energy into constructing his own historical legacy. "All you say sounds as if we had been writing or should write for others to see," she objected in a 1917 letter. Sara had the guy down: "Aren't you sorry you can't be in love with yourself and get your own letters?" she needled a few months later.

It didn't take much, then, for me to grasp Wood as a man of spectacular contradictions. He regularly lambasted U.S. imperialism overseas in the early twentieth century, yet he evidently never criticized his own role in the imperial conquest of Native Americans in the Pacific Northwest. He loved to glorify the "Common Man" but put a lot of work into making it very clear that his own cultural position was as unCommon as possible. His son Erksine recalls that "one of my father's favorite stores was Goldberg-Bowen" in San Francisco. "There he was a friend of the head of the department for wines and liquors and where he made his purchases, especially when this friend would tell him of some extra fine sherry that the store had just bought, or something of that sort." Most centrally, Wood railed in his writings and speeches against "monopoly" and "greed," but never put that together with the source of his own vast wealth, a huge land monopoly in Eastern Oregon owned and sold by one of the biggest banking firms in the world, on the proceeds of which he and his multiple retainers lived for the rest of his life.

An Amazon of Feminism,
And a Poet Besides, a Real Poet

SARA BARD FIELD, by contrast, was a bit more private, if still relatively easy to track down. I could find only the briefest of two-page biographies of her. But Hamburger's biography of Wood was full of information. I also had her own writings and, most importantly, a 661-page oral history of Field done in Berkeley between 1959 and 1963. When she was alive Field had clearly been much less self-promotional than Wood, yet she was just as famous for a brief time. She dwelled in their partnership in a careful balance of self-diminishing dedication to Wood and continued protection of her own work as a poet and political activist.

Sara Bard Field was born in 1882 in Cincinnati and raised in Detroit in a strict Baptist family. In a classic mistake, she tried to escape at 18 by marrying an even stricter Baptist minister thirty years her senior, Albert Ehrgott. The couple immediately set off to Burma and then India as missionaries, returning sooner than they'd thought when the birth of her first child damaged Sara's health. They landed in Cleveland in 1903, smack dab in the middle of the vibrant milieu of Progressive reform headed by Mayor Tom Johnson. As Sara raised their two children, her more adventurous sister Mary drew her into political activism. She heard lectures by Socialist presidential candidate Eugene V. Debs; she took up the ideas of Henry George; she decided she was a socialist. She started writing poetry.

But then Ehrgott took a job in Portland, Oregon, and Field immediately felt like she was suffocating. Life as a middle-class minister's wife in stuffy, isolated Portland was a long way from the exciting political swirl she'd enjoyed in reform-era Cleveland. She had a brain, but suddenly no way to use it. Ehrgott himself was unbending when it came to their daily life and faith.

98

In 1910, the famous lawyer Clarence Darrow, who Sara had known from Cleveland (and who was her sister's sometime lover) came to town, sniffed out her distress, and invited her to dinner to meet a friend of his, C. E. S. Wood, like Ehrgott thirty years her senior. She was immediately taken with him. Here was the wind she was hoping would sweep through her life. Wood, for his part, was pulled in by Sara's ability to match, indeed surpass him on the literary front, as well as her reserved beauty. Gradually he asked her to help him with his writings, and they fell deeply in love.

Sara's relationship with Wood liberated her as a political activist and poet. In 1911 she traveled with her sister to Los Angeles to report on the trial of the McNamara brothers, anarchists charged with bombing the *Los Angeles Times*. Darrow was leading the defense in a famous show trial pitting the elite Chandler family, owners of the *Times*, against the Los Angeles labor movement and Left. In 1911 and 1912 Sara traveled on her own across the state of Oregon, speaking in the tiniest of towns on behalf of women's suffrage, which passed the state in 1912.

Both Field and Wood had a little problem, though: they were still married to other people. Field couldn't stand it. In those days divorces were not only taboo but hard to get. In 1914 she announced to Ehrgott that she was leaving him and bravely moved with just her eight-year-old daughter—leaving two other children behind— to the town of Goldfield, Nevada, where you could get a divorce after six weeks of residence. Wood, meanwhile, was stringing her along. He only lived with his wife part of the time, and everyone (including his wife) knew he had mistresses. But he wouldn't break off his marriage to be with Sara. Nor did he give up his other women, while simultaneously writing passionate letters to Sara declaring his undying love and imminent intention to be with her. Hamburger argues that Field threw herself into long-distance suffrage work again and again in these years in order to get some clarity about, distance from, and power over Wood. She, too, like his other mistresses, considered suicide.

In 1915, in a healthier maneuver that would put her on the headlines of the nation's news, Sara embarked on a car trip and speaking tour across the nation, promoting a national amendment for women's suffrage. Accompanied only by a matching set of Swedish ladies named Miss Kindstedt and Miss Kindberg, one the driver, the other the mechanic, Sara gave speech after speech. By the time she reached New York she was so famous she was received with a ticker-tape parade. In Washington she and 500 other women presented a petition in person to President Woodrow Wilson. (Women's suffrage would eventually pass Congress in 1919 and be ratified in 1920.) In New York, she stayed a long while with Max Eastman and his partner Ida Rauh, at the center of the Greenwich Village bohemian elite.

After the trip Sara moved back to San Francisco, where her ex-husband nastily tried to keep her children from seeing her and where she awaited Wood's visits. Finally, in 1918, Wood's land-grant money came through, and he told his wife he wanted out. She wouldn't agree to a divorce—she wanted to keep her lofty social position as Mrs. C. E. S. Wood—but he gave her a third of the money and left for good. Together at last in San Francisco, Wood and Field launched their new life as a couple.

Then the worst happened. While driving her 18-year-old son's new car up a dangerously steep hill in Marin in 1918, Sara couldn't get the car into gear, and it slid backwards, off the road, and rolled down the hillside. Albert, her son, was killed; Wood and her daughter Kay were unhurt. Sara was devastated, her leg crushed along with her life spirit. She spent the next year in a deep fog of depression, as her leg mended, but not her soul. Eventually a deeply dedicated Wood pulled her out of her depression and into a world of progressive theater, poetry readings, and political engagement in the Bay Area.

They started their visits to "the shack" in Los Gatos.

In 1925 Wood and Field built their proper house at The Cats, where Field presided over the dinner parties that soon made their retreat famous. In adjoining studies up on the hill, the two of them wrote in private during the day, then joined later for dinner and social contact. Sara published two books of poetry during these years: *The Pale Woman* (1927) and *Darkling Plain* (1936). Both speak deeply of the meaning of love, of death, and of loss. The death of her son is as palpable as her appreciation of her new life with Wood. She also published a narrative prose poem, *Barabbas* (1932), the Biblical story of a man the Romans freed instead of Jesus, whose resultant anguish

C. E. S. Wood and Sara Bard Field [n.d.]. PHOTOGRAPH COURTESY OF THE HUNTINGTON LIBRARY.

led him to a Christian faith. During these years Field also regularly self-published small booklets of her poems and writings, such as annual lofty bits renouncing the commercialism of Christmas, or a long depiction of her daughter's marriage, *The Beautiful Wedding*, in which she described herself as a "An Amazon of Feminism and poet beside, a real poet."

But Field and Wood's most important creation, the two came to insist, was their love—what Robert Hamburger calls their "tendency to view their love, their lives, as an ongoing work of art, as a beautiful story." With Wood, nothing could be ordinary; so this late-in-life great romance had to be like no one else's. In 1934 the two commissioned Lawrence Tenney Stevens to sculpt a seven-foot-high, four-foot-square limestone portrait of themselves together, to commemorate their great love.

Sara appears to have been pulled into Wood's vision. But she was always much more reserved than he, more careful, less likely to pronounce and more likely to tastefully carry herself as someone with a great deal of dignity and a certain sense of style. Pictures of Sara in her later years show a still classically-beautiful woman with long, slightly wavy gray hair pulled back in a low bun; she always has a subtle, artistic edge to her collar or dress or necklace.

In 1933 ,Wood's wife died in Portland. Five years later, in a bow to convention, he and Sara were married in a simple ceremony on the hillside at The Cats. Wood was 86, she was 56. By this point the age difference was catching up to them, and she spent most of the late thirties and early forties tending to an ailing Wood until he passed away in 1944. She herself lived for another thirty years. "Although she tried bravely to carry on," her daughter later wrote, "her life, in its deepest meaning, ended with his."

By 1959, when a member of the Berkeley oral history project interviewed her extensively, Field was still better known in her own right as a nationally prominent suffrage activist than as Wood's partner, and the interviewer spent much of her time documenting Field's early life and exact opinions of various other suffrage activists. In the end, her fate wasn't all that different from Wood's: between the interviewer's questions about famous suffrage activists ("what was so-and-so like?") and her extensive queries about famous visitors to The Cats, at least half the final volume isn't about Field—or even about Wood—but about other, more famous people whose paths they crossed.

Upstairs, Downstairs at the Huntington

IT WASN'T SO HARD, then, to get a bead on C. E. S. Wood and Sara Bard Field and the broad sweep of their life at The Cats. But I wanted to know just as much about Vincent and Mary Marengo, too, Wood and Field's servants, who were still largely invisible in the biographies. Hamburger had based much of his book on Wood and Field's private papers, deposited at the Huntington Library in Pasadena, California. Pulling my head out of the books, I decided to make a pilgrimage to the Huntington and see what I could find.

Staying with friends in Santa Monica, out on the west side of Los Angeles near the ocean, I got up bright and early on a summer morning and drifted with the commuters along the Harbor Freeway toward downtown L.A. As the flow of traffic sucked me past the big, sleek high rises, I took silly pleasure in humming the theme from "L.A. Law," then got it stuck in my head for the rest of the week. I soon funneled out onto the Pasadena Freeway, which spat me out near downtown Pasadena after twenty minutes or so. Just after I turned right on California Boulevard toward the Huntington, I passed—believe it or not—"Marengo Avenue."

I'd heard of the Huntington for years, mostly from a friend who writes about California history. What is now a semi-public place was originally the very private estate of a man named Henry Huntington (nephew of the railroad magnate Collis P. Huntington), who in the first decade of the twentieth century made a fortune in real estate. On a 600-acre tract of land he built a series of Italian-villa-style palaces, gracefully arrayed across scenic lawns and surrounded by some of the most beautiful gardens in the entire world. Today the villas contain art galleries featuring Huntington's collections, gardens open to the public, and a famous research library specializing in books and documents from eighteenth-century Britain and the U.S. West.

Passing big, beautiful Craftsman-style houses with increasingly well-maintained yards the closer I got to the Huntington grounds, I drove up to the entry booth, explained I was going to use the library, and got waved in by the guard. He pointed me through the trees to its entryway, tucked between two big, white, vaguely classical buildings. Striding confidently into the doors marked "Library," I gave my name to the volunteer at the front desk and was seated in a floral-patterned chair in the front lobby. Even though I'd called ahead a few days before, I still had to wait fifteen minutes before someone came to fetch me. This was my first warning that the Huntington might not be the most welcoming place.

A hip-looking woman named Suzi Krasnow came out to meet me. She was pleasant and businesslike and led me down a long hall to a cluster of desks behind a little gateway. I had to fill out a form with my I.D. and references, and was eventually bedecked with a peach-colored name tag with "Reader" on it and my expiration date in big numbers.

After we used the tag to get me past a security guard, Suzi gave me a gracious tour of the research library. She showed me various card catalogs, a room full of shelved books, and pointed out the various reading rooms lining the sides of a long, quiet hall. The entire place was demarcated by different gradations of privilege, almost none of which I could enjoy. Upstairs were the offices given to Fellows who had year-long research grants and their names posted on a wall. To the right through noiseless swinging doors was a long, wood-paneled reading room arrayed with nests of long, flat wooden carrels and low green lamps. I wasn't allowed in there, though—that room was for the people with the six-month fellowships. We crossed, instead, into the Ahmanson Reading Room, a long, wide room with its own warren of carrels—assigned to other, shorter-term Fellows. Mere day trippers like me were allowed to use the three less-attractive tables in the middle.

This place made my skin crawl. The forbidden wood-paneled reading room, in particular, reminded me of an identical room at Yale, where I went to graduate school, which itself was modeled on Oxford and Cambridge. Women, even enrolled graduate and professional students, had been banned from the room until the 1970s, a few years before I got there. At the Huntington, the old-world caste system of graduated privileges seemed even more absurd than at Yale, here in the glaring sun of Southern California, surrounded by palm trees.

I waited obediently until Peter Blodgett, the curator in charge of the Wood and Field Collection, came out to meet with me. I'd known Peter at Yale, where he was several years ahead of me in the graduate program. He gave me various tips about mapping the collection, and I padded back into the reading room. It was full of maybe two dozen men in tweed suits and a few women with artsy eyeglass chains, poring silently over old books with leather spines and marble-paper covers, or documents on parchment written in illegible handwriting. In case I thought I was imagining things, I even spotted a light gray sweatshirt with "YALE" on it draped over the back of a chair.

With all the processing and delays, by now it was lunchtime, and we all got kicked out until 1:30. I was happy to emerge past the guards into the glorious gardens, with their Italian villa lines of sight and sculptures of nude men on pedestals. I strolled toward the tea room in the rose garden to buy lunch in the small cafeteria for Readers.

Waiting to pay the cashier, everything changed. The young man in his late twenties in front of me in line recognized me from my name tag. He and his wife, who I quickly met, were Yale graduate students in U.S. history; they knew my work. They pulled me immediately into a world of common friends and scholarly exchange, and brought me over to their table on the patio under the trees outside, where they enthusiastically encouraged me to join their group. It included two or three academic acquaintances of mine, and even one fellow labor historian, Alex Lichtenstein, who reminded me he'd been my student in a seminar I'd taught at Yale in the 1980s. In about three minutes I went from alienated outsider to a welcome insider who was a member of the club—the Yale club, at that. Here in sunny California, the institutions of intellectual elitism had long arms, and they were wrapped warmly around me.

As I returned to the Huntington on many days over the next year, though, I was always conscious of all the other people on the estate. Not the researchers, but the sea of people who, like Vincent Marengo, weeded and groomed and mowed those beautiful expansive gardens; the hive of aides who fetched boxes of documents for us in the library; and the endless security guards everywhere. I thought about Suzi, the intake woman, who turned out to be very cool; about the person who did my photocopying but whom I never met; about the cooks, dishwashers and cashiers at the tea room.

As I deposited my purse in a locker every morning before entering the research area, and then visited the locker room for various reasons during the day, I eventually became conscious that this was also a staff break room. While we Readers trotted off to the tea room for discounted gourmet food, the guards brought their lunches in paper bags and ate in this room next to vending machines. Reading a job notice on the wall one day, I asked the security guard next to me what he got paid. He said he started at $9.25 an hour, with an extra $1.10 for the swing shift. He estimated that maybe 100 people worked as guards at the Huntington. The majority of those I saw were people of color. As I put my purse away another day, I asked another man lightly: "How's the life of a security guard at the Huntington?" "Pretty good at times." "How is it as a job?" "Okay sometimes." He paused. "You know, in 27 years that's the first time anybody's asked me that."

Despite my insider status, I never felt like I fit in. Other academic friends of mine turned out to have the same experience: they all felt like outsiders who didn't belong, and were conscious, too, of the class and race politics of the place. Not coincidentally, they were mostly of Mexican descent. They all told me stories but insisted I change their names if I used them—they were afraid they wouldn't be allowed back in. "Queta Durazo" told me she'd arrived for her first research trip driving her dad's shiny copper pickup truck, references in hand, and announced at the front gate that she was there to use the research library. The woman in the booth had kindly informed her, "Honey, you know this isn't the kind of library where you can check out books." Another friend who did research at the Huntington on and off for years, said right off: "I never felt like I belonged." One day, he was at lunch in the rose garden with Ramon Gutiérrez, a famous Chicano historian who received a MacArthur "genius" grant. "I saw my roommate in college's father; he was a gardener here. It was an awkward moment. . . . Clearly he couldn't sit down at the table with us."

Before I even opened a single box of Wood and Field's papers at the Huntington, searching for their own invisible servants, I was replicating their lives myself: hobnobbing with elite intellectuals, following my own artistic interests, supported by a bevy of servants who disappeared from view. And however uncomfortable I might feel, however much I felt like an outsider, however much I wanted to identify with the workers at the Huntington, I was, in fact, inside, and a member of the club.

Highway Beautification

THE COLLECTION OF Wood and Field's papers in the Huntington was daunting. Its directory listed a total of 312 boxes plus another 43 in an addendum, containing altogether around 32,000 different items—photographs, drawings, manuscripts, diaries, clippings, scrapbooks, leaflets, and, especially, 193 boxes of correspondence. Peter, the curator, told me that the collection is very popular among researchers, not because they're interested in Wood and Field (and all those overblown love letters Wood wrote for prosperity, alas); but rather because they're interested in the more famous people like Bennett Cerf or Robinson Jeffers or Roger Baldwin or Muriel Rukeyser who wrote to them.

Right off it was easy to learn about my two stone cats. In the directory I discovered a file called "Clippings—The Cats." In the master list of correspondents I found Robert Paine, who Hamburger had said was their sculptor. Dutifully I filled out the order forms at the reference desk and waited for the page to fetch the two boxes. Putting their contents together with a few old newspaper clippings I later found at the Los Gatos Public Library, I was able to reconstruct pretty well the history of the cat sculptures and how they'd been created. Just this small piece of the story turned out to reveal a lot about Wood and Field—their artistic ambitions, their generosity, their self-importance, and the tendency of Wood, in particular, to overdramatize everything. I could see their ambivalence about "the People," who sometimes turned out to be bit ungrateful and unwashed. I didn't find Vincent and Mary, yet; but I was starting to get some clues about class dynamics up at The Cats.

At some point in 1919 or 1920, after they bought the property but before they built the main house, the Colonel and Sara decided to put up some kind of monumental sculpture near the entrance to their estate. "My wife and I had a sort of mania to prove that California was the American Italy—the very place for outdoor drama, outdoor sculptures and so on," Wood recalled in a 1931 newspaper article. Several other properties lay between the highway and their own estate, so they bought a small piece of land right where the dirt road turned off the highway. "We thought if we could put up on the highway . . . some very imposing and dignified sculpture in the cheap material of concrete, it would be an example that would inspire others to do likewise, and possibly towns and road districts would bring in sculpture as a decoration for parks and bridges and buildings."

Wood cast himself as benevolent instructor: "If we are to make youth of our country interested in art, they ought to live with it daily. It ought to be part of their common experience—not something set aside for the occasional visit to a museum or a park."

The poets were casting about among their Bay Area artist friends for a sculptor when Robert Paine approached them about commissioning a work. Paine had worked for the prominent American sculptors August Saint-Gaudens and Frederick McMonnies, helped out on sculptures for the 1893 Chicago World's Fair and the 1915 Panama-Pacific Exposition, and spent two years in Rome copying a famous statue of two chariots. He appears to have been most known for inventing a mechanical device used to exactly replicate sculptures. The only photograph of him I found shows a narrow-shouldered, long-faced man with blonde hair brushed straight back from his forehead and a pair of pince-nez spectacles perched on a long, straight nose. He's got just the hint of a smile, suggesting a mild-mannered amiability. Field described him as "an eccentric," "a rugged character," "a very odd and delightful creature." Wood just said he was "an anarchist."

According to Wood, Paine offered to design two sculptures at The Cats in exchange only for "the day wages of a mason" and lodgings while he designed and built them. Wood loved the notion that Paine was so dedicated to the project that he worked for almost nothing. Paine "believed that the artist who gained such joy from his work should not be paid large sums of money for it which make the artist's labor prohibitive for those of small means," wrote Wood on a subsequent occasion; "he insisted on taking only a day laborer's wage" (dropping, we can note, the wage rate in this version). But it seems just as likely that Paine didn't have any other work, saw an opportunity to execute an important piece, and wasn't averse to free rent and steady wages. In her oral history, Sara says that Paine "had never had a chance to do a heroic thing on his own."

Together the poets and Paine settled on two monumental cats. "We chose the cats as a figure," Wood later explained, "not because of any definite reference to this locality of Los Gatos—'The Cats'— but because at all times and everywhere the cat has suggested itself as one of the most beautiful forms for sculpture. We discussed bears, men, horses, bulls,—but finally, with the strong preference of the sculptor himself, we selected cats, and we did then select the wild cat in colossal form, because of Los Gatos."

In the fall of 1920 Paine moved from Los Altos to Los Gatos to live in the shack (Wood and Field were still living in San Francisco at the time). He'd already been sketching domestic cats and the big wild ones at the San Francisco Zoo. On December 2, Paine wrote Wood: "I will have a paper silhouette suggestion of the cats at one or both of two places following out your suggestion as to placing them as such seemed to me best, or at any other place you may have thought better." He suggested "the entrance to the place," where the cats could sit on a pedestal "of perhaps two thirds their own height." At this point—despite later pronouncements that he'd always wanted them by the highway—Wood was still considering a site farther up the road, where the road turned to cross a culvert.

Paine not only made sketches, but sculpted twenty or thirty little clay models of cats until he got what he wanted. "The feeling is the whole thing as you said it must be," he wrote Wood. "A cat is to me to be an appetite as ferocious yet as suppressed and unconscious as a tree's and must be done with a serenity more deep and enduring than a red-wood forest's." Paine then sculpted the first full-size cat in clay, from which a plaster mold to pour the final, concrete cat would be made.

By some point in late 1921 or 1922, Wood and his architect, Walter Steilberg, had settled on the site down by the highway. The cats were finally poured into two different molds, the casings removed, and they began their serene gaze out at the highway. Actually, one only is gazing, eyes wide open. The other has its eyes closed, its ears back. Contrary to my sure-bet memory, they aren't twenty feet high, but only eight. And they're made of concrete, not stone.

Wood and Field's cats quickly got the attention they'd wanted. The sculptures "soon became popular landmarks to travelers on their way to Monterey and Carmel," Hamburger notes. The problem was, they got some other attention, too. By 1930 the cats had been vandalized five times—with paint, with lipstick, with chisels. On Halloween night, 1930, the *San Francisco Bulletin* reported, Wood found them "painted all over in red and black, with the neck of one cat badly mutilated and an ear chipped from the other."

Wood and Field were irate, and not reluctant to show their own claws. In letters to and interviews with local newspapers over the next few days, they reiterated their own noble, selfless goal in erecting the cats—to bring art and beauty to the community—and decried the outrageousness of the cats' defacement: "Nearly everybody appreciates them as works of art, quite apart from civic pride. They have appeared in various articles all over the United States. We have received letters of interested inquiry from both foreign and domestic tourists, and their pictures have appeared to our knowledge in Los Angeles, Chicago, and Paris," Wood boasted. "Yet they are permitted to be destroyed." Writing later in the Los Gatos paper, he roared: "It is probably too much to expect them to be appreciated by the half-grown mind—childish, and perhaps moron intelligence of youth. These immature, childish intellectuals have seen in them only a subject for childish pranks." Apparently those he called the "latest defacers in this growth of rivalry in moronism" had failed to be sufficiently uplifted by art.

Wood soon toned it down a bit, only to cast a broader blame: "We know it is only by some small group of misguided young people without any knowledge of art; but also we know it has never aroused any real protest—any real interest—any real action by the people of Santa Clara County, to whom really the cats were intended to belong." Not so subtly, he suggested that he and Field might move the sculptures elsewhere if the people did not show their concern. "There is apparently not the slightest conception of Art in the community," he declared, or the cats would have been protected. "And let me conclude in saying it is not the thoughtless, foolish and ignorant people who are to blame, but it is the attitude of the whole people." Casting his supposed selfless dedication aside, Wood was furious, his contempt for the masses palpable. They had failed to keep up their end of some implicit bargain in which he graciously donated to the People, who in turn were supposed to properly revere his work.

The People, evidently shamed, did respond. Soon the Los Gatos Fire Department showed up to help restore the cats. The police department promised to station an officer in a car nearby every Halloween. For seventeen years the marauders were held back at the gate.

Then in 1947 they struck again; and this time it was Sara, on her own now for three years, who lashed out. On Halloween night someone poured red paint on one of the cats (rather artistically, it must be granted) so it looked like blood was dripping from its mouth and down to its paws. In a long letter to the *Los Gatos Mail-News*, Field let loose on city officials. "No police officer was near when the present outrage was committed." A week had passed, but "there has been no effort on the part of the community to discover who were the perpetrators of this vandalism . . . nor has the public shown the slightest interest in the matter." Equally important, "There has been no attempt, as there was before . . . to impress upon the children the honor due to works of art nor has the writer received any suggestion of community aid in restoring the sculpture if indeed, restoration is possible."

Field threatened to "take drastic action" and move or even destroy the cats if the public didn't protect them. She was also angry that cretins in town were profiteering from the cats. "The profit approach to art except in spiritual terms is distasteful to me but the fact is that the town of Los Gatos has had thousands of dollars worth of free advertising from the presence of these noble sculptures. With no benefit to us, indeed, without even our permission being asked, . . . picture post cards of the cats have been and are being made by the hundreds and are mailed all over the world."

She added proudly that she and Mr. Wood had received letters about the cats from European travelers "who recognize them as great sculpture." But Field was also clearly offended that the People, to whom she and Wood had given the cats, had their own independent, even profit-making ideas about how to celebrate them.

A few days later Field wrote again to "thank the people for their warm, understanding response not only through the written word but through the practical act of cleaning the defaced statue." Two employees of the city of Los Gatos had used cleaning fluid and paint remover to take off the offending paint. Sara also thanked all those who had expressed their love of the cats. "True works of art intimately associated with daily life imperceptibly become accepted as standards of beauty, and the cheap, vulgar, and ugly automatically rejected. In the nearly quarter century these cats have stood at the southern approach to our town I think they have silently taught some, at least, of a whole generation what noble sculpture in our very midst can do."

"Fate of 'Cats' Up to Wood's Buyer" announced the *Los Gatos Daily Times* in January 1953, when Sara put the estate up for sale. "I can't imagine that anyone buying the property would do anything to them," she told a reporter. "They are such an integral part of the place." She admitted that she "had been approached on several occasions with plans to move the landmarks into the town of Los Gatos," but preferred they "remain in the wooded hollow."

In 1955, Bruce and Diane Ogilvie bought the estate, and named the sculptures Leo and Leona. Vandals struck again in June 1964. For those of us who love the cats, the press photograph is painful to look at: this time they knocked off one cat's ears and the top of its head. The damaged cat looks eerily more ferocious than ever, with its slanted eyes wide open.

Although it's not clear when or how the Ogilvies restored the cats to their current incarnation; by later decades the story of the cats' original creation had taken on mythical elements that snowballed over time in the local papers. Paine, the sculptor, got more and more eccentric with each retelling; now it took him not two but three or sometimes four years to complete them. Now he had designed and built them for free out of pure dedication to art. "Mr. Paine lived almost as a monk" while creating the cats, one story in the late 1940s or '50s rhapsodized. "His diet consisted mostly of rice." Wood and Field weren't wealthy, we were told. The cats were now made of marble rather than poured concrete. One was now male, one female. And they'd always been named Leo and Leona, they were always chosen to reflect the town's name, and they were always going to be placed by the roadside.

In the end, C. E. S. Wood and Sara Bard Field weren't so misguided, really, in their highway beautification campaign. Generations of travelers did appreciate the cats, including a lot of children, including me. Like my own private redwood tree slice at Big Basin, my beloved cats were special to me and also to thousands of other people. I wouldn't have my private memory of either, in fact, if they weren't public objects, placed deliberately so children would be instructed. Even my photograph of my sister, my cousin, and myself was probably one of thousands taken as other families, too, picnicked at the base of the cats.

The sculptures embodied perfectly and for generations Field's and especially Wood's vision of themselves as artistic benefactors to the masses. But the cats' full story also turned out to reveal the poets' notion of themselves as a superior elite, more far-thinking, more generous, more culturally refined than others. And despite their self-deceptions, Wood and Field weren't entirely selfless. They expected recognition of their superiority and beneficence, or got incensed.

The Servant Solution

BUT WHAT ABOUT Vincent and Mary Marengo, the Colonel and Sara's servants at The Cats? I still hadn't begun to scratch the surface of their story. At the Huntington I pored over the guide to those 355 boxes in the Wood and Field collection, trying to figure out where they'd appear. In the "Correspondence" file, I did find one letter from Vincent to Wood, and two short notes from Mary to Sara. But the real gold mine was Wood and Field's diaries from the 1920s through the 1950s. Sitting in the Huntingon's reading room, day after day, reading the diaries, Vincent and Mary finally appeared at The Cats, woven throughout the two poets' entries. As I pieced together their daily lives and tried to figure out their different characters and relationships, it was fascinating to unpack who did what, and who thought what about whom.

But as Vincent and Mary gradually emerged into view, I had to keep reminding myself that I was seeing only the two employers' version of their servants. Except for those three brief letters, literally everything I learned was from the poets' point of view. Part of the fascination, though, was not just reading Wood's overblown, often delightfully witty if self-indulgent writing, but watching how Vincent's own personality and ideas—if not Mary's—popped through at times, if only fleetingly.

On May 5, 1923, C. E. S. Wood began his first diary entry at The Cats. "These books are dedicated by us . . . to our rough little mountain vineyard at Los Gatos and the rough little shack . . . which is the most wonderful home—every hour happiness." He and Sara were still living in San Francisco, and using The Cats as a retreat. "These little rooms and a stove-fireplace kitchen [are] the very heart of the home where we love to cook and eat and in the evening, by the fire read aloud some instructive moral book such as Anatole France or Rabelais—or poetry." Wood introduced the reader to Vincent and his labors in this very first entry: "Vincent is our Italian young man and all work—from plumbing to gardening, but chiefly he presides over *our* vineyard, prunes, ploughs, cultivates, suckers—erects scarecrows, scare-deer—scare-coyotes scare-jays and other devices for preserving a part of the grapes for us."

Clearly Vincent's life was indeed in many ways "all work." He lived in town in these years, but evidently worked at least six days a week up at The Cats. He dug, terraced, planted, and weeded the extensive flower and vegetable gardens that spiraled up and down the estate's steep hillsides, Wood's diaries show. He planted, pruned, and watered at least seven different kinds of fruit and nut trees. He built all sorts of walkways, structures, furniture, and devices, as directed by Wood or on his own. Although Wood never mentions it, Vincent must have cleared out the poison oak that would have originally covered those hillsides and continued to crop up. Erskine, Sara, and Vincent always had an assortment of dogs, and Vincent with great humor and affection fed, bathed, and doctored them. He even made them their own cement bathtub. He did all the vineyard work: planting the hillside; tending, weeding, and picking the grapes; and then bottling the red wine labeled "Princess" that Wood and Field drank and gave out as presents.

Vincent also seems to have done an awful lot of fetching: bringing up the mail every morning, running into town for groceries, moving objects up and down the hillside. "Vincent laid our milk and bread on the porch," Wood wrote of one lovely morning at the shack. In January, 1928, he wrote that he'd picked a basket of wildflowers and when the basket got too heavy, left it for Vincent to find and bring down to the house. And Vincent drove his employers around a lot: into Los Gatos, to the train station in San José and back, to friends and the opera in San Francisco, to doctors' appointments all over the Bay Area, to Wood's daughter, Lisa, in Marin County, and once even all the way up to Ashland, Oregon, to pick up the Colonel. During

Main house at The Cats, under construction, 1927.
PHOTOGRAPH IN COLLECTION OF MAY ARMANN;
REPRODUCTION BY VICTOR SCHIFFRIN.

nine months in 1924, while the poets were in Italy and New York, Vincent was responsible for running the whole place himself.

When they returned and decided to move permanently to Los Gatos, house construction began. Walter Steilberg designed a U-shaped, single-story structure tucked into the hillside, made of then-avant-garde cinder blocks (which turned out to leak for decades), with three bedrooms, a big living room in the center, a kitchen, a laundry room, and a solarium upstairs. The two wings embraced a courtyard with a fountain in the middle for which Wood and Field commissioned a sculpture of three little children, by Benjamino Bufano. A giant, bare-breasted two-story statue of "Maia," by Robert Stackpole, loomed two stories above a broad mural facing the patio. It wasn't a exactly a mansion, but more like a dramatic artists' retreat that was anything but a regular house. Vincent, aided by fellow Italian workmen from Los Gatos, did most of the work constructing the house and its outbuildings.

In these early years, when Wood and Field were living in the shack on and off, they apparently did their own cooking and housework. One night, Wood reported in his diary, they dined on "Turnips,—green peas—asparagus tips omelette from our own bed (the asparagus) and crisp bacon." Wood apparently did a lot of cooking himself and seems to have enjoyed it—at least he enjoyed reporting he'd done it. He made a cabbage soup for the construction crew one day, and soon after reported making his "daily pot of soup for the men." On another occasion he boasted, "I invented a new dish." Although she herself doesn't discuss it much in her own diaries, Sara cooked, too, baking a lemon pie and other desserts Wood mentions.

The exact division of labor between the two of them remains a mystery. It's clear, though, that Field consciously sought to do more than her share overall. In her oral history, the interviewer asked Field whether Wood was able to keep the "little practical things" going while he worked on his writing. Field replied: "Well, of course I took a great deal of that off his shoulders. He never, for instance, had to make out a check for a bill. Wherever I could see a person on a matter of mundane concern, I did it if I could to relieve him, because my one great ambition besides my own poetry was to give him all the help I could." "That probably meant that you had a little less time to spend on your own work," commented the interviewer. "Yes, it did."

In their life at the shack and after they first moved into the new house, Sara appears to have been the default setting for cooking—if only because Wood tended to crow about anything he did do. Wood did seem aware that cooking and housework were indeed work, and needed to be done—perhaps because he himself performed it at times. Once, in early 1925, he reported in a somewhat convoluted entry that upon his return from presenting a series of lectures in San Francisco on "Poetry in Drama, Drama in Poetry," Sara greeted him "with a gladness unspeakable—also with a fresh baked apple pie and gold cake—and a pan of Boston baked beans—so that when I recited my manifold activities in the city I could point to these culinary feats and say, 'I, too, have not been idle.'" He also once reported corralling unwilling houseguests into cleaning up. When a woman he referred to as "the crazy Helen Todd" visited, Wood reported that she "put on an apron on my command washed the lunch dishes—set the table." Another entry from this period, however, suggests that Vincent usually had responsibility for cleaning up: "We got our own dinner . . . . we piled the dishes for Vincent tomorrow—some people dont [sic] even pile them—and finished our reading of Shelley."

In late 1924, as they planned the new house, though, Wood was starting to rethink the arrangements. "We need more rooms," he wrote. "To live here we must have accommodation for a servant *and* for our books." By January 1926, he'd had enough of the romance of roughing it:

After washing dishes and doing the house work we went for a walk—this housework is a problem that must be solved or we will have garnered nothing by fleeing from the social demands of the City. By the time we have cooked—washed the dishes for two meals a day—made the beds—cleaned the house—there is neither that calm leisure for contemplation and creation nor the nerve strength which is needed—we have done almost nothing. It is a disturbing fact at present but I[t] is very plain that the real obstacle to creative work is going to be this household drudgery for which we should have a servant.

The servant problem wasn't so easily solved, though, even with servants' quarters. "Yet on this hill in the seclusion we want—no servant will—nor will want to walk up here and back in all weathers. Perhaps after all the only solution is as [Lincoln] Steffens insists—to live in Italy where you know nobody—and servants are abundant and cheap."

So much for living like the masses. Fortuitously, Vincent Marengo soon provided the solution to Wood and Field's housework problem. Italy came to Los Gatos—or, rather, had already colonized it. Enter Mary Gagliasso, formerly Benevelli, soon to be Marengo. And a second great love story.

On January 8, 1924—without any previous mention of Mary, Wood suddenly reports a truly amazing story: "Vincent brings us encouraging news today—He says that since 'Mary' sold to a husband in Italy at 18 and drudge breeder and wage earner for twenty years ran away some five months ago to get her freedom 12 wives have run away from their husbands in the Italian Colony of Los Gatos." "I know nine last month—myself," Vincent reported. Wood was just as astonished as Vincent, and unleashed his best literary excess: "Surely we have not lived in vain. But Mary—Mary to lead such a revolt—a jellyfish defying sharks—a jack rabbit spitting in the face of coyotes—a dove leading the dove cote against eagles—Mary the timid—the dumb—the gentle the spineless the obedient the subservient the coward—Well."

We never hear another word about the other twelve ladies and their feminist revolution in Italian Los Gatos. But Mary's story continues. A year later, Wood writes that Vincent and Mary would like to live at The Cats. "Well Mary's tragedy goes on and the romance hangs fire because of the difficulty of a divorce from a husband with the idea that he owns Mary." Here we get a hint of why she left (and a

Left: Mary Gagliasso (not yet Marengo) [n.d.];
right: Pasqually Gagliasso, Mary's first husband [n.d.].
PHOTOGRAPHS IN COLLECTION OF MAY ARMANN;
REPRODUCTION BY VICTOR SCHIFFRIN.

lot more of Wood's dramatic prose): "Love be damned. A wife is a man's sex joy and kitchen drudge and of children—let her add them to her cares—and if she earns wages they are his—and why not slap her if he feels like it—? Is she not his dog?" Mary's children, he reported, were caught in the middle: "And the frightened cowardly children—afraid of him, of the church and of the public opinion of the Italian colony—hang back and will not testify for her—hoping to force her to abandon the divorce suit."

By a final entry in late August, the plot had thickened further. "Tomorrow we intend to drive over to San José with Vincent partly to see his attorney . . . about the $100,000 lawsuit brought by Galassio—Mary's husband against Vincent for alienating Mary's affections." Wood loved the very concept:

> It certainly is comic—Mary was struck—beaten—reviled—
> worked hard for wages—her wages taken and when she
> wearied of this and struck [off] some one must be found
> who alienated her affections—I think a club is a pretty good
> alienator itself—that Mary & Vincent love each other may
> easily be—Vincent is kindly and chivalrous—decent—but
> alienating, bosh—nobody alienates affections.

By 1926 Mary was working days at The Cats, but not yet, evidently, living with Vincent. In the one letter I found from Vincent, dated October 31, 1926, he writes to Wood: "Mary called up Mr. Luise and he dind liket becouse she vase working up her he dindt think it was a good adea but I dont tink it is nothing bad because mary goese home avry night and the men bring her up in the morning and I take her down in the evening." I never figured out who this "Mr. Luise" was. But we can imagine the lovely walks home in the evening that Vincent and Mary shared, down the hill from The Cats through the oak forest into town.

We can also try to imagine all the work that Mary did during her days at The Cats. She was clearly cooking lunches and dinners from then on. Wood never again mentions or complains of cooking or cleaning. At one point Sara refers to Mary making the beds, cleaning the bathrooms. But the details of Mary's labors—unlike Vincent's—are starkly absent from both poets' diaries. All we get is an occasional praise of "Mary's spaghetti a la Milanese." Neither Sara nor the Colonel recorded the details of Mary's work in the way Wood recorded Vincent's. In part that was because Vincent worked for Wood, Mary worked for Sara, and Sara's diary entries were more terse. But it also could have reflected the general devaluation of women's work in the home—which was assumed to be women's natural, biologically assigned role or an act of familial love, not really "work" as in other jobs, and hence invisible.

In the years that followed, Wood and Field were famous for their dinner parties, often held outdoors. The literary figures and artists they invited would have eaten Mary's food, left her their dirty dishes. Sometimes they stayed for days, eating more food, dirtying more sheets and towels. Most days, though, the two poets preferred time alone to write, in their adjoining studios up the hill. As the fame of their estate spread, visitors increasingly arrived uninvited, interrupting them. Sara recounts that she and Erskine had their studios built deliberately far away from the main house, up the hill, so that Mary could tell drop-ins they weren't home and be telling the truth. We can imagine, though, that the drop-ins did interrupt Mary's work regularly.

One additional source gave me a glimpse of Vincent and Mary's labors in the years that followed. In a self-published 1927 celebration of her daughter Kay's wedding, entitled *The Beautiful Wedding*, Sara describes at lofty length the preparations at The Cats. First, she says, Vincent helped make the tiles to finish the new house's fountain and courtyard; then he and his cousin Dominic laid the tiles in the blazing hot sun. Then the two men cut a new path through the hillside, cleaned the whole place, cut and arrayed tree boughs, and along with Mary extracted "vases, bowls, porcelain, bronze and baskets from store rooms and made [them] ready for flowers." Vincent and Mary, she claimed, loved the work. "Had it been their own wedding there could not have been more ecstasy. Maria, to whom God has given two very great gifts, the arrangement of flowers and the making of delectable dishes, whether roasts, stews, pastries or cakes, saw at once a world for her to conquer and launched into plans." During the wedding itself Mary worked in the kitchen and Vincent directed traffic. The ceremony "was all bathed in love . . . with Vincent and Domenic [sic] working Sundays and after hours for no extra charge," despite horrible heat. Sara described Mary as "fluttering" like a bird "above a beloved nest."

In 1928 or '29 the poets built a gatehouse home for Vincent and Mary, finally solving the live-in servant problem. It perched by the side of the entry road, with a balcony overlooking the valley and a garage for Vincent's truck. Erskine and Sara, Vincent and Mary; the two loving couples lived together at The Cats for the next fifteen years. When Wood died in 1944, a newspaper clipping reported, he left $500 to Vincent in his will, $500 to Mary, $100 to Dominic, and the rest to Sara; his children already had their trust funds. The diaries get sparser into the 1930s and '40s—most years are missing, sometimes four or five in a row—but after Wood is gone Sara speaks more and more of Vincent and Mary in social terms, as they celebrate birthdays together on occasion or tend to each other when sick. She also reports regularly working with Vincent in the garden or sometimes with Mary on house projects, such as cleaning out the medicine chest. (Sara decided what to throw out, Mary cleaned and fumigated.)

Vincent and Mary stayed on nine more years until 1953, when Vincent's asthma got so bad he had to quit working and they moved into a house in town. "We bought them a little house," Sara said in her oral history, "and made sure they had, with their social security, enough to live on." On a few occasions in 1954 Sara records that Mary helped out with a dinner party or lunch for out-of-town guests. But mostly Sara laments her absence, especially when she returned from out of town: "No loving Mary with a fire, a drink, a simple well

Sara Bard Field and Mary Marengo, mistress and servant, 1931.
PHOTOGRAPH IN COLLECTION OF MAY ARMANN;
REPRODUCTION BY VICTOR SCHIFFRIN.

cooked dinner." Once or twice she came to dinner at Vincent and Mary's house in town. "Supper at the Marengos—just we three— with that easy relaxation of people who know each other well and assume the basic facts of friendship."

In 1953 and '54, Sara reports hiring a sequence of replacement couples, but it's clearly never the same for her. Two years later she sold the estate and moved closer to her daughter Kay in the Bay Area.

The poets' diaries told a beautiful story of an idyllic life, one I found myself longing for, full of warmth, humor, mutual respect, and literary expression, in a gorgeous Northern California setting nestled in the woods and fields with a view across the valley. There, one could be uplifted by sculptures and murals and clever, artistic, intellectual friends, with a chauffeur, lovely meals prepared by someone else, a fire glowing in the hearth, and no weeds to pull. I wouldn't even have to carry home the wildflowers I'd picked unless I found it romantically appealing to do so.

You Can't Get Good Help Anymore

BUT THAT WAS ONLY one story Wood and Field told in their diaries. The other was more complicated. It was more about the two poets themselves, more intense, more difficult to deal with, as their benevolent elitism—so implicit in their defense of the sculptures— became all too explicit in the way they talked about their servants.

Clearly Sara and Erskine had a vast appreciation for all the work that Vincent and Mary did for them over the years. Wood, as I've quoted already, went out of his way to praise Vincent's work over and over again, from his very first diary entry. That's how I could reconstruct what Vincent actually did. Sara, similarly, recalled in her oral history: "They made life possible for us up there; we could never have lived up there, with the need for outdoor and indoor help, without that marvelous couple." "We were completely taken care of by them." Wood and Field backed up this appreciation with concrete acts. When Vincent was sick, she brought him soup; once, early on, when he was stricken by a terrible flu, the poets brought him to stay with them in San Francisco. They evidently paid for his lawyer and doctor bills. They invited him in for a glass of wine at Thanksgiving. They also tried their best to be good employers—as when Wood piled up the dishes he left for Vincent.

Wood and Field's appreciation for Vincent and Mary, though, was always thickly romanticized. Here, for example, is Wood's 1925 description of winemaking on the estate: "Every Italian seems to know the art of winemaking—and all of it is beautiful—the bare armed men swinging and straining in sculpturesque attitudes at the press—even the purple stained tubs are beautiful and the mens [*sic*] arms—purple dyed to the elbows—a beautiful [???]nletion of the divine Dionysus." In Wood's mind, Vincent and his fellow Italian workmen were either straight out of classical mythology, romantic Italian peasants, or both. Wood's poems from these years are replete with images of himself lying idly in the sun or under a tree, "watching a ploughman and his white horse / High on the hillside, ploughing the vines." Much of his romantic appreciation of Vincent and other workmen is tinged with an implicit contrast with himself—a certain envy of the Manly Men who work with their bodies. "The cement men are all friends of Vincent's, all Italians," he wrote as the house was being built, "and so earnest in their job. That is true of the carpenters also. Every man works as if it was his pride to do a good job—I cannot help thinking how fortunate in society are these men who know how to build—know exactly what to do—than lawyers,—clerks and the idle rich." Of course, he himself was a lawyer to the "idle rich."

Sara had her own classical romance going too, although it was much more subtle. In *The Beautiful Wedding* she slipped in a reference to Vincent and Dominic as the "retinue of Pan." She, too, liked to write poems about happy simple workers picking grapes. *Vineyard Voices* (1930), for example, began:

The pickers, up at dawn, were through when noon
Summoned to salad, bread and cheese and wine.
The purple cleanly cut from every vine.
With spurts of laughter, talk or whistled tune
From guiltily stained lips they stumbled down . . .

And like Wood, Field is a passive watcher from above: "I overlooked all from the vineyard crowd / . . . . The merry pickers passed and all was still."

As both writers' positioning of themselves as reflective artists literally looking down on their employees suggests, though, Sara and Erskine's romantic appreciation of Vincent and Mary was mixed in with a vast, unquestioned condescension. Wood conveys his condescension—as well Sara's romantic posturing—in his very first diary entry. He's just described all the scarecrows Vincent has erected. "My wife won't let anything be shot because she says it is only natural they should want to eat our grapes and we might not want to work and raise grapes and tempt them."

Vincent confided in me confidentially—he gets that way
when we are off by ourselves— "Jesus we won'ts have no
grapes at all if Miss Field don't let me shoot some deer, foxes,
coons, coyotes, jays, quail and all dem other things what eat
the grape—Jesus if she say it natural they come eat our grape
I sweat for all summer, much expense to you ain't it natural I
shoot 'em?—Let 'em blame me—Ef that her 'ligion."

Wood has written in the margin: "How the Simple mind goes to the nub of any question," praising Vincent's acuity, only to then patronize him contemptuously.

Sara could be just as snotty. In her wedding story, she writes that Dominic, Vincent's cousin, described the temperature in the courtyard as "'more hottes as hell' (he has never been to Harvard, but speaks very good English)." Notice how she is not only mocking Dominic's inadequate English and distinguishing it from the Harvard-educated, but assuming that the reader—presumably sharing her own class perspective—will enjoy her little joke at Dominic's expense. She's more explicit in her oral history. The interviewer asks her: "Did Mary and Vincent take all your entertaining and your concerts in stride?" and Sara replies: "I don't think their taste was cultivated enough for them to come to all our gatherings, and they didn't." Elizabeth Elkus, wife of the composer Albert Elkus, attended many of Sara and Erksine's social gatherings in the 1930s. She told Wood's biographer that "she was rather put off by . . . the peculiar air of elitism she often encountered at The Cats."

Reading the diaries carefully, it gradually became clear to me that Wood and Field's condescension also had something to do with race. At one point early on Wood refers to "dear brown Vincent"; which wouldn't necessarily mean so much had not both he and Sara transcribed Vincent's and Mary's Italian accent in classic stereotyped Black "darky" dialect, with "de's" and "dems" and "ain'ts." "De snow never hurt nutting—it ain't de snow—it's de frost," Mary allegedly insisted. Vincent supposedly decried, above, "all dem other things what eat the grape" and absolved Sara "ef that her 'ligion." Wood put the same stereotyped words in the mouth of "black Emmanuel" in one of his poems, "Cradling Wheat": "De sweat of de just / Is de fat of de land." Vincent's own writing, by contrast, in the one letter I found, has lots of spelling and punctuation errors but is far from "darky"-speak: "Just a few line to let you now how we getting a long here," the letter opens.

Both poets also repeatedly referred to Vincent's big round eyes popping out when he got excited. Maybe they were big; maybe they did get bigger when he was excited. But combined with Wood and Field's transcription of Vincent's language, their package description of Vincent overall echoes racial stereotypes of African Americans widespread among otherwise progressive white people in the 1920s and '30s. While visiting Boston in late 1927, Wood described his hotel, for example, "with its charming gentle voiced negro girls in the elevators—A Loveable race—childlike—emotional—credulous—humble." It wasn't exactly that he thought Vincent was African American. But racial notions abounded in this period that cast Italians and other Southern Europeans as racially wilder, less "civilized," inferior, closer to Africans than to Germans or the English. Wood, like his peers, had a set of cultural notions about dark-skinned people available in his imagination, and when he went about describing Vincent, they tumbled out all too easily.

Wood pronounced in public that he wanted to "abolish all privilege," all distinctions between rich and poor, but the house he and Sara commissioned at The Cats, I discovered in the architects' letters, had a "service entrance." In 1927, Sara's shopping list included: "Carpet for Barda [a dog], uniforms for Mary, dish cloths." So Mary wore a uniform, and came in through a servants' entrance. Both were classic markers of explicit class hierarchy that were fading out in the 1920s in the face of a presumably democratic, egalitarian American culture uncomfortable with such "Old World" symbols. For all their radicalism, Sara and Erskine were in fact substantially retrograde in insisting on uniforms and a separate entrance.

Hamburger's biography of Wood, along with Sara's oral history, makes clear that the two had been waited on by servants for most of their lives. Wood grew up in Maryland with an African-American gardener, who he would later praise in stereotypical terms. Given the stature of Wood's family, and their location in the South, other African-American servants presumably served him in his youth as well. His wife Nan's household in Portland included, their son recalled, "two faithful Chinese servants—an old gardener named Louie and a houseboy equally old, named Ting." Sara recalled that while in Portland she herself "had a perfectly wonderful maid in those halcyon days when help from Europe came over not at all despising domestic service and capable of taking a great deal of burden off women who had something else to do." Their children had maids, too. Sara writes that her daughter Kay visited The Cats with "Rosa and Jenny her two maids." Both poets, then, were accustomed to full-time servants and had not really intended to do without at their estate in Los Gatos.

As Sara's remarks about the good old days of servants from Europe suggest, in her old age she would remember Vincent and Mary as the perfect servants, in contrast to the women who waited on her and nursed her in Oakland, where she was living at the time of her oral history. In one interview, as she first begins to discuss "the dear people who took care of us up there, Vincent and Mary Marengo," she actually says: "They just don't come like that any more; they're not even being born. They are just a different race of helpers that come along." Did Sara really mean what that sounds like? It does seem like she was praising the Marengos as racially more virtuous than the African Americans we can presume were working for her in Oakland in 1960.

From day one at The Cats, Wood and Field referred to Vincent as "faithful" and "loyal," over and over again—as in "dear faithful Vincent." Alternately, Vincent was "eternal," or "ever-responsible" or "all-seeing." Mary they merely described as "selfless." I kept asking myself what those phrases were all about. "Faithful" and "loyal," applied to servants, implied a continual willingness to put one's employer before oneself—as did "selfless" more overtly. The other words suggested a constant vigilance over the employers' interest— with the same suggestion of timeless dedication. "Mary never minded how many came in" to dinner, Sara insisted, "which most cooks do nowadays." Sara loved recounting how Vincent and Dominic had happily given up their days off to prepare for her daughter's wedding.

For all their class distinctions, condescension, and, yes, racism, both Sara and Erskine also simultaneously referred to the Marengos as "our dear friends," especially as the years passed. They seem to have meant it with deep sincerity and affection. Yet they could never quite separate that affection from their romantic obliviousness. In this respect, too, they were anything but unique. Historians, sociologists, and other researchers on domestic service have repeatedly found that employers tend to think of their servants as their friends, laboring out of pure love, while servants—whatever deep affection they might hold for their bosses—are well aware that what they are doing is a job, and they don't confuse appreciation for a good employer with their voluntary emotional relationships with their own friends and family members.

One of Wood's early diary entries is revealing of his almost willing obliviousness to the financial roots of his relationship with Vincent (as well as to Vincent's own point of view). Wood begins with a straightforward homage to his employee's loyal dedication: "Vincent certainly here deserves a word of recognition for his alert, faithful intelligent watching over our interests . . . always alive to our interests and what he knows of our wishes." But then he launches squarely into a denial of the economic nature of their relationship: "—the sort of service money never purchases. I think we have purchased it by believing him to be equally with us fellow prisoners on the planet and to be treated as a human being. Sara's care, thought, interest in all his problems and perhaps this—Sara's—sweet winsomness has brought to us what money alone never does."

And yet, the bottom line was that Wood and Field had, in fact, bought Vincent and Mary's love. Even Sara's love and charm, as depicted here, function as a means to obtain superior service. The kicker, though, is in the sentence that follows: "Vincent is hoping some day to inherit this shack." Of course Vincent was not an entirely selfless fool.

The diaries did, in fact, tell a final, more cryptic story, in that line and others, of what Vincent and Mary might have thought. Vincent does appear to have cared for his employers. On Sara's birthday in 1926, for example, he left a pot of ruby-colored cyclamen on the table, with a note, "From Vincent." In honor of Kay's wedding he built a love seat on the hillside. When he retired, he gave a beautiful speech thanking the poets. "Never shall I forget Vincent's talk," wrote Sara in her diary. "In a low, almost sad voice he spoke of how 'I came here a working man and was taken into the family.' He said Erskine and I had been Father and Mother to Mary and him. His love for all of us was so apparent. We were all close to tears."

However much Wood might think of Vincent as "our young man," though, Vincent was very much his own man, anything but simple-minded and stupid. As the diaries make clear, he had a vast range of skills, including the ability to manage a complex estate and, not to be underestimated, manage a complex couple of employers. He clearly had a sense of humor, too. It shines through at the end of his one surviving letter to Wood. "I am feling fine now and egoing [sic] my hot meals every day we have been diging the garage foundsome very hard ground had to [do] some blasting and we also did a little damige," Vincent reports. After reporting on Mary, he concludes: "I am getting fat and Bartha [the dog] is getting thin give my love to Kay an Jime Love from Mary and Vincent." He did evidently express his opinions on occasion. Walter Steilberg, the architect, wrote Wood while he was designing the gatehouse: "I was afraid that Vincent might curse me every time he drove in or out of the garage so I placed this element at an angle . . . thus making the approach to the doorway much easier."

Vincent also comes across as capable of asserting himself at times in negotiating his work load. Sara and Erskine originally had goats on the property, but gave them up when they went to Italy in 1924, because it was too much work for Vincent. Vincent also cautioned against overextending the gardens without an adequate water supply. He insisted on bottling their wine only when the moon was full. Wood, ever the romantic, loved this "superstition" but Vincent took it seriously, and got his way.

The evidence about what Mary thought was, once again, thin. The diaries offered no clues. But I did find two notes from her, both written after she and Vincent had moved into town, the first an Easter card tucked into Sara's 1954 diary. The cover reads "Wish We Could Be Together at Easter." Inside it has a printed message below which Mary has written, "Hope this Easter card finds you well. Hope you have a Happy Easter with your friends around you. Will be thinking of you. Love Mary Marengo. The second doesn't have a date, but was sent later: "Thinking of you," the cover reads. Inside Mary has signed "Love Mary Marengo" below another printed message. On the opposite side she's written: "Dear Mrs. Woods. Haven't heard from you in so long so I thought I would drop you a card and hope these few lines find you ever so much better. I am about the same, my hand and arm bother me [???] have a lot of pain. Hope I hear from you some time. Mary."

Once again, Mary's personality disappears into the woodwork she herself kept so gleaming. Wood called her "Mary the meek, the selfless," the timid dove. But she did, after all, leave an abusive husband, risk alienating her children, and serve as a role model for twelve other oppressed Italian wives in Los Gatos. It's not clear when exactly she and Vincent got together as a couple, but clearly she was brave enough to be deeply involved with him before she left her husband.

All in all, the diaries told a interwoven story of work and of leisure. The Cats could never have existed without Vincent and Mary, Dominic and the Italian cement men, and who knows how many others who worked for Wood and Field for shorter periods, along with Robert Paine, the sculptor. Sara and Erskine chose a literary lifestyle that mandated at least two other human beings serving them full-time for thirty years. Their dramatic house, their lovely gardens, their mediocre poems, their famous dinner parties, their private-label wine—all of the things that made them famous (or, rather, near-famous) were possible because of Vincent and Mary. In the end, I came to see, C. E. S. Wood and Sara Bard Field's cultural ascendance depended upon Vincent and Mary's institutionalized subservience—however bathed in love and affection.

The whole picture was so subtle: the two poets, Wood especially, were perceptive about so much. They were quick to praise Vincent and Mary and underscore how hard the two worked and what great servants they were and how they made their lives possible. But when push came to shove they were willing to take credit in public for what Vincent and Mary's work produced. Newspaper stories from the 1920s and '30s every once in a while mentioned Vincent, but usually they didn't. By the 1960s and '70s, the Marengos had dropped out of the poets' official story altogether.

I kept thinking about Bertolt Brecht's famous poem, "Questions From a Worker Who Reads":

Who built Thebes of the seven gates?
In the books you will find the names of kings.
Did the kings haul up the lumps of rock?
. . . .
Where, the evening that the Wall of China was finished
Did the masons go? Great Rome
Is full of triumphal arches. Who erected them?
. . . .
Caesar beat the Gauls.
Did he not have even a cook with him?

Who built The Cats? Sara Bard Field and C. E. S. Wood, or Vincent and Mary Marengo, Robert Paine, Dominic Bergamino, and the "Italian colony of Los Gatos"?

On March 5, 1925, after he was done admiring Vincent and the noble cement men pouring their foundations for the new house, Wood noted in his diary: "Sara gathered stones to throw into the bottom of the forms—so she could say she also had helped build our house."

They Weren't *That* Democratic!

THE DIARIES WERE overwhelming. I'd learned an enormous amount from them about daily life and daily emotions at The Cats; and Vincent—if not Mary—was starting to come into focus. But I was still trapped inside Wood's and Field's heads: almost every word, literally, was theirs, after all. I longed to escape the two poets' point of view, their individual interests, their overdramatizing, and find Mary and Vincent Marengo on their own terms, just as fleshed out and opinionated as the two poets.

At some point I'd heard from a friend that Cynthia Matthews, longtime Santa Cruz city council member, was the granddaughter of the people who lived at The Cats, and even had a film of life up there. So I called her up. She turned out to be C. E. S. Wood's *great*-granddaughter, and suggested I talk with her parents, Kirk and Pat Smith, who lived in Santa Cruz. They had the movie, she said, and would be happy to talk to me. So I bravely called them up. Kirk was gracious and friendly, and we arranged for me to come to his house a few days later.

When Pat opened the door and I walked in, I immediately faced an oil painting of C. E. S. Wood in his full gray-bearded glory, staring at me from the wall opposite. Next to it was a well-executed Van Goghstyle oil painting of a vase of flowers, signed by Wood himself. As I oohed and aahed, Pat showed me around the room, full of artifacts from The Cats, including a bas-relief white marble sculpture of three children (one of which was Kirk) and a tall, thin table of dark wood with intricate carved legs, set in a small, unpretentious living-dining room. As Pat and I chitchatted about the art, Kirk leaned in with a subtle grin and shook my hand: "Shall we begin the interrogation?"

The joke was, he meant a pre-interview interrogation of me, not mine of him. Kirk and Pat Smith wanted to know all about my project, the other books I'd written, what I taught. We ranged all over the place intellectually and historically as we settled into the living room. Kirk was charming and witty throughout, with a glint in his eye, a cheery style, and a clear, direct way of speaking. Pat was careful to deflect the conversation over to Kirk, although I kept wanting to ask about her family history, too—her father had been a literary agent.

Kirk Smith (officially Alan Kirkham Smith), was born in 1916 in Portland in the old Wood family home. His mother, Lisa—Nan Eliza Bryson Wood—was C. E. S. and Nan Wood's fourth child. She'd married Kirk's father, an insurance salesman, and moved the family to San Rafael in 1920. Kirk himself had gone to Stanford Business School, worked for Colgate Palmolive in the East, raised three children, and eventually settled down as a personnel manager for a wholesale pharmaceutical company in Oakland. He and Pat retired to Santa Cruz in 1972.

While he was growing up in San Rafael in the 1920s and '30s, Kirk and his family had visited The Cats regularly, he said—for Thanksgiving every year and for whole glorious summers. Wood and Field would come to San Rafael for Christmas. Lisa was the only one of Wood's children who lived in the Bay Area and the only one who accepted Sara, Kirk said, so the two families were especially close. Kirk remembered the earliest days at The Cats. "At that time, there was nothing there but what they called 'the shack,' a little summer house. They lived there while the main house was being built." The kids would sleep in cots on the porch.

Kirk remembered Vincent vividly, almost always wearing a white shirt and dark wool pants, no matter what he was doing. "Vincent was a great guy, always in good spirits. He was an all-around man as far as abilities were concerned, an excellent gardener and carpenter, making wine. He was very, very reputable and valuable; always pleasant and enthusiastic on his projects." While Vincent was working, "we'd tag along with him and Dominic. I *never* saw him in bad mood or utter a foul word." He remembered Vincent's chauffeuring, too. Wood and Field "had a big old Cadillac," dark green. "He'd drive them to San Francisco or to our house at San Rafael." I asked what Vincent did while his employers were at the house. "That's a good question. If it was a dinner party on the premises, he'd stay and wait for them." But Kirk otherwise wasn't sure if he'd gone somewhere else, or what. "Was Vincent invited in for dinner at Christmas?" No.

Kirk remembered that Vincent always called Wood "The Colonel"—never Erskine or even Mr. Wood. "They had a very good relationship. Their relationship was very informal and cordial. It wasn't a master-servant relationship at all. Vincent was always treated with respect." Kirk's memories echoed the diaries: "Both Vincent and Mary meant a lot to them personally. It was a friendly personal relationship."

What about Mary? "Vincent was much more outgoing that Mary. Mary was very, very retiring." But Kirk did remember her: she had a "very sweet face, a medium build, curly hair, a very nice smile," and spoke with an accent. "She always wore white, a blouse and a skirt. I never saw an apron on her." Mary was "very quiet, very sweet. She never got impatient with young kids pestering her in the kitchen" (suggesting, of course, that young kids did pester her in the kitchen). "We always looked forward to her breakfasts, delicious breakfasts . . . coffee cake, whatever you wanted, she'd get it for you. Mostly bacon and eggs and that coffee cake." I asked whether she'd cooked three meals a day. "I think they let her take lunch off. She may have prepared a spread."

Kirk described Mary and Sara's relationship as very different from the Colonel's with Mary and Vincent: "Sara always treated her with respect. I don't think she had the knack for the informal pleasantries that my grandfather had with Mary. He'd joke and make small talk. Sara was a very serious person. I don't recall her *ever* getting involved with humorous discussions." I asked him if Sara had worked in the kitchen. No, he said, "she never helped Mary cook or carry off the dishes." At Thanksgiving the kids would help clean up. He thought maybe there was someone else helping out in the kitchen for the holiday.

Kirk remembered wonderful dinners Mary cooked at The Cats: "roast beef, leg of lamb, always gourmet dinners, even though it was just the family there." Did Mary sit down and eat with you? I asked. "Oh, *no!*" Kirk shot back immediately, amused. "They weren't *that* democratic!!"

As their memories got slimmer and we all started to wind down, we moved over to the table and a small television with a VCR and DVD player next to it. Kirk and Pat, it turned out, had not just one but seven home movies from the late 1920s and '30s that Lisa, Kirk's mom, had shot. This was beyond my wildest historian's dream come true—actual live-action footage of The Cats. One of their grandsons had remastered old family films into digital form, so they were right there on a little silver disk.

Fiddling with the commands, we started with "Los Gatos—San Rafael—Typical Day 1928." Like all the films, it was in black and white, silent with a ragtime soundtrack that had been added later. It opened with various shots of dogs, kids, kittens, and puppies that Kirk said were in San Rafael, and a vague shot of Wood at the head of a dinner table. Soon the scene shifted to The Cats. Three teenaged girls (Kirk's sisters) in matching bobbed brown hairdos and light-colored shifts cavorted in front of the mural in the poets' courtyard, then played in the fountain. Kirk, maybe ten, appeared in clean white garb, then the Colonel showed up, explicating the mural to one of the girls. Along the murky way I could make out glimpses of the house's columns, tiles, and courtyard mural.

We skipped to Reel 4, "Gaga's 80th Birthday, February 20, 1932." It opened with Wood on a hillside with a stunning view of the valley behind him, carefully posed with a book opened in one hand, a hat clutched in the other. He looked up as a succession of women, some with artful furs draped around their coat collars, trotted down to kiss him. Sara appeared, white-haired, in an even nicer fur-collared coat, and they drifted down the steep hillside, only to greet more young people, and then climb back up. Wood was wearing a casual jacket and loose-fitting white shirt, with a short polka-dot tie. Then we cut to Sara, walking along curving, carefully swept walkways lined by lush plants, rows of tidy flowers, and white stones along the edges. I could actually see Vincent's garden, frozen in 1930s time.

But I was most excited about Reel #3, entitled "Mary and Vincent's Wedding 1931," two minutes and forty-three seconds long. I realized suddenly that I hadn't even known when or if they'd gotten married—and here I was going to see a film of their actual wedding. Alas, the film's lighting quality was terrible. It opened with a close-up of a hand cutting a big, round, flat cake. (Was the hand Mary's?). Next to it sit crystal glasses filled with red wine, and silver salt-and-pepper shakers. The camera moves across two or three tables, capturing a series of smiling, potentially Italian men in suits and ties, smoking and drinking. In a dark grey blur I could see a mustached man lifting a china teacup in a toast. We cut to Vincent and Mary's house, with good lighting and focus now, but the camera's frame is way off, and only captures the feet of some figures on the balcony above the garage. Then we see a couple laughing arm in arm as they saunter down a dirt road—not Vincent and Mary, though, but members of the Smith family.

Suddenly, in great darkness, we're behind The Cats' spiderweb gate, which opens up as a crowd of very darkly lit, unidentifiable people, some in pairs, seemingly all wearing black, move in a cluster past the camera. Then we get an interminable sequence of wealthier-looking adults and children from the Smith family loitering near an old car, then mysteriously pushing their way through an oak forest, cutting a few boughs—perhaps for decorating the couple's car? That was all. Vincent and Mary's wedding, but no Vincent or Mary that I could see. Did they even get married at The Cats—or was this the party afterward?

The most powerful film turned out to be a simpler one entitled "Tash Driving Vincent's Truck 1934." It opens with a shot of a dirt road, with Vincent off to the left, shot from behind, wearing a light-colored cardigan sweater with a bit of a collar, medium-colored pants, his perennial hat, and carrying a newspaper tucked under his right arm. A car starts down the road toward us, and as it passes we see its young woman driver; it's Tash, Kirk's sister. The film cuts to a shot of Vincent leaping into the car as the woman begins to start it up. As she fumbles with the gears Vincent turns to the camera and shoots a big grin back at us; Tash drives the car forward, and he smiles again and waves back at us with a rolled-up newspaper. He's got a long, thin, face; a long, sharp nose; and a look of amused patience on his face. As the soundtrack—a ragtime piano solo with a melancholy edge—winds down, we get one last shot of Tash driving the car up the road, with Vincent waving over his shoulder. Maybe it was just the music that got to me, but that smile from Vincent, with his head held slightly down with a self-effacing tilt, cut right to my heart.

So did a brief clip that followed, but from a different angle. We see a fancy dinner table with high-backed, dark wood chairs around it, outside in the courtyard, with a formal dinner set up. Wood, at the head, has his back to us; Sara's on the left, gesturing to a group of dressed-up people to the table's right, perhaps directing them to their seats. While this is going on and the guests are cheerfully settling in, a single figure, all in white with dark hair, passes between the house's columns at the back, then disappears deeper into the house. It's Mary, of course—a fleeting figure, at the edge of the frame. The image made me think of Bruce Robbins's book, *The Servant's Hand*, in which he talks about servants in nineteenth-century English novels as half-invisible figures, mysteriously but powerfully popping up around the edges of the text. I wanted a smile from Mary; I wanted her to talk.

I did get that smile. When I watched the first "typical scenes" film again at home, deep in the footage I caught a brief clip: Vincent is sitting down, reading a newspaper, his hat tipped down over his face, when a figure appears from the left and hands him a little platter with grapes or some other fruit. He selects one to eat, chatting, smiling. The camera moves slowly up to capture Mary, talking, too, looking down at her partner with a lovely, shy, but wide smile.

The best film of all I'd already tracked down myself, "Grape Picking and Crushing in the C. E. S. Wood Vineyard 1930," another of Lisa's ouevre. Robert Hamburger had referred to it in one of his footnotes, and I got a video copy of it from the Oregon Historical Society in Portland. Kirk, Pat, and I watched it together; they helped me identify the characters and settings. At eleven minutes it was much longer than the others, more complex in its story, and captured perfectly the dramatic preposterousness of life at The Cats.

It opens with an old pickup truck silhouetted against the Santa Clara Valley. We can see Dominic standing up in its bed, as Vincent, Sara, and the Colonel hand boxes up to him. They all climb into the back, including Mary—in white blouse, skirt, stockings and black shoes—and Vincent drives the truck away. Then we see them unloading the boxes by the vineyard. Vincent, in a white shirt and a straw hat with a black band, kneels down, cuts a bunch of grapes, crushes them in a pot, and tests them with some kind of tubed instrument, perhaps making sure the sugar content is correct.

Next we see a long sequence of various figures moving to and fro in the vineyard, picking grapes, putting them in large baskets, and unloading them into wooden boxes, interspersed with sundry shots of dogs and cats, all framed against stunning views of the valley. Sara feeds some grapes to one of the dogs. She's wearing a dressy dress of thin, light-colored material, with a long pleated skirt and long sleeves dangling from her wrists. ("She always wore these filmy dresses," inserted Kirk.) Wood holds up a bunch of grapes, leaves attached, and romantically holds them up to his mouth to nibble at. He's in a white shirt with a loosely-tied black necktie and giant conical straw hat. All these people dressed up in white to pick grapes on a dusty hillside—I kept wondering why they didn't wear something more practical. And who would do the laundry afterwards?

Then the show gets more comical, and Wood's silly romanticism kicks in. Vincent and Dominic load the boxes onto a sled and pull it like mules with long ropes, up, across, and down a hill to the house. On the return, they've suddenly sprouted giant grape-leaf antlers from their hats, and are pulling Wood, seated on the sled with his own antlers stuck in his hair and a bunch of grapes held up high in each hand—posing as some imaginary Zeus-meets-Bacchus figure—replete with happy peasants pulling him along, right out of one of his poems.

Finally, it's grape-crushing time. Dominic's got his feet in rubber boots, squishing the grapes in a half-barrel. In the next barrel Vincent's using a long wooden mallet. Nothing so simple for the Colonel: we see him take off his shoes. In the next shot he's got his shirt off, his pants rolled up, and, with one hand on an amused-looking Vincent's shoulder, is jumping up and down in a barrel, 78-year-old chest jiggling away.

I had a great time watching the films with Kirk and Pat. They even let me take their disk with me so I could make my own copy. On my way out we went on a tour of their back yard, stretching on and on into a wonderful garden at the back with enormous rows of raspberry vines and two giant raised beds full of winter-squash plants. As I left, Pat generously gave me two original Christmas missives from Sara, an original cover of the July 1911 *Pacific Monthly* with a painting by Wood of Mt. Hood on the cover, and one of the poets' actual wine labels. It reads "Princess" at the top in red, with "The Cats—Los Gatos, California" at the bottom, framing a black-and-white wood-cut rendition of their mural, grape vines curling along the sides. I felt like a member of the family.

My visit with Kirk and Pat changed so much for me. Here were two real people, very much alive, with actual memories of Vincent and Mary, Sara and Erskine. I could hear a bit about each of their four personalities and hear about the social bonds and social boundaries between employers and employees. Kirk confirmed what I'd read in the diaries: Vincent and Mary were *almost* "members of the family" but not quite. Sara and Erskine were caring and cordial, but they didn't invite Vincent and Mary to the dinner table.

And those films: Now I knew what Vincent and Mary looked like; and it was great to see Erskine and Sara in action—the Colonel with his charm, Sara with her grace. The grape-picking movie, especially, underscored Erskine's preposterous fantasies of himself. The films also gave me Vincent and Mary in action laboring for Erskine and Sara: In Mary's case, setting and clearing the table discreetly out of view, dressed all in white, at Sara's behest; in Vincent's case, picking, packing, and pummeling grapes dressed in a silly hat, at the Colonel's behest. I could see Vincent with his lilting smile, teaching their daughter to drive. And Mary—well, she still slipped away. But her own timid smile, like Vincent's, was worth a thousand diary entries.

How the Other Half Remembers

I COULD HAVE stopped there. I was already in far deeper than I'd ever intended, and the whole thing was getting less jolly and a lot more serious. But I also had to face the fact that I still hadn't escaped the poets' viewpoint. Kirk Smith was *Erskine*'s grandson, after all. Even the films—what might seem like an "objective" view of life at The Cats—were shot by Lisa, Erskine's daughter, who owned the camera and chose where to point it and when. Vincent and Mary only showed up when they were at work—never inside their own living room, with their own families, or in Los Gatos away from the gaze of their employers. Even the film of Vincent and Mary's own wedding never quite showed Vincent and Mary themselves. As for the private smile between Mary and Vincent, it was nonetheless shot by Lisa's prominent camera. I was still on the poets' side, looking down.

If I stopped now, I'd be complicit somehow in replicating the very inequality I was trying to investigate. So I took a deep breath and started all over from the other side.

I still had my ace in the hole, whose phone number was sitting on a piece of paper in my filing cabinet: Robert Balzer, my linoleum guy, Mary Marengo's grandson. For five years I'd known he was out there with the family photos he'd promised me. I'd been afraid to call him, though, afraid the photos had all burned up or been thrown away, afraid he couldn't remember anything; frankly, afraid he'd died or somehow disappeared. But when I finally called him he was very much alive and well, booming through the phone. "You should talk to my sister Betty. She's older and remembers them much better."

So I called up Betty and explained to her how I was interested in Vincent and Mary Marengo and their relationship to the Colonel and Sara. Betty and I arranged to meet at her house in Campbell, between Los Gatos and San José, on a weekday morning in July. It was hot and glary when I finally found it (I got my Mapquest map turned upside down and ended up on the completely wrong side of the freeway), a classic 1960s Santa Clara Valley tract house. Betty was friendly, warm, and laughed easily—as anxious about talking with a history professor as I was about interviewing a complete stranger. We chatted a bit about the house and its history as she led me through a living room to an addition at the back of the house. Like Kirk and Pat's, Betty's house had a huge lot stretching out in the back, with fruit trees, flowers, and lawns farther than I could see.

Before I could even sit down and pull out my notebooks and tape recorder, I was—Bammo!—on the other side of the story, as Betty burst out: "They worked my grandmother to death. She was the only one up there in that huge house. She did all the cooking and all the cleaning. They had all their children and grandchildren up there and she took care of all of them."

Betty Ann Balzer Weltz was born in 1925, the daughter of Ida Balzer, Mary Marengo's youngest child, who'd married Betty's father at fifteen. Betty had visited Mary at The Cats throughout her childhood. She remembered Mary as a kind person, reserved but happy. "Grandma was very sweet to us. But we hardly ever saw her." Betty was quick to point out the contrast: Mary spent a lot of time taking care of and feeding Sara and Erskine's grandkids, but barely saw her own. "She didn't complain, but we didn't see her as often as she would like to have because she was always busy." As she got older, Betty and her mom would sometimes work at The Cats, too, cooking and serving food. "Every once in a while grandma would have a big party and mother and I would go up and help her." She'd help at dinner parties with 14, 16, maybe 20 people.

I asked her what Vincent and Mary's gatehouse had been like. "It was very nice, but they hardly spent any time there," she said, "because they were working for the Woods all the time. I think they just went down there to sleep." Did they take vacations? Not that she could remember. Every Christmas, Mary gave each of her grandkids a dollar in an envelope. "That was your Christmas. She didn't have any time to do anything else." Did she join her daughter or grandchildren for Christmas dinner? "She would be too busy."

Betty was explicit about Mary's relationship with Sara, too—and her own. "Grandma was a hard worker. I think Mrs. Woods [*sic*] expected her to do it." Sara, she said, was "tighter than a tick." "She was lovely. She was very polite. But grandma was help." "And, then, too, we always felt she always looked down on us a bit. Grandma knew her place, and I'm sure Mrs. Woods [*sic*] made sure she did." Later, Betty repeated: "She had her place and she knew it. I think that was about grandma, too"—meaning that Mary herself accepted the strict demarcation of mistress and servant. Mary, she said, always called Sara "Mrs. Woods" (with an extra "s") who, in turn, called Mary "Mary." Erskine called Vincent "Vincent," who called him "Mr. Woods" to his face, "the Colonel" to everyone else. (As for the grandkids, "we always called them the Weird People.")

The Colonel, by contrast, was always nice to the kids, Betty said, and would show them around his study or the property. Vincent had a different relationship with Wood, too, than Sara's with Mary. "I think he respected the Colonel very much." Betty quickly qualified that, though: "But when you were working in those days, you did what the man you were working for told you to do. Whatever Woods asked him to do, he did. He never said no. Neither did Grandma."

Betty also told me about Pisqually Gagliasso, Mary's first husband and Betty's own grandfather. Pisqually, she said, worked as a gardener, too. He and Mary had had their first daughter, Marguerite, in Italy. The grandkids hardly ever saw him. "We'd walk to the movie theater with him, and he'd pay for it," but he never came in. "So, he tried; I think he was trying to be nice to us because of grandma." "To me, to this day, I'm still amazed that this Italian lady, who was Catholic, got a divorce in her day and age, because that was unheard of." Betty and her siblings had never been able to get anything out of Mary about the divorce, although they did know that it had been an arranged marriage. "It was hush hush. Italians and Catholics just didn't get divorced. I think it was wonderful that she did."

I read Betty the Colonel's diary entries about Mary leaving Pisqually and prompting the revolution of Los Gatos ladies. She was, needless to say, floored. "You really made my day!" "That explains why she wasn't ostracized. We thought she was all alone." Betty immediately started ticking off the names of the other Italian ladies of her grandmother's generation who she'd grown up with, trying to guess which ones had left their husbands. She couldn't wait to get on the phone with friends and sisters to figure it out.

I myself thought about my own grandmother, Marie Bogio Frank, who was born in the Italian Piedmont in 1886, about the same time as Vincent and Mary. Her mother and father had had an arranged marriage, too. But after Marie's father died when she was eight, her mother, Tecla, sold a piece of land and used it to elope over the mountains to France and then to the United States with Mark Cavaletto, the distant cousin she'd always loved, taking my grandmother with her. In my grandmother's papers we found a turn-of-the-century photograph of a mysterious sister of hers in Switzerland, somehow left behind or shipped off in the deal. Like Betty, I wanted to know what the real story had been of my great-grandmother's private love.

I also started to see the poets' story in a different light, along with their relationship with Vincent and Mary. Erskine and Sara, like their two servants, had left their legal spouses and "lived in sin," as it was called in those days, during the 1920s and '30s. While they were in Portland, many of their set had ostracized them quite actively. According to Wood's son, even when they lived in San Francisco they'd had to run a gamut of social exclusions. That was one of the reasons they chose to move to the relative middle of nowhere in

Los Gatos. Mary and Vincent, for their part, also apparently lived together as a couple for a few years before she was divorced, since they moved into the gatehouse in 1929 or '30 but weren't married until 1931. I realized there was another story here: some perhaps entirely unspoken acceptance between the two couples of their mutual illicit status.

Betty remembered Vincent fondly as "a big, tall man," thin, always wearing white shirts. "We never called him grandpa—we called him Vincent." "He came to town a lot. Grandma never did." He did all Mary's shopping, and was responsible for opening the gate when company came to The Cats. Vincent had loved the dogs up there—Prince, the nice one, and Corda, the mean one. When

Vincent and Mary Marengo's wedding, 1931; left to right: Judge Bell, Sara Bard Field, Vincent Marengo, Mary Marengo, C. E. S. Wood. PHOTOGRAPH IN COLLECTION OF MAY ARMANN; REPRODUCTION BY VICTOR SCHIFFRIN.

he rode into town he'd always have the dogs in the back of his pickup truck. "Everyone knew Vincent and his dogs. He was very well known in town. He wouldn't let anybody near his dogs." What about his relationship with Mary? I asked. "She really looked up to Vincent. . . . They got along very well. . . . She was happy. They were content and happy to be doing what they were doing."

But Betty didn't just remember her grandmother as a quiet, dedicated worker and wife. "When she was with her Italian friends she was an entirely different person." Betty would go visit Mary after she had retired. "She laugh, and she'd talk. She was in her glory when she was with her Italian friends. They all got loud and noisy. (Now I want to know which one of those ladies left their husbands.)"

Vincent, too, had a different life and identity in town, Betty said. "There was a card room in Los Gatos. He'd go to the card room, and that's where he did his business. He loaned money. It was all the time that they were up at the Woods's." Vincent was a fixture at the card room throughout the 1940s and 1950s. "If he wanted to do business with someone, he'd send them there." After he retired, "he was with his cronies a lot," in the card room. Or else "they'd sit and talk at each other's houses." Betty remembered Mary and Vincent's later house in downtown Los Gatos. "It was lovely . . . set back on the street, with a big living room, dining room," a new kitchen at the back and a creek running behind the house. But Vincent's asthma was terrible. "You could hear him breathing all the way into the next room."

As she brought in a tray of cheese and crackers, Betty showed me two cards saved from Vincent and Mary's memorial services. Vincent's had a picture of a redwood tree, with a streak of light slanting down from above. He'd been born, it said, in Lecquo Tanoro, Italy, on October 28, 1887, and died in Los Gatos, California, October 12, 1965, age 74. Mary Benevelli Marengo's memorial said she'd been born September 9, 1885, in Momforte d'Alba, Italy, and died September 3, 1974, at the age of 88.

Finally Betty brought in a large picture frame with two dozen photos in it. There in the bottom right corner was a picture of Vincent's mother, Lucia, who had also lived in Los Gatos, it turned out. She had Vincent's long sharp nose, long gray hair pulled back in a bun, and a skirt down to her ankles. Sara Bard Field may have recorded in her diary that Vincent, in his retirement speech, had said that "Erskine and I had been Father and Mother to Mary and him," but neither she nor Wood ever mentioned that Vincent had his own mother living nearby in town all those years.

At the very bottom of the picture collection was a shot of Vincent and Mary. They're sitting on a low wall in front of the gatehouse, with a view of the valley behind. It's 1938. Vincent's got on his hat, dark

Lucia Marengo, Vincent's mother [n.d.].
PHOTOGRAPH IN COLLECTION OF BETTY WELTZ;
REPRODUCTION BY VICTOR SCHIFFRIN.

pants, and a black tie, and is wearing roundish black eyeglasses with
his head tilted back a bit. Mary, much smaller than Vincent, has curly
graying dark hair, pulled back. She's wearing a dark, short-sleeved
dress with polka dots and a V of white lace at her neck, and dark,
medium-heeled shoes with a fashionable white strip across along the
middle, her feet neatly crossed at the ankles. One of Vincent's hands
is behind her back, curled around her left side; the other rests on
his right knee. Mary, smiling at the camera, has her own right hand
resting comfortably on Vincent's other knee.

My visit to Betty brought me immediately to the other side of the
story, and deep inside it. I could suddenly see Vincent and Mary's
independent lives, their identities outside the long shadow of their

Vincent and Mary Marengo, 1938, at the gatehouse
to The Cats estate. PHOTOGRAPH IN COLLECTION OF BETTY
WELTZ; REPRODUCTION BY VICTOR SCHIFFRIN.

employers' notions of who they were. Vincent with his cronies in the card room, cutting deals; Mary laughing noisily in the kitchen, "in her glory." They had their own lives. Yet they also, Betty underscored, knew where their bread was buttered. They "knew their place," as she put it. To Wood and Fields, the Marengos were "our dear friends." But for Vincent and Mary, the two poets were "our good employers," to whom they were grateful for work. They knew that those at the bottom spent Christmas cooking big family dinners for others, or Thanksgiving sitting in a car in a driveway three hours away, thinking about their own loved ones—wife, husband, children, grandchildren—who they barely saw.

History from the Bottom Up, Literally

I STILL WANTED to talk with Betty's brother Robert, my linoleum guy. I decided to talk him into installing new vinyl in my kitchen. It wasn't entirely a pretext: the flooring was definitely looking dismal. Plus this way I could spend money on a new floor and tell myself that of course I had to do it for research reasons.

Robert showed up and immediately started prowling my kitchen with a measuring tape, running the numbers, talking vinyl shop talk. I myself whipped out my tape recorder and hoped he'd forget it was there. Just as I remembered, he was a hoot—laughing and talking from the minute he walked in.

"I'll tell you what I know about Vincent. He was the most fearless guy I ever met. I was terrified of him." Like Betty, Robert never called the man "Grandpa"—he was introduced to him as Vincent. Robert, too, remembered the white shirts, always ironed, the hat, and "baggy-ass pants that he'd have to keep pulling up, for god's sake. . . . I remember his pants being around his goddamn . . . " "See that hat?" Robert said, when I showed him the videos. "I think that was the same goddam hat he always wore." He loved the grapes film, laughing at the Colonel: "Look, he's picking it, vines and all!" Especially the dogs. "They're Italian dogs! What other kind of dogs would eat grapes?"

Robert remembered hanging out at The Cats when he was little with his sister and his cousin Georgia Dean, the daughter of Mary's son George. But "you never saw [Vincent] very much because he was always working in the gardens." Like Betty, Robert, too, remembered Pisqually Gagliasso, his actual grandfather, taking him to the movies. "Pisqually was a little shit, compared to Vincent." Vincent was "a big tall guy."

And Mary? "I can't remember her talking to us much. Nodding, smiling; just a sweetheart. . . . She didn't talk much." Mary was a "great cook. . . . She used to cook zucchini blossoms. She'd put batter on them." Robert echoed Betty's description of Mary: "My grandmother—all she did was work. She used to sweep the goddam sidewalk. I think she *looked* for work to do. . . . She was always busy. I never seen her sit down and relax."

Twelve years younger than Betty, Robert mostly remembered Vincent and Mary after they'd moved into their house in town. "When you came in the front door, you could hear Vincent wheezing out in the back yard." "They had a lot of meals with *their* friends and family. Big polenta feeds."

When he told his favorite Vincent story, Robert was suddenly transformed into a terrified high school kid: "At University and Main there was a tobacco or cigar store. When I bought my first car, my mother said, 'you go see Vincent,' because he was loaded." When he walked in the store where Vincent hung out, "all I could hear was his wheezing. I'm scared to death when I'm talking to him. He says, 'This is how it's gonna be. You tell me the day, the month,'" when Robert would pay him back. When Robert did deliver the money on that day, "he gave *all* the interest back, because I paid it that day."

Fifty-five years later, Robert was still impressed by that interaction. Who knows what Vincent had been thinking?

Mary sure didn't. "My grandmother didn't know whether [Vincent] made five cents or ten," Robert said. After he died, "the banks got ahold of my grandmother, and shit, they had money here, they owned part of this property, that property, all over town, and she had no idea that Vincent had done that with the money when he was working. He just didn't tell her anything." This Vincent was a long way from Wood's simple peasant speaking in dialect—more like the savvy man who told Wood he was hoping to inherit the shack someday. He'd taken care of his wife, financially, after his death; but he hadn't exactly told her about it, either.

Now I was cooking with gas: I had Vincent the operator, the loan shark, the real-estate speculator right there in his card room, a sharp guy, just like his grandson. And Mary? Well, she was a great cook, and worked hard. I even got a new little glimpse into their relationship. I could feel a piece of both of them alive and well in Robert, too, laughing away in my kitchen. And I was also going to get a new floor.

I've Seen the Mountaintop

"I'M GOING TO send you to one more sister," Robert announced. His younger sister May Armann, he said, had all the pictures. So two weeks later I was in Santa Clara, driving through one of those 1960s tract-house neighborhoods I had grown up near, the kind where the ranch-style houses repeat themselves and you can lose your sense of direction. Betty opened the door when I found their cul-de-sac and pulled me into the house, where I met her sister May. May sat me down immediately at the kitchen table, where she and Betty had already laid out a picture display like the one I'd seen at Betty's, but with a different set of pictures, plus a pile to the side of clippings and more photos.

Half the fun at May's was having both her and Betty there, while they zipped through the photographs and debated what they could remember. Pretty quickly I gave up on my formal set of questions and sat back to enjoy what they had to offer. Only afterward did I realize what I was really learning—and what I wasn't.

Mostly I got more details about Mary's life and character. May insisted: "She was very well educated." "She spoke Italian to the Italians in Los Gatos. She always spoke English in front of Mother, and the grandkids." Betty qualified: "Grandma did not speak what you'd call fluent English." But Mary was "not Sicilian." "Grandmother married beneath herself when she married Gagliasso. She was from the North, and he was from the South."

Again, this sounded like my own great-grandmother, and the enormous unromantic class and cultural divides between Northern and Southern Italians. My great-grandmother Tecla hadn't originally been allowed to marry her beloved because he was of too low a class background (her father was a policeman, not a mere peasant). Later, in Illinois, my aunt Leona overheard Tecla snarl at her husband, "In my country, my people would spit on your people." My aunt, growing up in an Italian immigrant coal-mining community, was allowed to play with the African-American kids but not the Sicilians.

May and Betty said they'd tried many times to get their grandmother to talk about Italy and her voyage to the United States, but she'd always refused. Once, May remembered, "she said it was a horrible experience." But every other time the kids had asked about Italy, "she'd just walk away."

Was that because things had been so awful with Pisqually Gagliasso back then? We know theirs was an arranged marriage; we know it was abusive. "He was short and fat, and always wore a black suit every time we saw him," Betty said. In the one photograph of him,

I could see a small man with a sharp nose and a thick mustache, in faded overalls and a cap, with his pants tucked into high-laced boots and chickens at his feet.

"When grandma came here she was adamant about becoming an American," May said. She produced an undated newspaper clipping, "Colonel Wood Has Patriot Reception for New Citizens," that offered a few final clues about Mary, Sara, and their relationship. "Mrs. Mary Marengo Saturday evening was hostess at 'The Cats,' home of Colonel and Mrs. Charles E. S. Wood, to a group who were instrumental in her attainment of citizenship," the article began. Vincent was "host." Guests listed included the high school principal, Mary's citizenship teachers, Miss Dorothy Tonietti (one of Vincent's sisters or sisters-in-law, Betty thought), and George Denison and Frank Ingerson (two neighboring artists who Betty remembered as a gay couple). "Mrs. McClure entertained with her delightful pianologues," the article reported. "C. Minor Moore made a gem of a speech, telling of Mrs. Marengo's faithful work as a citizen in his class, preparing for citizenship, and Sara Bard Field read some verse, a salutation to her in her new status. Colonel Charles Erskine Scott Wood, noted writer, gave a dramatic account of early citizenship in Virginia and elsewhere."

Culturally, the content sounds a lot more like Wood and Field's world than Vincent and Mary's, as does the guest list.

I went back to see what Sara had said about Mary's citizenship in her oral history. As usual, she revealed as much about herself as about Mary, though she does give us a touching glimpse of Mary: "Mary decided she wanted to get citizenship, so she went down to school nights. . . . Vincent would drive her down. Then I would coach her at the house, and finally she felt she was ready." The day before Mary's hearing, Sara and Erskine went to visit the judge and asked him to go easy on Mary, since she was so timid. "The judge called on her the very first, and the only thing he asked her was what form of government we have. I can hear her little voice saying, 'Of the people, by the people, for the people.' And that was the only question." Sara described the party afterward: "We had all the teachers from the school who had helped her and a few others that she loved, and we had dinner on little tables in the living room, and on every one there was an American flag and the various dishes would come in with American flags in them. . . . One of my friends played some amusing songs that they would enjoy and understand." Sara's account, as usual, is full of love and concern, cultural condescension, and a subtle silence as to who exactly brought those dishes in, if not Mary.

May showed me beautiful shots of the gatehouse, set idyllically in the oak forest with a balcony overlooking the valley. "But grandma kept telling us, 'Now remember, this is not my house,'" Betty said. "She told us she was never there. She told us she'd leave early in the morning, come back late at night. I don't know how they stayed married." (May slipped in: "Maybe that was how.") Once again, Mary knew exactly where her bread was buttered, and who owned what; and she also explicitly wanted her grandchildren to keep that clear.

Most shocking among the pictures was a faded color shot of Mary as an old woman. I realized I had her stuck permanently in my imagination at around 35. May also produced Mary's 1974 obituary from the San José *Mercury News*. The obituary said she came to the United States from Italy in 1902, and was survived by 12 grandchildren, 26 great-grandchildren, and 7 great-great-grandchildren. She was born in Monforte d'Alba, in the Piedmont region, maybe two hours from my grandmother's little town on the opposite side of Torino. We could be related.

Vincent's obituary, which identified him as a "gardener and chauffeur," said he had died at home at the age of 77. "He was a member of the Italian-Catholic Federation, Branch 184, and the Los Gatos Italian-American Club," it reported. I thought about the classic film, *Imitation of Life*, the original 1934 version, with its story of an African-American live-in maid and her white mistress. At the very end, when the maid dies, the mistress tracks down her funeral and discovers, to her surprise, that the maid had played a prominent role in the local African-American community. All those years the mistress had thought she knew the maid, but she hadn't had a clue as to who she really was.

During the late 1940s and '50s, my grandmother worked as a tailor doing alterations at I. Magnin's, the luxury department story, in Beverly Hills. She also made dresses on the side for rich ladies she met at the store. Thirty years after she died, we found a box with two beautiful sleek shifts inside, with "Mrs. LeRoi and Mrs. May" marked on the outside—as in the wives, evidently, of the actor Mervyn LeRoi and the namesake of the May Company, southern California's equivalent to Macy's. Like Mary, my grandmother called them "Mrs." to the end; but I'll bet they called her Marie. And I'll bet neither Mrs. knew much about Marie Bogio Frank beyond the gray braids twisted across her head and her quiet, proud demeanor.

Did Sara and Erskine ever quite know who Vincent and Mary were? Not really. Equally importantly, did I? The grandchildren opened a whole world to me; they took me far away from the diaries. I could see Vincent's sense of humor, his reticence and his volubility, his love for the garden and for Mary. I could get a sense of Mary as a dedicated worker, a loving cook, and a scarred immigrant. I could see both of them as family members who didn't confuse their own family with Wood and Fields'. I could see all sorts of photos of them with their family, even watch them age. I could read their obituaries.

But that was it. That was the mountaintop, and I realized, as May served up cream pie, that I'd reached a limit in learning about Vincent and Mary, and it was probably all downhill after that. I had a lot of revealing little tidbits, but it was hard to put them together. I was getting Vincent and Mary, and the poets, too, from grandchildren's point of view: benevolent characters at the dinner table, keepers

Mary and Vincent Marengo at the wedding of Mary's
granddaughter May Armann, 1955. PHOTOGRAPH IN COLLECTION
OF MAY ARMANN; REPRODUCTION BY VICTOR SCHIFFRIN.

of tales never told. They sounded more and more like my own grandmother, a mixture of benevolence, mystery, and a vague, never-recovered Italian past. They dissolved into anyone's grandparents; into Family History. For the great-granddaughter who hovered in May's living room, Mary Marengo was only some vague person the older folks were interested in. After a certain point, the harder I worked, the further away I would get from Vincent and Mary.

Local Girl Goes Local

I WASN'T QUITE done, though. I had one more set of tricks up my sleeve—or so I thought. I was, after all, a social historian, with a Ph.D. focusing on ordinary people in U.S. history. I had a whole set of professional tools still at my disposal to learn about Vincent and Mary. And I could use them to try to learn about the Italian community of Los Gatos, too, to go deeper into their world.

All this time I hadn't talked with a single person in Los Gatos. So I started by looking for a history museum. Right off I found a web site for the Museums of Los Gatos. The first page of their newsletter advertised an upcoming Valentine's Day art sale called "Touch my heART: That's Amore!" at which attendees could win a trip for two to Italy; Michelangelo's David gazed across the pages: "David says: order your . . . tickets today!" This wasn't exactly the Italian Los Gatos I was looking for. Nor were the results of my Google search under "Italians Los Gatos," which yielded listings of choice Italian restaurants in town along with local couples' reports of their recent trips to Italy.

I called the museum number and got redirected to the Forbes Mill Museum of Regional History. The woman who answered the phone there was incredibly efficient in answering my queries about research sources. She sent me to Peggy Conaway, who turned out to be a big find. Peggy was the director of the Los Gatos Public Library and, it turned out, very deeply engaged in local history and excited about my project. We arranged to meet at the library the next week.

I headed over Highway 17 again, dragging my friend Gerri Dayharsh with me just for fun. We waved at the white cats as I made the slightly nerveracking left turn off the highway into downtown Los Gatos. Immediately we noticed big vertical banners hanging from streetlamps with the silhouette of the cat sculptures, and a giant painting of them on the end of an apartment building. As we entered town I started remembering trips to Los Gatos in the early 1970s, when it represented the outer reach of my high school bike-riding forays from Los Altos. Now, as Gerri and I curved through town across the freeway, by a series of Victorian business blocks, I gradually transported my visual imagination back still further into the 1920s, trying to picture the town when Sara and Erskine, Vincent and Mary first moved there. We pulled over in front of the library and I looked back at the hills to point out to Gerri where The Cats estate must have been, up above.

We stopped across the street from the library to order a very tasty lunch of gazpacho, gyros, and blueberry smoothies. "I'll have the Italian coffee," requested Gerri, loyally. It was great to have a friend with me on a research trip—usually it's a pretty solitary endeavor. Over lunch I tried to explain to her some of the differences between the kind of academic history I was trained in, and the world of local history. Professionals usually disdain most local history as "antiquarian"—that is, concerned only with the past for the past's sake, preserving factoids or events simply because they happened. I didn't go that far, but I was conscious that the pull of local history is naturally toward things that happened inside a narrow geographical range. Big national or global developments like the New Deal, World War I, or mass immigration tend to drop out of the story, while local entrepreneurial elites loom far larger than their actual historical importance. And, of course, any kind of economic development is usually by definition Good.

I'd found one book on Los Gatos history, and it epitomized these pitfalls: *History of Los Gatos, Gem of the Foothills*, a coffee-table book published in 1971 by George G. Bruntz, a local high school teacher (and, coincidentally, Mary Marengo's citizenship instructor). "It covers location, climate, beauty; it tells of the struggles of the pioneers to bring about industries or expand horticulture and agriculture; and the building of mountain roads; advent and demise of railroads; and finally the arrival of today's freeways," Bruntz opened. "Schools, churches, service clubs all are given their fair share of attention. In fact the entire spectrum of life comes under the purview of the writer in this absorbing story." Actually, Bruntz's spectrum missed a whole lot: the entire ethnic history of Los Gatos, for example, including immigrants from China, Japan, Europe, and Latin America. We got the history of the fruit-packing industry, but no sense of the daily life of the people who packed the fruit or what they did after work. Completely out of the picture were the lives of servants like Vincent or Mary, for example, or the daily life of women cooking meals and raising children. This classic "celebrity entrepreneurs" approach to local history lived on most recently in a 2005 museum exhibit in Los Gatos entitled "Grist, Gumption, and Genius," which showcased "a few innovative businesses, products and ideas that were born and at least partially raised in Los Gatos" such as gopher traps, pet rocks, and "early high-tech products."

After lunch Gerri and I tromped across the lawn and into Los Gatos Public Library. I left her upstairs with the novels and wove downstairs to find Peggy, who turned out to be incredibly helpful. We shared ritual offerings: I showed her some of my choice photocopies from the Huntington and told her about the videos and grandkids; she handed me a folder of clippings about The Cats she'd already generously copied for me.

Peggy also gave me a copy of a new book she'd just published on Los Gatos history, part of a standardized national series of local histories commissioned by Arcadia Publishing. It was a picture book in the old-fashioned genre, with an explanatory paragraph under each shot, but in contrast to Bruntz, Peggy had done a great job of including ordinary people. We could see farmers delivering wagonloads of fruit at the train station or women workers pitting peaches inside a cannery. She'd been careful to include diverse ethnic groups, along with shots capturing daily life on the street, inside stores, or at cultural events like the "Whiskerino Celebration" and the "Pageant of Fulfillment."

Peggy led me into a tiny hallway in the back designated the Local History Room and set me up to poke around to my heart's content. As usual, it was easy to learn lots more about Wood and Field. Peggy's folder had all sorts of newspaper articles and miscellaneous documents from the twenties through the present, like a 1944 story, "Author's Will Hits 'Insanity' of Capitalism" or a column from the 1960s or '70s entitled "Col. Wood: A Traitor to His Class."

Looking around the materials in the room, I had to keep asking myself: where would the Italians be? I tried a big filing cabinet on the left and three rows of blue binders above it full of newspaper clippings and photographs. They were organized around topics like "Droughts," "Vehicles," "Downtown Buildings," or "Pioneers." (My favorite was "Permanent Citizens," a misspelling of "prominent".) Elites were everywhere. The closest I could get to Vincent and Mary in those files was a bit about the history of their Catholic church, St. Mary's, mostly the comings and goings of successive priests. I tried a binder marked "History 1885–1971," but only gleaned news about banks, clubs, and businesses, or enticing stories like "20,000 Visitors Saw Baby Show on May Day" or "Apricot Kernels Bring High Price."

Then my detective skills kicked in. Over to one side were a series of dull-looking books called city directories, from various dates beginning in 1919. City directories are extremely important to social historians because they provide information about ordinary people. Before phone books displaced them, directories listed residents, their addresses, and occupations. Pulling 1925 off the shelf and flipping through the alphabetized names, I finally hit pay dirt: "Gagliasso Pasquale lab h 511 Univ." That told me where Gagliasso had lived, and that he was a "laborer." Then I found "Marengo Mrs. Lucile h 146 College": I had the address of Vincent's mother's house. In the appended "rural" section, I found "Marengo, V. PO box." Not much there; but a little historian's shiver nonetheless went up my spine because I'd found Vincent's actual existence in the middle of all the bankers and inventors. The directories were chock full of Gagliassos, but nothing much more on the Marengos. In a 1950 phone book I did get Vincent's number, "El gato 4-1394".

If I'd wanted to, though, I could have used the directories to reconstruct all sorts of things about the Italian community the Marengos had been part of. "All these Italians lived on University Avenue," Betty had told me. "We called it Little Italy. Of course the Italians were all close together." Indeed, the city directories gave me "John Vedova Cement Contractor" at 226 Bachman Street—the same street on which Mary and Vincent would live in the 1950s. Or "John Traina: Fruits and Vegetables" and "Mrs. Luella Traina, Confectioner," along with St. Mary's Catholic Church and the "Los Gatos Pool Room" at 35 N. Santa Cruz Avenue—perhaps the place where Vincent cut his loan deals. Going over those directories, year after year, I started recognizing some of the most prominent Italian names, like Barbaro, and wondered which of those families produced the Italian women who left their husbands in the 1920s. I also, somewhat eerily, started recognizing names from my high school, not so far away to the north; Italian ones like Traina but also other ones like Silva or Lepetich.

My Los Gatos trip got me going again—what about all those Italian friends, relatives, and purveyors to Vincent and Mary? Back in the UC Santa Cruz library, I tried another social historian tool, the manuscript census. Most people, when they think of the census, think of the aggregate numbers. I could look in a bound book from the Fourteenth Census in 1920 for example, and learn that there were a total of 6,285 Italians in Santa Clara County. But the really cool stuff lies in the original pages on which the census-taker wrote down detailed information, house by house, street by street, about specific individuals. Copies of these manuscript pages are available on microfilm up though 1930. Depending on the year, they can list not only an individual's name and address, but their citizenship, education, race, age, gender, marital status, age at first marriage, literacy, place of birth and that of each of their parents, occupation, relation to the "head of the family" and whether or not they rented or owned their home. Hard-core social historians use these entries to reconstruct entire communities in minute detail.

I, too, could have used the manuscript census to learn an enormous amount about Mary and Vincent's world. But with the clock ticking, I settled for whatever I could learn about Mary and Vincent themselves. After an irritating three hours searching tediously through microfilm pages for all Santa Clara County— sometimes impossible to read because they were poorly filmed or because I couldn't read the census taker's handwriting—the shiver shot up my spine one last time: There was Mary Gagliasso in 1920, age 32, and her three children, Marguerite, 15, born in Italy; Ida, 14, and George, 12, born in California. That meant Mary had been maybe 17 when Marguerite was born. Mary said she entered the U.S. in 1905. Putting the details together, that meant she might have been pregnant with Ida on the ship crossing—imagine the morning sickness. Pasquale, I could see now, had been ten years older than Mary. In the 1920 census I found both Vincent and his mother. He

told the census taker that he became a naturalized citizen in 1913—
at least two decades, then, before Mary did. (Sara, by contrast,
told her interviewer that "Vincent never changed his citizenship,
although he didn't like it.") The 1930 census offered a few more
tidbits: Mary was now Mary Benevelli, no longer Gagliasso, but
not yet Marengo. Sara and Erskine, for their part, told the census
taker they were married (which they weren't—at least not to each
other) and that her name was "Sara Bard Wood." So much for the
historical accuracy of the manuscript census.

It was certainly thrilling to see all their names there in the census
taker's original handwriting. Mary and Vincent, in particular, were
somehow more "real"; I'd proven their existence, somehow, in the
official (if suspect) historical record. But I wasn't learning much that
I didn't already know. It was more like I was confirming what the
grandkids had already said. For all my professional tricks, it felt like
I was back in the land of diminishing returns.

Still looking for Los Gatos Italians, I tried a Web site for the
Italian American Heritage Foundation of Santa Clara County,
but it mostly just offered me a "Historic Photo Collection" that
"recognizes prominent Italian Americans who, from the earliest of
recorded time in Santa Clara County, have contributed significantly
to its development through farming, various businesses, professions,
community service, events, and organizations at least fifty years old."
I was circling back to what's known as Great Man History, only
Italian style.

In a last burst of scholarly energy, I tracked down a whole pile
of books with titles like *From Italy to San Francisco* or *Italian
Immigration and the Development of California Agriculture*; articles
like "Italians of Los Angeles: An Historical Overview"; and even,
looking for Mary and the other women, "Breadwinners and Builders:
Stockton's Immigrant Women," with a section on Italians. But my
heart wasn't in it. The academic studies would be terrific on the big

picture of why people like Mary and Vincent came from Italy in the first place, why they ended up in places like Los Gatos, and why they specialized in trades like winemaking. But as individuals, my friends would disappear.

I'd run out of time, and spirit, and it was time to close the books and accept some kind of little defeat. I sent the books back, shut my filing cabinet, and admitted to myself that the trail had run truly dry. The school year was starting and I had other duties.

Just before classes began I went on a little trip to Providence, Rhode Island, to give a talk at Brown University, and had breakfast with my friend Paul Buhle, a well-known historian of the American Left. Paul is legendary for his encyclopedic knowledge of Left history trivia. Sitting in the car with him in his driveway, I started to tell him about my research on C. E. S. Wood. "Here's a trivia test you'll enjoy: I'm writing about an anarchist in Los Gatos . . . " Before I could finish my sentence, he jumped in: "Ah, that was where they might have published the Italian anarchist newspaper, *L'Adunata dei Refrattari*, in the 1920s, after the editors had to leave New York and go underground because they advocated the armed struggle."

Well. Maybe the real anarchist in Los Gatos wasn't Wood, it was Vincent. Maybe Vincent was part of a secret underground anarchist cell. For all I knew, Vincent could have been listening to his boss mouth off all day about anarchism and never uttered a peep to him about the anarchist newspaper someone was cranking out across town, in Italian. There were only about 200 Italians in that town in the 1920s. Vincent had to have known about the anarchists. No hint of any leftward tilt on Vincent's part ever popped up in the diaries. But the clever servant might have been keeping things to himself. Who knows, today, what was going on in that card room? I don't really think Vincent was an anarchist—it would have come out, I think, in the way he helped raised Mary's children, and the ideas he passed on to them. But I can't be 100 percent sure.

On the plane to a conference in Toronto a few days later I sat next to Jennifer Guglielmo, who was finishing a book on Italian anarchist women in New York and New Jersey in the early twentieth century, called *The Anarchist in the Kitchen*. I told her the details of Vincent and Mary's story in detail and what Paul had said. As we flew across the Canadian border, Jennifer and I suddenly had the exact same thought: why Vincent? What if Mary had been the secret anarchist, laughing in the kitchen? It was completely implausible, but still tantalizing.

Gated Communities

I DID HAVE one last ritual visitation to make before I closed up shop. All the months and months I'd been researching The Cats, I had never made it up the road, inside the gate to actually see the original buildings and surrounding estate.

My plan was to look up the owners' names on the deed in the county public records office, write the owners, explain my project, and hope they'd invite me up. I knew from Sara's diaries and oral history that the house had been sold in 1955 to Diane and Bruce Ogilvie. I knew from driving by The Cats in the 1970s, '80s, and '90s that they or some subsequent owner had gradually added a curving stucco fence, two oak barrels, a metal gate and, later, a hanging green light. But I had no idea who currently owned the place or lived up there.

Ken Christopher, a friend at work, had told me his friend Sallie Johnson used to live at The Cats. I called Sallie, who turned out to live around the corner from me, and she stopped by. She told me she'd rented the gatehouse at The Cats with her husband and son for a year or so beginning in late 1967. The big house up on the hill, she said, was cut up into studios and rentals; the outbuildings had been rented out, too. The place was all overgrown. "You could get lost in the chaparral." Wandering around the property, Sallie had found tucked away in the undergrowth all kinds of clues to the poets' former heyday: stone benches with inscriptions like "we had a wonderful picnic here today," the remains of an abandoned vineyard on the hillside, and a sculpted portrait of Sara Bard Field built into an exterior wall of the big house.

The owners and landlords since the 1950s, Diane and Bruce Ogilvie, she said, had lived in the main house. Bruce was a professor of sports psychology at San José State; Diane was a torch singer, "a faded rose," as Sallie put it. In the late sixties she was still getting bookings in Los Gatos—singing Judy Garland songs and the like. "She'd stop by the gatehouse on her way in to the gig, to show off her feathered splendor." Their son Doug lived up top in the big house. "Doug was a physical specimen. He lifted weights every morning in the solarium. You could hear the weights clanking." Sallie didn't know much of what happened later, though she thought the Ogilvies still owned the place. But she'd given me a glimpse, if a somewhat depressing one, of the post-poets Cats. At least the place hadn't been torn down to build a Silicon Valley executive mansion as I had feared.

I talked to Peggy Conaway, the librarian, about my dream of seeing The Cats. She'd tried various angles, she said, but never gotten in. But a professor from Arizona who'd come through town a while back, researching Wood and Field, had told her that she'd heard Diane Ogilvie still haunted the bar and restaurant next door, also called "The Cats." The professor had said she was going to try to stake out Diane in the bar.

I decided it was time for a last supper of sorts at the Cats Restaurant. The place had its own set of urban legends to outrival my sculptures, usually involving illicit sex. In *Highway 17: The Road to Santa Cruz*, Richard A. Beal writes that "the Cats Roadhouse served as a way-station for the horse-driven wagons on their way to San José, as well as a rowdy social club. . . . At the time the road was first paved, around 1920, the Cats was one of the more notorious speakeasies and bordellos." In the 1940s and '50s the place toned down to host a gun shop and real-estate office, then reopened in 1967 in its latest incarnation as a semi-restored bar and restaurant. Several people I talked with mentioned that it had been a gay bar in the 1970s; others said it was a straight pickup joint.

Somehow I myself was under the impression that the Cats Restaurant was currently a straight biker bar. So I invited my friends Carter and Thomas, both very tall, very substantial guys, to escort me as protection (hoping the bikers wouldn't notice they were a couple). As we pulled into the parking lot in Thomas's gold PT Cruiser the other cars weren't Harleys, though, but Mercedes and Jaguars. Inside, the bar was lovely and dark, with a mishmash of oak counters, wood paneling, Tiffany lamps, and framed clippings about Diane Ogilvie's nightclub act. That evening's clientele of clean-cut heterosexual couples in polo shirts and khakis suggested slumming yuppies, not leather guys, gay or straight.

My scheme was to gradually win over the bartender and with my charm and detective skills eventually gain access to Diane Ogilvie. But the minute I subtly broached the subject to our superfriendly waiter Alan, he cheerfully announced that Diane came in every night, in about an hour, and he'd be happy to send her to our table.

The menu offered various renditions of big hunks of barbequed meat, served atop tables with song lyrics decoupaged into their yellowing varnish. Midway through the roast beast, Diane plopped herself down next to me. I couldn't have made her up. She had to be at least in her late seventies, and was wearing a red glittery top under a creamy satin blouse, with spiral dangly earrings, long white hair pulled back into a red scrunchy, and sleek black satin pants, all ready for the stage. The joke was on me: I'd thought it was going to be hard to get her to talk, but she couldn't stop talking—entirely about herself. "I had a husband who was fabulous," she gushed. "I only married him because he was gorgeous," she announced, whipping out an ancient 5-by-7 photo of the two as a young couple. He was in fact very handsome, in an Erroll Flynn way. Diane said he had died in the 1990s.

Diane confirmed that she and Bruce had bought The Cats estate in the '50s. Then she kept talking about what else she'd bought, built, or developed since then, including all the property between the sculptures and the original estate, the bar/restaurant we sat in, and various houses and cabins extending up the hillside. She also made it sound like she owned half the real estate in downtown Los Gatos. She gushed on and on. But I couldn't get her interested in anything about The Cats before she owned it, or the fate of its various structures.

Nor did I ever get the gumption to pop the question of whether I could come visit it. I just didn't like the ethics of chatting her up only to advance my own research purposes.

I told Kirk Smith, Erskine's grandson, and his wife Pat about my hopes of someday seeing The Cats. They were interested, too, and knew someone who knew Diane's daughter, who also lived on the estate. But, again, I felt manipulative asking them to help get me in, and let the idea drop. The Ogilvies had their own private family now at The Cats, and this time I hadn't been invited in. Perhaps the hillside was gorgeously manicured; perhaps it was overgrown. But as Pat pointed out, "They might not have a wonderful Vincent" to keep it lovely.

The gates stayed shut. In the end, it was like an adventure movie, in which the heroes intrepidly wend their way deeper and deeper down a tunnel only to discover there's another brightly lit door deep inside, sealed shut.

Who Built History?

THE GATES OF my historical imagination, though, had swung wide open. I had started out vaguely curious about who'd built my stone cats, and found out more than I'd thought possible, not just about two bohemian poets and their estate on the hill, but about their two lifelong servants, and their lives together as masters and servants. My private memory had opened up into a wider narrative about class, deference, and dignity in a country built on myths of equality.

Sara Bard Field and Charles Erskine Scott Wood were wonderfully attractive people, with fascinating creative lives that splayed across the western landscape and, especially, in their later years, the Los Gatos foothills. I didn't doubt that Erskine, especially, believed what he said about democracy, equality, and liberation; I didn't doubt that they respected and cared about Vincent and Mary Marengo. For thirty years the two couples' lives were intertwined at an intimate and daily level, in houses not far apart, eating the same food, looking out at a garden lovingly tended. But Sara and Erskine's benevolent appreciation of their servants was always swimming in condescension, in paternalism, in stories they told themselves about how they were subtly but assuredly smarter, more valuable, ultimately simply better than the two working-class Italian immigrants with whom they lived.

Were Mary and Vincent their equals? Of course. They were human beings, with hopes, dreams, parents, children, and a joyous love for each other that wasn't that different from Sara and Erskine's. And yet, on that hillside they weren't. All day, every day, the two poets explored their respective inner essences while Vincent and Mary picked up the mail, rooted out the weeds, washed the sheets, and shooed away unwelcome visitors. Six, sometimes seven days a week; ten, twelve, fourteen or more hours a day or more, they did what their two employers told them to do, well aware, especially during the Depression, that they were lucky to have good work. Vincent laughed at the Colonel's jokes; Mary put on those white, painstakingly ironed uniforms every morning and had dinner on the table every night—on Sara's table, not her own. Even the house Mary and Vincent lived in wasn't theirs, as Mary was quick to remind her grandkids. Vincent and Mary watched patiently over the Wood and Field grandchildren, but rarely saw their own.

Are they equal in the eyes of history? My upstairs, downstairs story at The Cats was ultimately a saga of the unequal politics of history. Sara and Erskine jumped out of the historical sources, waving furiously at me. I could have kept learning more about them for the rest of my life, literally: I'd only opened a dozen of those three hundred boxes of their papers at the Huntington. I could spend years on a literary analysis of their hundreds of published books, poems, book reviews, editorials, speeches, letters to the editor and assorted rants. For every letter they'd received, carefully hoarded, they'd sent two or three others; I could track down those thousands of letters in the archived collections of their vast web of correspondents. Then there were all the additional sources I could draw on to reconstruct Erskine's time harassing Indians or Sara's trip across the country promoting women's suffrage.

Wood and Field, I came to realize, had created their own historical importance rather brilliantly. "How determined they are to carve their names on the walls of fame," wrote a local columnist about the two in 1929. They'd left all those documents, schmoozed with all those famous people, and that on its own made them historically important. They wrote those voluminous diaries self-consciously for posterity, too, pulling me into their world view. Most obviously, their sculpted cats by the side of the road, erected in part to stress Wood and Field's own importance as artistic benefactors, had quite successfully roped me into writing about them seventy-five years later.

Sara Bard Field and C. E. S. Wood could put up those cats, and produce all those documents only because Vincent and Mary Marengo were doing the rest of their work. As Wood himself put it so honestly, "the real obstacle to creative work is . . . household drudgery for which we should have a servant." Both the poets' artistic production *and* our memory of it depended on the servants in the wings.

Vincent and Mary, by contrast, slip away, out of the story. They owned no movie cameras. I think I spent so much time knocking on doors, barking up often fruitless trees, because for me they came to stand for all the invisible people in U.S. history who never make it into the history books, who do the work, then disappear; who lead ordinary lives while making other people's lives easier, more creative, and more historically memorable. Just as I was finishing my research on the Marengos, my own father died, the son and grandson of Italian immigrants. I had less than an hour to sum up his entire life in a 243-word obituary. He left no three hundred boxes of papers, just a bundle of letters he'd written to his mom during World War II. Would he, too, disappear from history?

For all the skills I could muster, I couldn't make Vincent and Mary equals to Erskine and Sara in the historical record. I could only peer into the microfilm, piece together tidbits, and speculate. I also had to accept that Mary, in particular, wanted some things to remain private forever, especially her time in Italy and her first marriage. She had closed one historical door herself. Maybe she and Vincent were not as passive in this story as I'd cast them. Maybe they wanted their privacy. As they scrubbed the floors and the Model T, year after year, did they also "know their place" not just at The Cats, but in history?

But then I myself stepped in to change the story. Writing this, I made their private story public. Would they, perhaps, become famous now because I wrote about them? Or rather, would I, local girl writing this, "make history," instead, because I wrote a story honoring them?

Who exactly came out ahead here? After all, like Wood and Field, I was a leftist, feminist, vaguely bohemian writer who didn't have to clean houses all day. I was a member of the Yale club, an insider at the Huntington, not the security guard.

MY LINOLEUM GUY, Robert Balzer, Mary's grandson, came back when the vinyl arrived to put in my kitchen floor. He brought along his son Jeff, a big, broad-chested guy who installed floors up in the Sierra foothills, in Placerville, where he was building a new house. As they cut and laid the floor, I listened to their affectionately competitive father-son banter about who knew best about how to cut corners or lay seams. Robert called his son "Junior" the whole time, although Jeff was at least a whole head taller and crossing into middle age.

As we waited for the glue to dry and I passed Robert and Jeff a substantial roll of bills, I read them the passage from Sara's autobiography in which she describes Vincent and Mary as the kind of perfect servant you just can't get anymore. I read the part, too, where she buys them a house in Los Gatos. I pointed out that Jeff and Robert, Mary's grandson and great-grandson, were now working for me, the bohemian intellectual.

"They were good subservient servants, and she built them a house in Placerville," mocked Jeff.

"I'm not buying you a house," I protested.

"You just did," he pointed out. "You just bought a little piece of it."

I like to think Vincent the card shark would smile at that.

The Pulgas Water Temple when it was first constructed in 1938.

CHAPTER 4

I HEARD IT THROUGH
THE PULGAS WATER TEMPLE

ON TRIPS NORTH TO San Francisco, if we weren't in a hurry, instead of taking the Bayshore Freeway my father would sometimes follow a series of back roads along the eastern base of the hills that march up the peninsula. One of those, Cañada Road, wound along the side of Crystal Springs Reservoir. As you passed the reservoir, you could just barely see the Pulgas Water Temple off to the left, where the city's water supply bubbled up after passing through dams, pipes, and tunnels all the way from Yosemite's Hetch Hetchy Valley in the Sierra Nevada, and then flowed out into the reservoir.

We'd stop there sometimes on the way to the city during the early 1960s. The temple was nestled off to the left in the oak trees—white, somehow Greek-looking with a circular array of columns atop a pedestal. It had a lovely grassy slope leading down to it and a long reflecting pool in front. In the middle of its columns, behind a low wall, lay a deep, well-like hole lined with aqua blue tiles. If you peeked down over the wall you could see the water come rushing up into it dramatically, bubbling in from a hole in one side with a loud roar and then swirling out a tunnel on the other side, on its way to the reservoir. Once, I remember, my dad grabbed me by the waist from behind and pretended he was going to throw me in. I was terrified, and for years afterward thought he shouldn't have done that, even though I knew perfectly well he was the most mild-mannered man on the planet and didn't mean to scare me so much.

When I was in the eighth grade or maybe a freshman in high school, a story went around about the Pulgas Water Temple. According to the story, there were these guys who would jump down into the temple and ride the water out through the tunnel to the reservoir. They had to calculate it just right. If the water level was too high, they'd drown in the tunnel. But if the water level was too low, they'd hit bottom when they jumped in and break their necks.

I always remembered the story of those jumpers, partly because I was so impressed that they'd actually leapt in, partly because I liked the bit about the exact water level calculation, and, most of all, because once I heard about them, I secretly wanted to jump into the temple myself, too. I knew perfectly well I would never have to guts to do it, but for years and years I imagined what it would be like. The story also stuck with me because I never, ever knew if it was true. Did those heroic guys actually exist? *Was* it possible to jump into the temple and survive? Or was their story just an urban myth, floating up and down high schools on the San Francisco Peninsula?

A few years ago, I started asking around among my friends who'd grown up in the area, trying to figure out if my story of the jumpers was true. I hit up my friend Casey Carlson, who'd grown up in San José. "Do you remember any stories about the Pulgas Water Temple? "That's where my mom said they put LSD in the water supply," she answered immediately, though she'd never heard about anyone jumping in. I tried Stephen McCabe, father of my "nieces" Becky and Ramona; he grew up in Santa Clara. "I never heard about anyone jumping in," he said. But he'd heard that the water in the temple made it all the way from Hetch Hetchy to Crystal Springs purely by gravity—although he'd never been quite sure if that was true.

My friend Cathy Buller said she'd heard there were people who ran naked through the pools in front of the temple.

I tried my best friend since I was four, Judy Shizuru, who'd gone to my same schools and might have heard about the jumpers. She hadn't, but said that when she was a kid, she'd thought there'd originally been a town under Crystal Springs Reservoir, before the dam. "I remember going there and you'd look at the town where it had been flooded. There was the temple and there had been the town." Laughing, somewhat embarrassed, she confessed: "I always thought it was a temple they put up to honor the people they flooded in the town. When I was little I thought they flooded the town with the people in it."

What was it about this place? Everyone had a story, and all the stories hovered right on the border of true or not true (well, except for the last bit from Judy about the live drowning people). They could all be urban myths or they could all be "true," for all I knew. I decided to find out.

What I eventually learned was often unsettling, preposterous, or merely silly, and the line between truth and fiction was consistently porous. I got a good sense of how the Pulgas Water Temple—sitting there so serenely in our imaginative landscape—has served as a charming but powerful pawn in the grand scheme of California's environmental politics; and I figured out, too, how its attractions had converged so perfectly with the culture of the 1960s and my own generation to make it the ultimate hippie symbol of mystical timelessness. Perhaps most importantly, I came to understand why we told and retold these particular stories about the Pulgas Water Temple, and what our urban myths revealed about the imagined California in which they they helped us believe.

Hydrology Worship

I THOUGHT I'D start with Steve's story about the water making it all the way from the Sierra to the peninsula on gravity alone, rather than using pumps or any external power. Several other people had heard this story too, and I figured researching it would get me into the basics about the temple itself and its construction. I soon found several books on the origins of the Hetch Hetchy system, which moves water from Yosemite National Park all the way into the city's water outlets. In the archives of the San Mateo County Historical Society I also found a gold mine of newspaper clippings on the temple itself, spanning sixty years.

The Hetch Hetchy system is certainly very famous, first, because it was an enormous engineering feat. As San Francisco expanded in the late nineteenth century, the city's water demands quickly started to outgrow its supply, since it was at the tip of a peninsula with no direct watershed to draw on. Beginning in the 1860s, the City bought water from a corrupt private enterprise called the Spring Valley Water Company, owned by local elite businessmen, which itself bought up watersheds and built reservoirs all over the greater Bay Area—100,000 acres from the lower peninsula to Pleasanton, far away past the East Bay hills. By 1900, even Spring Valley's water wasn't enough, though, and a group of San Francisco entrepreneurs got the idea of shipping water down from the Sierra Nevada. They landed their sights on the Hetch Hetchy Valley in newly formed Yosemite National Park. After a massive propaganda campaign, these promoters successfully passed a $45 million bond act in which the people of San Francisco voted to move in on Hetch Hetchy and build a massive set of dams, pipes, and tunnels to transport its water to their doorsteps. In 1913 Congress passed the Raker Act making it legal for the city to appropriate a large piece of the national park.

By 1934, the system was complete. Looking at the maps, I was astonished to see quite how much was—and is—involved in moving all that water: a huge dam in Hetch Hetchy; two other smaller dams at Lloyd Lake and Lake Eleanor; the big ugly power plant and electrical lines that snake up the bald mountainside by Priest Grade at Moccasin Flat on the way in to Yosemite; fifty miles of pipes across the San Joaquin Valley; a 25-mile-long tunnel under the Coast Range; mystery pipes that parallel the Dumbarton Bridge on their own trestle, then plunge under the Bay along the sea floor; big white pipes on stilts snaking through residential neighborhoods in Sunnyvale, Palo Alto, Redwood City, and San Mateo; and all the water in Crystal Springs Reservoir, waiting to flow north into even more reservoirs and water stations on the way to San Francisco and inside it. Gray Brechin, in *Imperial San Francisco*, underscores the vast regional domination the Hetch Hetchy system achieved, as the city reached out in tentacular fashion not only to snatch up the Sierra snowfall, but to buy and transform huge hunks of land all over the state to transport and store its water and then use it to generate electricity.

San Francisco's water system is even more famous among environmentalists for its destruction of the stunning Hetch Hetchy Valley—which was, after all, part of a national park supposedly dedicated to the preservation of nature's wonders for all eternity. During the 1900s and 1910s, as San Francisco elites plotted to build O'Shaughnessy Dam at Hetch Hetchy, John Muir and other conservationists mounted a losing national campaign against it. Environmentalists have called for the dismantling of the dam ever since, and the issue is very much alive today.

The Pulgas Water Temple was built as a propaganda tool in this ongoing battle. Its backers got the idea from the Sunol Water Temple, built much earlier in 1910 near Pleasanton in Alameda County. As conflicts between San Francisco and the the Spring

Valley Water Company had heated up at the turn of the century, the company had erected this first temple in order to deflect attacks on its monopoly power. Edward F. O'Day, writing in an architectural journal in 1922, rather baldly summed up the domination it both symbolized and sought to ameliorate: "In the water temple at Sunol all the waters from the Alameda source of the Spring Valley Water Company—sources that represent control of six hundred square miles of watershed—meet and mingle for their long journey to San Francisco." According to Brechin, William B. Bourn II, president of Spring Valley, "modeled the structure after the Temple of Vesta at Tivoli, northeast of Rome ... to make explicit the connection between the Sunol temple and the means by which the Eternal City had annexed *its* neighborhood" (i.e., the expansion of the Roman Empire) and thus to "allay the decades-worth of friction."

O'Day reported in 1922 that the Sunol temple's waters originally met and bubbled up "in a rude shed" in which "display of the volume and crystal purity of the water was impossible except by dropping flaming newspapers through the trap-door of the shed." (We can imagine august water entrepreneurs having a good old time reverting to adolescent bad-boy behavior). "President Bourn appreciated the desirability of a more dignified treatment of this important point of water control."

Willis Polk, the temple's architect, drew on Greek and Roman inspiration to design a sixteen-foot-high, 25-foot-diameter round temple, with 24 columns holding up a conical top, plopped down in the middle of a wide-open plain near Pleasanton. A biblical quote scrolled loftily around the top: "I WILL MAKE THE WILDERNESS A POOL OF WATER. THE STREAM WHEREOF SHALL MAKE GLAD THE CITY." Actually the Temple Fathers patched together two disparate quotes, one from Isiah 41:18 and the other from Psalms 46:4, to suggest that God had personally commanded the Spring Valley company to build dams for San Francisco. Playing off the same noble-classical theme, the water company in its 1912 report captioned a large photograph of the temple, "THE MEETING OF THE WATERS."

When the Hetch Hetchy system was finished in 1934, San Francisco wanted its own temple, too. Cleverly responding to environmentalist attacks, the water system's managers elevated their "achievement" by fusing a celebration of their own engineering brilliance with images of classical dignity, imperial grandeur, and water worship in a second pseudo-classical temple. The original 1934 Pulgas Water Temple was an exact, smaller, papier-mache replica of the Sunol temple. The name "pulgas," which means "fleas," came from unhappy Spanish settlers' name for the site, eventually known in the Hetch Hetchy system as the Pulgas Outfall. This 1934 Pulgas Temple, unlike the later, permanent temple, was constructed directly alongside the reservoir, straddling the point where the Hetch Hetchy waters dumped out of a flume into the lake. It was built as a public-relations device, a stage for a giant press conference that took place on October 28, 1934, the day the waters first flowed. Secretary of the Interior Harold Ickes showed up to give a nationally broadcast radio speech, and the city got its grand occasion into the national press.

I could never find out what happened to that original, temporary Pulgas temple—presumably it ignobly melted in the winter's rains and was carted off by maintenance workers. Two years later, in 1936, the *San Francisco Chronicle* reported that "a block of granite will be transported to the outfall and suitably inscribed. A clear pool of mountain water will shimmer beneath playing fountains." By 1937–38 the Public Utilities Commission had authorized a permanent temple on the site "and the conversion of this area into a grander spot where visitors may view the water from Hetch Hetchy pouring into the Crystal Springs reservoir, at the end of its long journey from the high Sierras." The current version of temple was completed in July 1938, and evidently opened without any fanfare at all. Made of cast stone, granite, and concrete, it was a circle of ten sixty-foot-tall columns, topped by a ring, open to the sky in its center. Assorted grape leaves, zigzags, lion's heads, and other neoclassical froufrou were carved into the stone. Its own Bible quote curved around the top: "I give waters in the wilderness and rivers in the desert to give drink to my people" (Isaiah 43:20). Inside, maybe twelve feet down, the water roared up in a greenish-blue tiled basin about ten feet wide, with a curved round weir in the middle, with tunnels for the water to enter and exit on opposite sides.

The newspaper clippings I found betrayed a vast confusion about who had actually designed the temple. "No one knows who designed this . . . structure," declared Carolyn Adams of *The Country Almanac* in 1978. Tim Goode, in the *Peninsula Times-Tribune,* repeated Adams's assertion in 1991. One theory attributed the temple to Willis Polk, who'd designed the buildings at Filoli, Spring Valley president Bourn's estate down the road. Another theory gave credit to San Francisco architect John Reid, Jr. In *Sacred Places of San Francisco,* Ruth Willard concludes that "Pulgas was actually designed in miniature by artist William Merchant." A prominent stone-carver, Albert Bernasconi, she says, then "scaled it up to the size he thought best, and built it, using California granite, cast stone, and concrete." Bernasconi had worked on all sorts of famous buildings, including San Francisco's City Hall, Opera House, Grace Cathedral, and parts of the University of California, Berkeley. The sculptor allegedly said he forgot these other buildings after a while, but declared: "This is one I don't forget. I built the temple, myself."

The sources were even fudgier about the temple's exact architectural style. Willard said it was "modeled after the *tholoi,* or round temples sometimes built near their waterways by the ancient Greeks." A 1972 newspaper columnist likewise promised that "a visitor may get a glimpse of ancient Greece" upon visiting the temple. Others went for Rome. Gray Brechin quotes an undated

Chronicle story describing the temple as "a little bit of Rome out there in the California meadow, a sort of reminder of the aqueducts that made Roman civilization." Similarly, the *San Mateo County Times* in 2002 reported that "The Pulgas Water Temple looks like a gigantic stone gazebo plucked out of ancient Rome." My favorite commentator, in 1954, depicted the noble temple in its opening line as "standing like a Roman carport." From "Roman" some observers unwittingly slid over to "Romanesque," an entirely different architectural style from the Middle Ages. On the architectural front, commentators also loved to knowingly point out that the columns were Corinthian—an echo of the days when all educated persons memorized the difference among Doric, Ionian, and Corinthian columns. (I tried in my youth but could never get it.) Many, begging the historical references, simply went for "classical," "neoclassical," or "Greco-Roman."

Whichever the exact style, the temple's originators were using the power of imagined classical imagery to legitimate their domination of the California landscape. Wrapping themselves in the Greco-Roman flag, they set themselves up as august personages bringing order, peace, spiritual harmony, and crystalline water to the masses, who would now see the virtue of the Hetch Hetchy project while they watched the waters flowing from the temple. Their cleverness in drawing upon classical imagery, though, could not fully disguise the bizarreness of plonking down a round, white Greekish temple in the middle of Northern California's oak grasslands. Those of us who are from California think it's normal that our landscape is littered with anachronistic monuments like Hearst Castle, San Francisco's Palace of the Legion of Honor, or the Huntington Library and Gardens, in which western elites imported their own renditions of the classical world and presented them as somehow normally present in the twentieth century, in order to shore up their cultural authority. Those who didn't grow up here, by contrast, are more likely think these landmarks are a bit less normal. My editor at City Lights, Elaine Katzenberger, for example, who grew up in Connecticut, thought it pretty strange that San Francisco's water officials had erected "this weird pagoda" to justify their machinations.

Although the temple's promoters envisioned the Pulgas Water Temple as a monument to their superior wisdom and triumphal engineering feat, its evocative architecture and placid, natural setting soon, however, trumped tunnel-and-dam worship. The *Chronicle*'s 1936 article heralding the new temple had hoped that "the people should be allowed to see, and let their imaginations dwell upon the

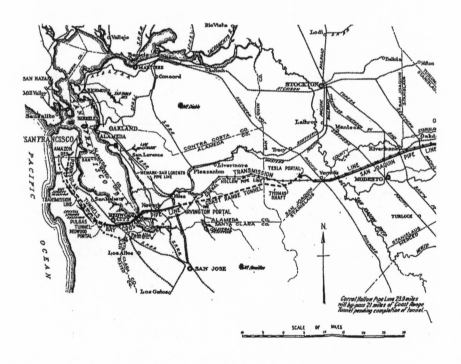

200 miles of pipe-line and . . . tunnel, constructed and bored through hard rock at great human sacrifice, through which the water has rushed to local storage reservoirs." But the people's imaginations dwelled instead on neoclassical paganism and what might lie in the picnic basket. "Water Temple attracts visitors, offers a place of contemplation," ran a subhead in the 1994 *Examiner*. "It's a good place to come meditate," confirmed Mr. Fried of Foster City. After supervising the site's groundskeepers for twenty years in the eighties and nineties, Gary Fisher concluded: "Mostly it's a place where people come to reflect."

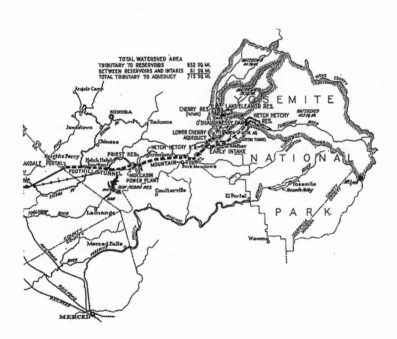

Official map of the Hetch Hetchy System, 1931.

FROM M. M. O'SHAUGHNESSY, THE HETCH HETCHY WATER SUPPLY
AND POWER PROJECT OF SAN FRANCISCO, 1931.

Crystalline Springs

BUT WHAT ABOUT the gravity story? It wasn't about lofty thoughts; it was very concrete. It enshrined in popular culture the very engineering feat the temple's designers had sought to celebrate. But with a twist.

I called up Bob Curry, longtime hydrology expert at UC Santa Cruz and now ensconced at Cal State Monterey Bay. Someone told me he knew about the Hetch Hetchy technology. Bob was great: jolly, helpful, and immediately on my wavelength about the urban myths question. He said that he'd been in touch with San Francisco water department people on other business, and that the gravity story was only half-true: because the Hetch Hetchy system generates hydroelectric power along the way, "there's no *net* power consumption. It generates more than it uses." I asked Bob how, exactly, he knew that? He said one of his former students was a Merced Water Company employee, and she got her boss to come speak at his class in Monterey, and he'd specifically used the word "net." "Does that make his story 'true'?" I half-jokingly asked, and Bob laughed. "Would it be 'true' if that guy put it in writing somewhere?" I continued. Bob said he'd seen it in writing somewhere in some documents in the Berkeley library.

With my first story I was already lost in an urban-myth ambiguity thicket. I didn't really mind not knowing who the temple's architect was, or whether it was Greek or "Romanesque," but I wanted to nail this thing about the gravity. Instead it spun me into new legends. "The story derives from myths in the Santa Cruz mountains," Bob told me. "It actually comes from Santa Cruz. There was this bottled water company. I can't remember the name. Scotts Valley somewhere, with a name like Crystal Springs but not. It had on its label a springs." When Bob first came to UCSC, his students would bring him bottles of this water and tell him that "it came from the Sierra Nevada all the way under the San Joaquin Valley and bubbled up in these crystal springs in the Santa Cruz mountains. And the proof of this, they claimed, was the that springs flowed all summer long. There was no snow or rain [then], so it had to be coming from the Sierra." The students didn't know about surface tension and underground wells as a summer water supply—therefore the water *had* to come from the Sierra, where there was still snow to melt. "What did you tell them?" I asked. "I told them it was absolute nonsense!"

This story about the Santa Cruz springs was pure urban myth, I could obviously see. But it also seemed derived from the Hetch Hetchy system "reality," too, with its Sierra-derived snowmelt water, transport across the San Joaquin Valley, and name referring to crystal springs. And there was, indeed, a Crystal Springs Water Company.

Bob suggested I call Sandy Lydon, retired Cabrillo professor and guru of Santa Cruz County history, to get the name of the water company. Lydon replied with an e-mail the next day. He thought Bob Curry's story came from yet another local myth: "There was . . . a guy that owned the Spring Hills Golf Course out on the north side of the Pajaro Valley who believed—and told everyone who would listen—that there is an underground river flowing from the Sierra to the sea passing beneath the Pajaro Valley. He wrote me many letters to that effect when I had my local history column in the *Sentinel*." I'd sort of traced Bob's myth, then, only to spiral over to another story—and another: "This is similar," Lydon continued, "to the one that marine scientists still sometimes tell (and believe?) about the fresh-water 'boils' in the middle of Monterey Bay. They claimed that nineteenth-century ship captains could stop in the middle of the bay and put buckets over and get fresh water." I have to say that one sounded like some ancient sailors' tale I think I read in a nineteenth-century novel like *Moby Dick* or *Two Years Before the Mast*.

I called up the San Francisco Public Utilities Commission, which owns and manages the temple, to find an "expert," and got directed to Joe Naras, Watershed Resources Manager. We met at his office in a warehouse district in Burlingame, right across the freeway from the San Francisco airport. He was extremely helpful, although it was subtly clear that he needed to be off doing more important things than confirming or refuting urban myths about the Pulgas Water Temple. "It's a gravity feed the whole way," he volunteered right off. "There's no pumping station." I asked him how he knew (verging into rudeness, since he after all was in charge of a big hunk of the water system). He said politely and definitively that if there were pumps on the way to Crystal Springs, he'd know about them. He did say there was localized pumping after the water arrived inside the City, to get up certain hills. On the way out he gave me a big full-color map of the Hetch Hetchy system. In official black letters in a gold box at the bottom, it stated "the water is moved only by gravity 167 miles from a reservoir in the Sierra Nevada mountains into San Francisco."

Okay, so the gravity story was "true." I'd successfully tracked down my first myth. On the other hand Sierra water didn't, I assume, bubble up in Scotts Valley or the middle of Monterey Bay.

But Judy Shizuru's drowned town did exist—sort of. A February 9, 1961 clipping from the *Redwood City Tribune*, discussing Searsville Lake in Palo Alto, reported that "this area was once one of the earliest towns in the county" until entrepreneurs in 1887 plotted to dam it and connect the water with the Spring Valley system. "The dam was built, and the town site flooded, but the pipe was never connected with the Spring Valley system." The article reassured, though, that "every vestige of the town was removed before the area was flooded by the Crystal Springs Reservoir, the town didn't even get its feet wet." I felt much better about the drowning live people, until I realized the story was full of internal contradictions: which lake was it, then, Searsville, or Crystal Springs? If the latter, then the water *was*, in fact, part of the Spring Valley system. Robert Righter, in *The Battle over Hetch Hetchy*, writes that Spring Valley cast its acquistive eye on the Searsville town site in the 1870s. "When the residents of the tiny town . . . lost their court case in 1879, they saw their homes inundated by fathoms of water." He said Spring Valley never did connect the lake to its broader system, and eventually sold it to Stanford University. That straightened out the which-lake question. But his line about the townspeople seeing "their homes inundated by fathoms of water" did suggest the people were at least nearby at the time, potentially subject to wet feet, if not drowning. Nobody, though, seems to have honored them with a temple.

Cleanup Operations

WHY, THOUGH, DID the gravity story get repeated? It must have had some attraction to both tellers and listeners or it wouldn't have moved around among my friends, true or not.

At a basic level saying "I heard that the water makes it all the way to the peninsula from the Sierra purely by gravity" is about appreciating the engineering accomplishment of the Hetch Hetchy system—precisely the goal the Pulgas Water Temple's promoters originally had in mind. But on another level the story is also about the water arriving *purely* by gravity. Implicitly, this engineering achievement is cool—and therefore worth sharing with a friend— because no pumps or industrial processes were necessary for the water to arrive. The story, in part, is about "pure water."

And the temple has always been about pure water. When the city fathers planned a memorial at the temple site in 1936, they envisioned "a clear pond of mountain water" and a place where "visitors will drink undiluted snow water." Over fifty years later, the *Examiner* described the temple's "torrent of pure Tuolomne water rushing to its destination." In 2001, fusing the temple's engineering with the water it carries, the *Chronicle*'s Web site insisted that "Pulgas is one of the purist water systems in the world." Indeed, much of the contemporary apparatus of the Hetch Hetchy system is dedicated not to moving the water about but to making sure it stays clean through a complex and ever-updated maze of diversions, bypasses, and filters.

The temple's "pure" water reputation spawned another story I picked up. While talking to my linoleum guy, Robert Balzer—Mary Marengo's grandson—about The Cats, I mentioned I was also researching the Pulgas Water Temple. "Have you heard any stories?" I asked, since he'd grown up in Los Gatos. Robert had heard people went to the temple to drink the water and be cured. "They think there is this mystery water, and I'll be damned, I haven't thought about it in years." Robert, not coincidentally from a Catholic family, added a new dimension to the pure water theme with his story. Now the Pulgas Water Temple was a shrine at which visitors could be cured of their ills and washed of their sins.

The "purely by gravity" story, in its own way, purified the Hetch Hetchy system by erasing the immense industrial processes central to its construction and ongoing function. It takes a huge amount of "impure" industry, after all, to produce a drop of "pure" water moved "purely" by gravity—but that happens off stage: blasting, bulldozers, dust clouds, raw hillsides. If it's only gravity, by contrast, the system gets purified, cleansed of its industrial taint. The water that flows out of the temple and into the city's taps can then pass for natural and clean, as well as classically and nobly San Franciscan. My editor Elaine tells me she was out to lunch one day with Lawrence Ferlinghetti, other City Lights staffers, and Kathleen Alioto, of the legendary San Francisco political family. When the waiter ceremoniously queried whether those at the table would like tap water or imported bottled water, Alioto piped up loyally, "I'll have pure Hetch Hetchy."

This faith in hydrological purity isn't just about Hetch Hetchy water, moreover. A 2007 story in the *Chronicle* points out that consumers who pay for expensive bottled water are often unwittingly buying ordinary tap water that has merely passed through further filtration. "The irony is that, while the packaging of purified water frequently evokes natural settings and often features the word 'pure,' it is distinct from ordinary tap water precisely because it has been run through sophisticated machinery. It is, in other words, anything but natural." By the same token Hetch Hetchy Water isn't pure and natural either—it's just purified, both industrially and politically.

In her famous essay "Holy Water" in *The White Album* (1977), Joan Didion picked up on the contradiction between Californians' yearning for an imaginary natural landscape and the reality of our industrialized daily lives. While confessing to her own private obsession with the vast hydrological systems that move about the state, Didion underscored California's dependence as an arid land on artificial water systems. "The apparent ease of California life is an illusion and those who believe the illusion real live here in only the most temporary way," she charged. Didion subtly juxtaposed the romance of the "natural" with the practical realities of uncontrolled water: "I know as well as the next person that there is considerable transcendent value in a river running wild and undammed, a river running free over granite, but I have also lived beneath such a river when it was running in flood, and gone without showers when it was running dry."

Industrialized water, in other words, flows throughout the romantic California landscape and into its residents as well, whether we drink it from a plastic bottle or from the tap in our kitchens. Yet despite extraordinary evidence to the contrary, we want to believe in the myth of its naturalness. So we repeat the "purely by gravity story" not only because we think engineering can be cool, but because we want to believe in "pure water."

The Pulgas Water Temple, then, has partly served its creators' purpose in the end. It promotes a popular appreciation of the San Francisco water system's vast engineering complexities, but in a curiously reversed version, in which the city's sin of destroying the Hetch Hetchy Valley is expiated—cleansed, shall we say—by the curative water of the temple.

Impure Water

OKAY, BUT WHAT about the plot to put LSD in the water supply at the Pulgas Water Temple? Surely that wasn't "true." Casey, my first source on this one, said her mother had been obsessed with the LSD threat in general, and warned her about the temple plot. Three other people who'd grown up in the South Bay area told me they'd heard about it. "It used to be so simple," my dad speculated. "There would be nobody there, and there was the water supply." It still seemed far-fetched, though. Tracing this one pulled me deep into the 1960s, the nature of urban myths, and some intangible quality about the temple that attracted all this stuff.

Everyone I talked to agreed that the LSD story came from Abbie Hoffman's supposed threat, during the protests at the 1968 Democratic Convention, to put LSD in Chicago's water supply. Hoffman, Jerry Rubin, and the "Yippies" were the quintessential fusion of 1960s youth rebellion, New Left opposition to the Vietnam War, and experimentation with hallucinogenic drugs. Hoffman loved to thumb his nose at established authority with over-the-top rhetoric and street spectacles. In 1968 Chicago, during a planning meeting for the protests, he pointed to a conservative-looking stranger, presumably a police agent, and jokingly announced: "We are all cops here. The cops know all our plans. We're going to put LSD in the water supply. Right?" Mayor Daley supposedly took the threat seriously, and posted guards 24/7 at the city's reservoirs.

Hoffman's threat exploded into popular consciousness in the United States. Not only did thousands of people believe he'd actually planned to do it, but the legend morphed into thousands of alleged threats to drop LSD into the water supply elsewhere (the stories always include that crucial phrase "water supply")—capturing popular fears that sixties, hippie leftist drug culture was somehow threatening the American way of life. Television comedy shows picked it up and made related cracks for decades. A Web site I found called "The Video Beat! 1950s & 1960s Rock n Roll Movies," reported a December 12, 1969, episode of "Get Smart," for example, entitled "Is This Trip Necessary?": "Evil scientist Jarvis Pim (Vincent Price) spikes the water supply with a mind-bending, hallucinatory drug (even stronger than LSD!) that sends Max, 99, and the Chief on a wild hallucination-filled trip! Trippy visual effects!"

I plugged "LSD water supply" into Google and landed in a limitlesss sea of stories stretching back into the 1950s and all over the world. Clearly the World Wide Web is the true home and nurturer of urban myths today, outflanking anything the social networks of my youth could conceive of in their wildest dreams and blurring any remaining lines I could draw between truth and reality. I didn't just get TV episodes; I got an avalanche of stories about allegedly real plots by the CIA to put LSD in the water supply long before Abbie Hoffman, supported by all sorts of evidently official documents on CIA activities in the '60s. I also learned about plots by the Russians to do it, thwarted heroically by the CIA. A special 2002 report in *Counterpunch*, a Left media-watch Web magazine I respect a lot, entitled "Sex, Drugs and the CIA," by Douglas Valentine, dated stories back to 1951 "when the CIA received an unsubstantiated report that the Soviet Union was about to corner the world market in LSD." According to Valentine, "the CIA reeled at the prospects of Russian agents dumping LSD into New York's water supply, and then using Communist propaganda to turn drug addled American citizens against their own government." In response, the CIA started its own experiments with LSD in a project called MKULTRA. From that factual base, all kinds of Web stories spiraled off to report plots by the CIA to manipulate innocent Americans with water-borne hallucinogens.

LSD stories are alive and well today in Web postings by healthy paranoiacs of every stripe. One unattributed diatribe I found charged that "parents, doctors, and school officials have been duped by a nationwide hoax" perpetuated by "police and health departments, warning of a new drug problem in the form of tattoos impregnated with LSD (sometimes laced with Strychnine)." He or she said that drug-hysteria rumors were spreading "like a virus" through schools and law enforcement agencies. "The alleged worldwide distribution of LSD stick-on tattoos has now been around for two decades, or more." This way-out-there Web stuff really challenged my scholarly standards for evidence. Could I count this obviously dodgy source as "reliable" evidence if it was only reporting, and criticizing, other, even dodgier rumors?

After September 11, 2001, LSD-in-the-water-supply rumors have morphed into alleged plots by terrorists, now made quite plausible by supposedly real schemes during the sixties and more recent actual releases of anthrax into the mails and poisonous gasses into the Japanese subway. In 2002, the *Sacramento News and Review* reported that a man named Marc Keyser had set himself up "as executive director of his own registered nonprofit, Neighborhood Terror Watch," in which citizens volunteered to maintain eternal vigilance over the Elk Grove, California, water supply, lest terrorists poison it. "What if the terrorists pumped a cocktail of deadly poisons in the outgoing water line, including radioactive waste, and it contaminated the plumbing and everything the water touched in people's homes?" warned Keyser. I got a little scared myself, although in the light of day it did seem a bit implausible that strategically sophisticated international terrorists would target the quiet suburb of Elk Grove—so well guarded by Mr. Keyser. Joe Naras, the Pulgas Temple's manager, alluded to new post-

September 11 security measures in the Hetch Hetchy system, but of course wasn't going to explain them to an outsider.

Walking on thinner and thinner evidentiary ice, I decided to see what academics had to say about urban legends. I pulled a pile of books and articles out of the library, hoping they'd help me understand this Never-Never Land I was getting increasingly lost in.

Most of the academic studies of urban myths, I soon learned, were concerned with demarcating persuasive differentiations between rumor and myth, gossip and legend, or any given combination of the four. Patrick Mullen, in "Modern Legend and Rumor Theory," an oft-cited source, in turn knowingly quoted Gordon Allport and Leo Postman's *The Psychology of Rumor* (dedicated to "Edward G. Boring"): "A legend may be regarded as a solidified rumor." Jan Harold Brunvand, in *The Vanishing Hitchhiker: American Urban Legends and Their Meanings*, reassured readers, "Urban legends belong to the subclass of folk narratives, legends, that—unlike fairy tales—are believed, or at least believable, and that—unlike myths—are set in the recent past and involve normal human beings rather than demigods." This was helpful, but I got confused about that belief bit—didn't kids believe fairy tales? And what about his sudden shift from "believed" to "or at least believable"? The scholarly discussions of urban myths inevitably opened by pointing out that, of course, "urban" was a misnomer, since these stories circulate in rural areas (and presumably suburbs like Elk Grove), too.

For all their silliness, the urban-myth studies helped a lot. Professor Brunvand pointed out (albeit somewhat obviously) that "urban legends are told both in the course of casual conversations and in such special situations as campfires, slumber parties, and college dormitory bull sessions." I could suddenly remember all the scary ghost stories I'd heard—and told—at Girl Scout sleepovers in somebody's cabin. These professors, inevitably based in Indiana or Iowa in the 1960s or '70s, knew all about the stories that went around my California slumber party world: the rat someone had found in the Coke or Seven-Up bottle (if you, too, found one and sent it in, you'd get a lot of money from the company), or what Brunvand called "The Hook," the one about the couple making out in a car in a deserted place up in the mountains. In the more-or-less classic version I learned, they heard a scratching noise on the outside of the car. Scared, they spent the night in the car (somehow keeping each other entertained and warm); and in the morning when they opened the door, they found a disembodied artificial arm dangling from the door handle. I hadn't heard the one Brunvand discussed about the spiders in the woman's beehive hairdo, but my next-door neighbor Hamsa heard it in the sixties growing up in Alaska.

According to the theorists, a successful—i.e., repeated—urban myth needs to be ambiguous. "With most rumors the ambiguity of the original situation is resolved so that the rumor eventually dies," argued Mullen. "But when a situation remains ambiguous the chances are greater that a traditional legend will survive." All my stories about the Pulgas Water Temple, indeed, hovered on the cusp of uncertainty. Did someone jump in? Did they die? Could you get the water all the way there without gravity? Was there a hippie plot to spike the water? The scholars said the other key element is plausibility. "Reality and plausibility must be present for a story to be accepted," argued Mullen. Yes, exactly: my stories were fishy, but *potentially* true.

One classic urban myth the theorists discussed was about the alligators in the sewers. According to this one, somebody's pet escaped in the bathroom and multiplied in the sewers of New York City (or, alternately, one's own metropolis). I heard and more or less believed this one in the mid-sixties, although where I lived we had neither alligators nor sewers. (We did have little four-inch "alligator lizards" as pets, which always died off quickly but which we could easily imagine slipping into the toilet and growing large on a diet superior to our iceberg lettuce.) The alligators-in-the-sewers myth was both plausible and ambiguous—and somehow related to my Pulgas Water Temple stories. Like LSD in the water supply, or guys jumping in and swimming out, it was about impure, intrepid things moving underground in pipes, out of the control of proper authorities. Like my stories, too, it carried an element of danger and sensationalism—another key element of urban myths. "Urban myths gratify our desire to know about and try to understand bizarre, frightening, and potentially dangerous or embarrassing events that *may* have happened," noted Brunvand. So they're plausible, weird, but there's "always some element of doubt."

My urban myths, then, bubbled up from some collective underground network, like the gravity-driven Hetch Hetchy water. They surfaced to thrill, while pulling us into the never-quite provable, but always enticing possibility that maybe, just maybe, they were true.

Fountain of Youth

BUT THERE WAS something else about the temple and the LSD story. Somehow this myth was connected to a kind of harmonic convergence between the Pulgas Water Temple and the culture of the 1960s. I heard lots of other stories about sixties hippie culture and the temple. My friend Cathy Buller, my sister, a friend of hers, and several others had all heard about naked people running through the ponds, for example. I also garnered firsthand stories of things people I was talking with had actually done at the temple during the sixties. "I remember going there and smoking a joint," Andy Butler, who'd grown up east of the temple in Atherton in the 1960s, told me. "We rode all the way out there on bikes and back so the wind would get rid of the smell and my mom couldn't smell it on me." I also heard about lots of sex. "That was my old boyfriend's favorite place to have outdoor sex," the man who rang up my purchases at City Lights Books told me.

The newspaper clippings confirmed all these sixties, hippie, youth-drugs-sex stories. On June 23, 1968, according to one report, "San Mateo County Sheriff's deputies shooed more than 200 young people out of the Pulgas Water Temple area . . . last night shortly after a 'be-in' broke up at El Camino Park." As I recall, a "be-in" was a kind of giant collective high, involving a lot of hugging, incense, dancing, rock music, tie-dyed clothing, bad hair, drugs, and spiritual transformation. According to the report, no one was arrested but "the people were asked to move along because some 'were in varying stages of dress and undress,' according to the sheriff's office. Others were splashing in the small reflecting pool."

Another newspaper reported a November 1969 hippie wedding performed by "an ordained Universal Life minister, before 120 amused guests." This was the kind of minister famous in those days for being ordained through the mail. The photo showed a bearded groom in a tux with wire-rimmed glasses and hair past his shoulders, joined in holy matrimony with a long-haired bride dressed, like her bridesmaid, in the kind of long "granny dress" we loved to trot around in during the late sixties.

A third clipping, from August 27, 1970, headlined "Pulgas 'Bomb' Wasn't," reported that "a crudely-made device, suspected at first to be a bomb" had been found near the temple. "After a few anxious minutes" officials concluded it was "non-explosive." Eugene Stewart, assistant sheriff, reassured that "there was no danger at any time to the drinking water supply in the nearby Crystal Springs Lakes . . . speculating that the device might have been made by youngsters as an experiment." Notice how Assistant Sheriff Stewart leapt rather quickly from the discovery of an ineffective bomb to "youngsters" and then to threats to the water supply. Maybe *this* was the origin of Casey's mom's story of a plot to put LSD in the temple.

Oliver Stone picked up on this sixties vibe at the Pulgas temple when in 1990 he decided to shoot a scene there for his movie *The Doors*. The scene takes place in 1968; the band is playing at night on a stage lined with columns. Swarms of spaced-out hippies, naked and clothed, dance in front of a bonfire as Jim Morrison sprawls through a song. Way off in the distance, in the dark behind the crowd, you can catch a glimpse of the Pulgas Water Temple. Stone and company built the stage at the highway end of the temple's landscaped area, looking out across the pool toward the temple and the reservoir. According to Joe Naras, the watershed manager, the stage was a replica of the Greek Theater at Berkeley, where the original Doors concert had taken place, but Stone wasn't allowed to shoot there. The

The Pulgas Water Temple as movie set for Oliver Stone's *The Doors*, 1990. PHOTOGRAPH COURTESY OF THE SAN MATEO COUNTY HISTORICAL MUSEUM.

film's scene opens, though, with titles reading "San Francisco, 1968." A shot of the temple I found on the Web, by contrast, headlined "filming locations," assured that "the Hollywood Bowl scenes were actually filmed at the Pulgas Water Temple." Where was the original concert, then? Here I was again in woo-woo land.

Naras told me he'd been at the temple when they filmed the scene. "It was pretty strange." The crew had constructed a bunch of cut-out figures out of plywood, painted like hippies to intersperse among the crowd in order to lower the cost of extras. Joe said it was weird to walk between and behind them; reality and illusion started to blur. "I just had this feeling like being in *The Twilight Zone*. I thought, what if all those people in the crowd were plywood people?" There it was again—the temple attracting, and producing, mystical experiences. And more nudity. According to the newspaper, "One actress who declined to be identified said extras were paid $40 if they were clothed or $80 for removing their clothing."

By pure accident, I met someone who put it all together for me. One wet Thursday evening in October, I was huddled in the bleachers at San Lorenzo Valley High School in Felton watching my niece Ramona play a water polo game. Another parent-type nearby, someone I hadn't seen in a while, asked me what I was working on these days. When I mentioned stories about the Pulgas Water Temple, a complete stranger sitting two rows down volunteered: "Oh, I grew up in San Mateo in the sixties and we did all kinds of things there." I whipped out my pen and got her phone number.

Nine months later I called her up and she suggested meeting at the White Raven, a wood-paneled coffee shop in Felton. "Zamora"—the pseudonym she decided to use—told me I could recognize her by her "piercing blue eyes," and I did. She was wearing a necklace with a little ivory moon and stars dangling from it, to match the assorted Tarot cards, herbal handbooks, and witchcraft tips arrayed on the shelves around us.

"This was a wild time," she opened, speaking with a slightly clipped, formal, Europeanish accent that I couldn't place until she said that her father had been from Romania (her mom was a Swedish Lapplander—hence those eyes). During her high school years, she said, she'd hung out regularly at the Pulgas Temple and nearby dam with a crowd of teenagers, some of them in school, some dropouts. "We were all loaded. Smoking weed." Without a bit of prompting on my part she went straight for the sixties youth-rebellion theme: "We were the rabble-rousers, the people who didn't fit the society. At the time there was an internal revolution and creativity and defiance. Everything we were supposed to do at that time we didn't want to do. It was a resistance against society. If there was a rule, we were against it." Part of the ethos among her friends, she said, was a wonderful creativity and openness about their bodies. "We waded in the pools

Maxfield Parrish, *Daybreak*, 1922. Private collection.
PHOTO COURTESY THE ARCHIVES OF ALMA GILBERT-SMITH.
USED WITH PERMISSION.

naked at night when no one could see us." Yes! I'd nailed another one of my stories.

Zamora spoke of the Pulgas Water Temple as a unique place that nourished this spirit. "It's almost like a Maxfield Parrish painting," she said. "It was amongst the fairies. . . . We were caught up in a spirituality that was almost disconnected from reality. The clothes we wore, our hair, the energy, it was magical."

Zamora's comparison with Maxfield Parrish was right on the mark. During the 1910s and '20s Parrish produced lavish, lurid scenes of semi-clad nymphs draped across Greco-Romanish urns, reflecting pools, and columns. They were very popular in the sixties on dorm-room walls, capturing, for thousands, the psychedelic freedom promised by hippie culture.

What exactly was it about the Pulgas Water Temple that attracted all this?

"I loved the Pulgas Water Temple. It was so mysterious," volunteered Dave Iermini, who works at Logos Books in Santa Cruz and grew up in the area in the same period; "just sort of out there, so unexpected. It had an appealing air of mystery." Jozseph Schultz, famous Santa Cruz chef, rhapsodized, "It's lost in the mists of time." Ruth Willard, in her official piece for *Sacred Places of San Francisco*, concluded, "Coming upon Pulgas Temple unexpectedly while driving . . . is an awesome experience, like suddenly finding oneself in an ancient land." Elaine, my editor from Connecticut, might see merely a "weird pagoda," but we sixties locals fell for the magical and the mystical.

I think the mystical appeal of the Pulgas Water Temple transcends the local and the '60s, though. In part it's the temple's isolated, natural setting, in sharp contrast to the very urban Bay Area humming just over the ridge to the east. In part it's about the contrast between classical architecture and cookie-cutter suburban shopping malls. But it's also about some deep programming in western culture, a lingering fantasy about the image of the white, columned temple standing alone, symbolizing for centuries—and in thousands of paintings, travel guides, movies, and television shows—a mystical, timeless access to an alternative reality. The sixties *zeitgeist* merely tapped into the temple's already "timeless" appeal: the site served as some kind of mystical magnet for anything that was creative, mysterious, or otherwise out of the ordinary.

The temple's mysterious aura didn't just spawn lovely contemplative fairies, though. It also produced the drowning villagers, and a lot of murder stories. "I gather there have been a few bodies dumped in the area and whatnot but I cannot find any real accounts of anything like that," apologized a Mrs. Alhadef from the Redwood City Public Library to my phone machine. At an academic conference I met a professor from the University of Iowa named T. M. Scruggs, who'd graduated in 1969 from Millbrae High School, by the San Francisco airport. He'd been the leader of a garage band called "Free Beer." (They'd figured people would show up at their concerts, looking for the beer.) Professor Scruggs told me he'd heard that "someone was murdered there. They dumped them in there." By the time a body eventually showed up in the reservoir, its fingerprints would have soaked off "and it wouldn't be associated with the temple."

By the 1980s the happy hippie heaven of the Pulgas Water Temple's youth rebellion was in fact dissolving into a very unromantic, edgy nightmare for the temple's maintenance officials. In April 1980, San Francisco Water District spokesman Gilbert Benoix announced that "the parking lot was closed earlier this month because of muggings and pretty heavy juvenile drinking parties." According to Benoix, "Two high school classes met in the parking lot . . . for a fight last spring." Closing the lot didn't fix the problems. In August, a columnist reported that "unruly groups still congregate at the temple resulting to [*sic*] calls to the sheriff's department for many drug-related emergency measures." Mr. and Mrs. E. R. Bottomore, in a letter to the *Sun-Times* on the matter, contrasted these "undesirables that would gather in large groups with their drugs, liquor, extremely loud music, knifings, and muggings, and dogs running wild," with "the family-oriented people" for whom the temple area should be made safe.

I wasn't sure which side I was on here in the family-picnickers vs. rowdy hoodlums rumble, until I read a story headlined "Pulgas Water Temple being overrun by teenage vandals" in the *Peninsula Times Tribune*, reporting that "rowdy youngsters . . . bring pills and booze on Fridays and by Monday they leave behind felled pine trees, broken bottles and temple water that is contaminated with urine." I drew the line there. Urinating in my temple; cutting down trees; suddenly the frolicking rebels were, indeed, "hoodlums."

Two years later the situation was still out of control, not just at the temple but at the reservoir's dam as well. According to the *Half Moon Bay Review*, "The locations at the dam and at the water temple have been described as 'Hophead Heaven' where the reek of marijuana smoke has been detected." After "heavy drinking" the "hoodlums" "have been known to hurl rocks at cars and engage in brawls," the sheriff's department reported, successfully arguing for a ban on alcohol at the temple. It appears to have had little impact. In June 1983, sheriffs had to chase off "about 1,500 high school seniors from the Annual Nude Relays." Lieutenant Richard McKillip reassured, however, that "the name of the event . . . has become somewhat misleading: The students weren't nude and the only racing being done was with their cars." In 1987, Ed Fonseca, manager of suburban operations for the San Francisco Water District, complained that the temple still "attracted vandals" and that teenagers were "ruining it for the general public" with their beers, cars, and stereos. Rather than getting in touch with their inner Greek, these later visitors preferred to worship what one newspaper called "the beer gods."

All these newspaper clippings were, needless to say, disturbing to me. They took the temple out of Maxfield Parrish land and into a mundane world of petty rebellion and petty authority. They also, in a new way, disrupted my sensibility about what was real and what wasn't. In contrast to my evocative world of orally transmitted stories, the clippings were cold, hard, supposedly "true."

Deadliest of all were newspaper stories reporting closures of the temple altogether. In 1967 the authorities closed the temple for 45 days in order to construct a new bypass tunnel. From 1972 to 1974 they closed it to build a new power station. After 1980, the parking lot remained closed as an anti-hoodlum device, only to open timidly in 1993, on weekdays only, from 9 to 4. Then, in 2002, the temple's handlers shut it altogether for two years in order to divert the water into a new 10,000-square-foot treatment plant to remove chloramine from the water. "Pulgas temple reopens, but kiss the water goodbye" announced the *Chronicle* on October 26, 2004. The water doesn't bubble up into the temple at all anymore, but instead, rushes out two pipes into the flume toward the reservoir 150 feet to the west. Only a bit of that water has been left to cosmetically lap at the temple's depths.

However sobering, these later clippings nonetheless confirm the temple's continuing pull for visitors of all ilks. In their very existence, after all, the newspaper stories underscore that readers throughout the Peninsula and Bay Area were interested in learning about the fate of the Pulgas Temple.

For over 65 years the Pulgas Water Temple's old black magic has kept doing its work, attracting visitors interested in crossing over to some other mysterious time and place through a variety of cultural approaches, whether meditating, partying, or prancing. I realized the temple worked on two levels: first, in attracting this kind of activity, and second, in spawning stories *about* about this kind of activity. Its most creative visitors have usually been adolescents—precisely those most likely to relish hearing and repeating stories about what might or might not have happened there. The 1960s were hence the Pulgas Water Temple's great moment of glory, when youth rebellion, hallucinogenic drugs, parental alarm, and, above all, an enthusiasm for the otherworldly all converged in the temple's rushing waters. I myself, just entering high school in 1970, was part of the generation that converged on the temple, both literally and in our imaginative reconstruction of what might have happened there. Maybe there wasn't LSD in my water supply fifteen or twenty miles south, but something was in the air, at least, that made it to my wholesome suburban school.

The Gods Must Be Crazy

SO THE STORY about the LSD in the Pulgas Water Temple wasn't true. But the one about the water making it there on gravity alone was, along with the one about the naked people in the ponds. That left my heroic guys who'd actually jumped into the temple and swum out.

Lots of people had heard about them—not just on the peninsula but in the Santa Clara Valley and around Santa Cruz. One woman in her eighties I met in the History Room at Los Gatos Public Library told me she'd heard stories about possible jumpers at Stanford during the 1950s. Robert Righter opens his 2005 study, *The Battle Over Hetch Hetchy*, with the story of visits he made with to the temple with his dad in the 1950s. "My father, a Stanford graduate, told me that freshmen students who joined an eating club had to walk blindfolded on a two-by-twelve-inch board across the abyss as part of their hazing ritual. Whether or not this was true, I resolved that I would never attend Stanford University."

My jumpers story, I now knew, had all the classic elements of a popular urban myth. It was plausible, ambiguous, sensational, and contained an element of danger. It moved around among my adolescent age-cohort just like the experts said, and hovered enticingly on that border between real and unreal. Lending it a further legendary aura, my jumpers story also had elements of classic Greek myth: noble youths who cast out into adventure, risking their lives with a potentially fatal willingness to brave danger.

"That one's true!" insisted my sister Laura at a Thanksgiving dinner debate. "How do you know it wasn't an urban myth?" I pressed. "Because I heard it several times!" But my dad had heard the story, too, he said—which suggested my guys might in fact be real, because he wouldn't have heard it through our youthful rumor networks; he would have had to have read about it in the newspaper.

I figured I had two ways to prove or disprove this one: find someone who jumped in, or find a newspaper story reporting them.

At a party at my friend's Judy's home (she of the drowning live people), I met the novelist Mike Koepf, author of *The Fisherman's Son*. He said he'd grown up in Half Moon Bay, just over the hills from the temple, and had driven there once in high school with friends, planning to jump in, but they had chickened out. Later he confessed that they'd mostly just talked about it to impress their dates.

I kept asking around for maybe five years, but only turned up more rumors, more collateral myths; no jumpers.

Then, one hot September day, eating lunch outside Zoccoli's delicatessen in downtown Santa Cruz, I ran into Matt Farrell, who's married to a union activist friend of mine named Connie Croker. He asked me what I was working on these days, and I told him I was collecting stories about the Pulgas Water Temple. He let drop casually, "Oh, Connie knows some people who used to jump in there."

I beat a fast track to the telephone and made an appointment with Connie. We met in her office in the UCSC library, high up in the hills with big glass windows looking out at the redwoods. As I listened to her story it felt like I was participating in some sacred ritual.

In 1969 or '70—it was during the summer, she remembered, because the day was warm—Connie was eighteen or nineteen, living away from home for the first time while going to the College of San Mateo. In those days she was part of a crowd that hung out at the Pulgas Water Temple and engaged in mild forms of sixties-type activities. "We were young, we had time." That particular day, "there were a few people hanging out. And these two guys walked up, obvious friends. And they were hanging out talking about jumping in." Both men were young, white, thin, with longish hair; one had a ponytail. Clearly they were prepared somehow. "Everyone was just in awe. Oh God, I wonder if they're going to do it! Your first reaction

Inside the Pulgas Water Temple, looking out the tunnel, 1938.
GEORGE FANNING/SAN FRANCISCO PUBLIC UTILITIES COMMISSION.

was that it was a really cool thing to do. Then you hope no one gets hurt. . . . You could hit your head, and there would be no one there to rescue you."

"They didn't hesitate. They took off their shirts and shoes and just went in. Once they started they just climbed up and jumped in. They didn't linger at all. They just went boom! boom! one after the other. . . . And they were just swept into the tunnel. And they were just gone." Afterwards, only the incredibly loud roaring of the water was left. "It happened so fast you were like, Whoa! Did that really happen? Then it's back to that rushing. They became part of that momentum." No one said a word, wondering what had happened to them. Then the two guys reappeared, presumably having popped up in the flume or the reservoir and climbed out. "They came back, got their stuff, and just left."

Connie had the feeling they'd done it before. "They were so confident and relaxed," and had their technique down. "The idea is—and this is exactly what they did—to go in feet first, with your feet facing toward toward the tunnel, so that water coming in from the sides sweeps you into the tunnel, so you don't hit bottom . . . . Obviously you have to hold your breath until you pop back up."

Connie cast the moment in now-familiar sixties terms. "It was a beautiful place. It had a certain feel to it. . . . It's a trip. The whole look of the place creates a kind of ambience. Plus, most people that went there were kind of young." I asked her if she herself had considered jumping in. No, she said, although she had liked the idea. "No one thought they were going to die back then. It was a time period when we tried anything." Over thirty-five years later she vividly remembered those jumpers. "You don't forget something like that."

I sat there, listening to Connie's story, a little stunned. She, too, understood the solemnity of the moment. Her astonishment at watching the boys jump, my search for the answer to the mystery, and the cool dark of the redwoods outside somehow came together for both of us on an otherwise ordinary summer day in the library. As she carefully told her story, though, I slowly realized I hadn't actually wanted to hear it. I'd finally tracked down my story. It was true: I had an eyewitness. But I'd killed the myth. I'd taken my potentially heroic gods—powerful, I realized, in precisely their mysteriousness— and turned them into mere foolhardy kids.

When I later interviewed Joe Naras, the all-business Watershed Manager, I asked if he'd heard about anyone jumping in. He said that maybe ten times, when he'd been introduced to people as someone who managed Crystal Springs, various guys had told him they'd jumped in. He hadn't learned any further details, though, because the self-identified jumpers usually told him about it with an edge of aggressive belligerence, enjoying asserting that they'd done something *verboten* on his territory, so he'd changed the subject.

My mystical informant "Zamora," though, had all the details. She told me she'd seen about four different people jump in, some naked, some clothed, all young men. "Number one, you either had to be stoned or drunk or insane to make the jump," she began. "It was a kind of spontaneous insanity." Once she started to describe the actual jump, it was almost as if she'd done it herself. "You had to position yourself exactly so you didn't hit the tiles. . . . It was an incredible rush to make the plunge. But after you made the plunge, it pulled you with such force that therein lied the rush." She said you had to remember to hold your breath for seven seconds before you made it out the tunnel and popped up in the flume. It was dangerous: "Sometimes you could get in that damned whirlpool in there. It was just like a waterfall, where the turbulence can roll you." But the whole thing was "such a rush," that "they'd get stoked and then go do it again. You do it once, you'd do it again."

For Zamora, leaping into the temple was a deeply symbolic act. To jump was to revolt, to be free." "It was our way of rebelling, of making a statement, and in a sense making a revolution of the new generation. . . . It made us ageless."

I had two firsthand accounts now, plus Joe Naras's braggers. But nothing in writing. Somehow, I still needed that printed word to make my jumpers fully "real." I'd thought it would be near-impossible to troll through years of the *San Mateo Tribune*, the *Palo Alto Times*, the *Chronicle*, and the *Examiner* to try to find obscure mentions of jumpers. But the San Mateo County Historical Society's archives had three folders of stories, all neatly clipped and saved over the years, and there, too, were my jumpers—if merely passing references. Mostly they dated from the 1980s, referring to an earlier period. "There were several incidents of people's taking dares to jump in and ride the water down the flume" ran a typical one-liner. A little clipping stamped July 18, 1967, though, reported that "Eight soaking wet teen-agers were lectured and sent home by San Mateo County Sheriff's Deputy John Hammerstrom after a strange caper at the Pulgas Water Temple." According to the sheriff, "the youths, aged 16 to 18, tied a rope to one of the pillars and were taking turns letting themselves down into the rushing waters." I liked that about the rope. Why hadn't I thought of it?

Those clippings really killed the mystery, though. They were so matter-of-fact, so disapproving, so factual. "I could tell you some stories," offered Cliff Brown, a volunteer behind the counter at the archives, who was helpfully photocopying my clippings. He grew up in San Carlos; he and his friends would go up to the temple in the 1940s and '50s and neck with their girls. He'd heard stories about jumpers all his life—and was entirely disapproving. "There were guys that went down there; some of them didn't make it. It was dangerous. A lot of kids that jumped in got really badly hurt or killed." I asked him if he knew any concrete evidence that anyone had been hurt. He said he'd heard about it in high school. Had he ever wanted to jump in? "Shoot, no—that's dangerous. Anybody who did that would be *stupid!*"

I started to notice a pattern: lots of people I talked to about the jumpers who'd grown up very close by didn't think it sounded noble or thrilling; they were hostile. "We used to go there and see it churning around and say 'I'd never jump in that,'" a local artist told me. In the UCSC library, searching an old microfilm copy of the *Chronicle* for stories, I ran into Greg Herken, a fellow historian and author of several books on the development of the atomic bomb. He'd gone to Aragon High School in San Mateo, it turned out, and had heard all about the jumpers. "I remember going up there myself at night and thinking there was no *way* I was going to jump in. What I was worried about was if you jumped in, you'd get stuck somewhere." Like Cliff, he'd heard someone had died there, but had no concrete evidence of it. And like Cliff he separated himself thoroughly from the jumpers. "The circle of people I ran with were not the type that would jump into the Pulgas Water Temple. We were nerds. Nerds would never do that."

In 1973, more or less (I couldn't quite pin down the date), the Water District stopped the jumpers once and for all by installing a round grate over the top of the temple's rushing waters. Later they added a finer-mesh web over that, to stop people from tossing in foreign objects (if not hallucinogens).

I knew I was hostile to that grate. I did sympathize with Greg and Cliff's point of view—after all, they'd been actual local teenage guys subject to real pressures to jump in, so they had a right to be sensible. But I didn't want to be sensible. I had always wanted to jump in. I wanted to be like Connie and Zamora, although I had to admit that they were girls and hadn't actually had to jump in— they could watch the thrill of jumping in, endorse it, but keep their respectability without ever been expected to actually jump. (I never did hear a single story of a woman jumping.)

When I was far along in my research, I told David Sweet, a retired history professor friend of mine, that I was writing about urban myths. "Are you for them or against them?" he asked, laughing. I knew at that moment I was for them. I might be a professional historian myself, and know perfectly well I was supposed to be on the side of the newspaper clippings, the statistics, and the manuscript census, and against unreliable oral history and memory, let alone often preposterous urban myths. But this was my own history we were talking about, my own slumber parties, my own perhaps too vivid high school imagination. I wanted it back. I didn't know what to do with the "truth" of the jumpers—nor did I want to know about the protruding pipes or the riptide allegedly down there. I didn't want my heroic guys to deflate into reckless adolescents out for a good time, too drunk or stoned for their own good, not Greek gods.

I wanted Pandora back in the box. I'd killed my own private story, cherished for over thirty-five years.

Let the Mystery Be

A BIT WARY, with the lowest of expectations, I took my niece Ramona, now almost sixteen, to visit the temple. I hadn't been there myself since maybe 1965, although I had an old photo of it my dad had taken, framed and perched on top of my filing cabinet.

We drove up on a Wednesday afternoon in August, almost missing the modest, old-fashioned little sign off Cañada Road. Only one other car was in the parking lot; no one else was to be seen. Ignoring the signs directing us through the trees I took off to the right instead, down through the big open grassy basin where they'd built the *Doors* movie set, so I could get the best long-shot visual approach to the temple. And there it was off to the left, seated on its circular stone platform, with a big cawing raven on top. Between us stretched the long, flat, rectangular reflecting pool in fifties pale aqua, lined by a row of scraggly but nonetheless picturesque Italian cypresses on either side.

The temple was much, much more beautiful than I remembered. It was big and white with a clean design that set up gorgeous visual angles, especially through its circular open top. The opening where the water had roared up and out was much smaller than I'd remembered—maybe eight feet across. We leaned in and down as far as we could, and there, deep in the murky wet dark we could see a few of the bluey-green tiles of the weir. If we squinted and tilted our heads exactly right we could just barely make out dark semicircles where the tunnels came in and out. Way deep down there we could hear the roaring of water, somewhere far within. The water we could see, though, was entirely still. It had a deep, old, wet scent. Outside, we could see past a chicken-wire fence to where the new, filtered water poured into the flume maybe 200 yards down, toward the reservoir. That must have been where the roaring came from, some underground echo through the tunnel.

Ramona and I were both exhausted that day—she from the beginning of water polo practice known as "hell week," me from my own hell of home improvement—and the place was deserted, so we lay on our backs in the sun on the temple's platform, gazing up through the columns to the open blue sky and admiring the carved leaves and vines. As we lay there, bits of brightly lit cottonwood seeds floated in, up, and out, sometimes caught in the air currents and dancing slowly round. Two pale yellow butterflies wandered through. Then a jet from the San Francisco airport passed over, leaving a luminescent vapor trail that exactly bisected the temple's circular opening, then slowly, slowly, drifted sideways and out.

I could feel it: The Pulgas Water Temple was as mysterious as ever, and Ramona and I were floating away to another time, another place. I hadn't killed the mystery at all. And after all, I still had plenty of ambiguities to embrace: who, in fact, designed this lovely structure? Was it Greek, Roman, pagan, or Romanesque? Did, in fact, anyone ever die here—whether jumping in, or murdered? Had there been a town over there under the lake?

Two young women dressed all in black showed up, then disappeared. A middle-aged bicyclist sporting a DayGlo yellow top leaned briefly against one of the columns. "Have you heard any stories about people jumping in here?" I queried, in one last research gasp. "No," he said. "Have you?"

Yes, I indeed had. I knew all about those guys, I could proudly think to myself. I also realized suddenly that I never found an actual jumper guy to talk with. I still had that mystery, too.

Ramona and I gradually roused ourselves and started messing around at the opening to the temple water. I had a sudden urge to throw a rock down there, getting it past the wire mesh. Ramona pointed out that a piece of the wire cover had been pulled back at one corner, and that if we tossed the right-sized little stone just right, we could get it in. She obligingly and rather athletically lay on top of the circular wall and leaned down to roll the rock in and produce a tiny plop down below. I just barely stopped myself from suggesting she lower herself down onto the grate—only, after all, three feet below the wall—from which she could very easily climb back out.

There was the temple's magic again: I went from transcendent to trangressive in about five minutes, from floating hippie spirit to proto-hoodlum; all, somehow, part of the appropriate spirit of the place.

"You're a representative teenager," I said to Ramona. "What would you do if you were here with your friends? Would you have jumped in?"

"I'd probably be the one saying to my guy friends 'don't do it,'" she said. "I mean the other girls would be thinking it; I'd just be the one vocalizing. But actually I don't think my guy friends would do it. I hope not. But you never know." No, you don't.

I realized, in the end, that we tell our stories, especially as young people, in part because we want them to be true. We want life to be full of adventure and creativity and daring that might, just might, be real. We want to believe our water is pure and untainted and purged of industrial processes and environmental destruction. And in repeating each story, we made it real, at least in our little piece of imaginative California. Maybe my jumpers didn't, in fact, ever exist. Maybe I'd imagined them into being, along with all my friends, because we loved the Pulgas Water Temple and loved the other, magical world it might, just might, offer an entry point into, if we closed our eyes, jumped feet first, and counted slowly to seven.

It was almost closing time, so Ramona and I walked slowly back to the parking lot through manzanitas, live oaks, madrones, and scorched golden grasses, the beloved landscape of my childhood. I like to think Ramona, too, will now have a story to tell about the Pulgas Water Temple, as she turns sixteen next month and imagines her own Caifornia history.

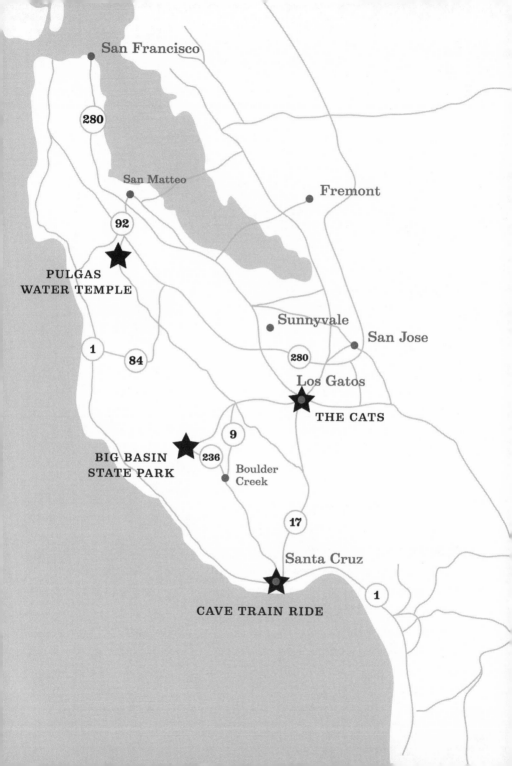

DIRECTIONS

Big Basin State Park and its Log

FROM SANTA CRUZ:

Take Highway 9 North up the San Lorenzo Valley to Boulder Creek. In downtown Boulder Creek, turn left at the stop sign onto Highway 236/Big Basin Way. Follow 236 nine miles all the way into Big Basin Redwoods State Park. As you arrive in the center of the park, the log slice is on the right, just to the right of the Park Headquarters Building.

FROM SAN JOSÉ, THE EAST BAY, OR
THE SAN FRANCISCO PENINSULA:

Take Highway 17 South over the mountains toward Santa Cruz. After the highway flattens out in Scotts Valley, take the Mount Herman Road exit. Turn right onto Mount Herman Road through Scotts Valley and on into Felton. When Mount Herman Road ends at a signal, turn right onto Graham Hill Road and then right (north) again immediately onto Highway 9. Follow Highway 9 fifteen miles to Boulder Creek. At the stop sign, turn left onto Highway 236/ Big Basin Way. Follow 236 nine miles all the way into Big Basin

Redwoods State Park. As you arrive in the center of the park, the log slice is on the right, just to the right of the Park Headquarters Building.

Alternate, much curvier route: Take Highway 9 from downtown Saratoga. Continue on Highway 9 for twelve miles. Turn right onto Highway 236 and follow it for nine miles into Big Basin Redwoods State Park. As you curve into the park, the log slice will be on the left, just after the Park Headquarters Building.

FROM SAN FRANCISCO OR THE PENINSULA, ALTERNATE, CURVIER ROUTE:

Take Highway 92 West off Interstate 280 in San Mateo; at the top of the pass, turn left (south) onto Skyline Boulevard. Follow Skyline Boulevard to Highway 9; turn right (south) onto Highway 9. Take Highway 9 until it intersects with Highway 236; turn right onto 236 and follow it for nine miles into Big Basin Redwoods State Park. As you curve into the park, the log slice will be on the left, just after the Park Headquarters Building.

The Cave Train Ride

FROM SAN JOSÉ, THE EAST BAY, OR SAN FRANCISCO:

Take Highway 17 South toward Santa Cruz. As Highway 1 exits on the right, stay in the left two lanes and follow the signs for "Ocean Street—Beaches." Highway 17 will turn into Ocean Street After several blocks, watch for the light at Broadway; take the next right turn after it onto Barson, then turn left onto Riverside Drive and cross straight over the river. Continue forward until Riverside ends at Beach Street and the Boardwalk; turn left on Beach Street to find parking. The Cave Train Ride is at the far left (east) end of the Boardwalk, on the lower plaza. It's generally closed in the winter, open on the weekends in the spring and fall, and open every day in the summer.

FROM SAN FRANCISCO, ALTERNATE ROUTE:

Take Highway 1 South toward Santa Cruz. Continue on Highway 1 as it turns into Mission Street; turn right at the light at Bay Street. Follow Bay Street until it ends; then turn left on West Cliff Drive, which will carry you straight down onto Beach Street in front of the Boardwalk. The Cave Train Ride is at the far left (east) end of the Boardwalk.

FROM MONTEREY:

Take Highway 1 North all the way to Santa Cruz. Stay in the left lane as you go around the big curve at the end, and then merge (quickly and carefully) onto Highway 17. Immediately keep to the left lanes and follow the signs for "Ocean Street—Beaches." Highway 17 will continue straight forward and turn into Ocean Street. After several blocks on Ocean Street, watch for the light at Broadway; take the next right turn after it onto Barson, then turn left onto Riverside Drive, and cross straight over the river. Continue forward until Riverside ends at Beach Street and the Boardwalk; turn left on Beach Street to find parking. The Cave Train Ride is at the far left (east) end of the Boardwalk, on the lower plaza. It's generally closed in the winter, open on the weekends in the spring and fall, and open every day in the summer.

The Cats

FROM SAN JOSÉ, THE EAST BAY, OR SAN FRANCISCO:

Take Highway 17 South toward Santa Cruz. After the second Los Gatos exit (Exit 20A, East Los Gatos) and two overpasses, watch for an on-ramp coming in from the right, and then just after that a short, wide road exiting to the right. The cat sculptures are tucked back up that road to the right. To return Northward on 17, enter Southbound 17 in front of the cats (very carefully), then proceed on 17 a short distance to the Alma Bridge Road exit; exit and cross back left over the highway, and re-enter 17 traveling north.

FROM SANTA CRUZ:

Take Highway 17 North towards San José. After Lexington Reservoir, when the road straightens out along the spillway to the right, watch for the cats on the left, tucked back into the hillside just before the Los Gatos off-ramp exits leftward from the highway. To actually drive up to the cats, take the Los Gatos exit off-ramp to the left, turn around in town, and take Santa Cruz Avenue back down to return southbound onto Highway 17. The cats will be on the right, set back down a short road, immediately after you enter the highway. (Watch out for fast traffic zipping around the corner as you enter and exit 17).

The Pulgas Water Temple

FROM EITHER SAN JOSÉ OR SAN FRANCISCO:

Take Interstate 280 to the Cañada Road/Edgewood Road exit. Turn west (toward the mountains) on Edgewood Road, then right onto Cañada Road when Edgewood Road ends. Traveling north along Cañada Road, the Pulgas Water Temple is off to the left a short distance after the sign for "Filoli." The temple and its parking lot (easy to miss as you drive past) are only open weekdays between 9:00 a.m. and 4:00 p.m. For those seeking to merely drive by for a peek at the temple, Cañada Road is itself closed on Sundays to all traffic except bicycles from 9:00 a.m. to 3:00 p.m., November to March, and from 9:00 a.m. to 4:00 p.m., April to October.

For those interested in further reading, a brief list of sources for each chapter follows. Scholarly researchers seeking exact citations are welcome to contact the author.

Chapter 1: Redwood Empires

For the history of Big Basin Redwoods State Park and redwood preservation, see Carolyn de Vries, *Grand and Ancient Forest: The Story of Andrew P. Hill and Big Basin Redwoods State Park* (Fresno: Valley Publishers, 1978); Willie Yaryan, "Saving the Redwoods: The Ideology and Political Economy of Nature Preservation," unpublished Ph.D. dissertation, University of California, Santa Cruz, 2002; Willie Yaryan, Denzil Verardo, and Jennie Verardo, *The Sempervirens Story: A Century of Preserving California's Ancient Redwood Forest, 1900–2000* (Los Altos, Calif.: Sempervirens Fund, 2001); J. D. Grant, *Saving California's Redwoods* (Berkeley, Calif.,: Save-the-Redwoods League, [n.d.]).

The archives of the California State Parks, Sacramento, California, including General Plan Files, State Park Files, and Central Files, include correspondence, maps, clippings, cartoons, and other materials regarding the history of Big Basin. Historical photographs are located in the California State Parks Photographic Archive in West Sacramento. The archives at Big Basin Park itself also offer a rich array of photographs, correspondence, and other materials.

Historical works on the redwoods and their larger importance include Richard St. Barbe Baker, *The Redwoods* (London: George Ronald, 1943); Walter Fry and John R. White, *Big Trees* (Stanford, Calif.,: Stanford Univ. Press, 1930); John Evarts and Marjorie Popper, eds., *Coast Redwood: A Natural and Cultural History* (Los Olivos, Calif., Cachuma Press, 2001); Jeremy Joan Hewes, *Redwoods: The World's Largest Trees* (Chicago: Rand McNally, 1981); Harriet E. Huntingon, *Forest Giants: The Story of the California Redwoods* (New York: Doubleday, 1962); Ralph W. Andrews, *Redwood Classic* (New York: Bonanza Books, 1953); James Clifford Shirley, *The Redwoods of Coast and Sierra* (Berkeley: Univ. of California Press, 1937); "California's Coastal Redwood Realm," *National Geographic* 75 (February 1939), 133–84; Theodore M. Knappen, "The Undying Redwood Tree of Our Western Coast," *Review of Reviews* 67 (March 1923), 293–98; "The Sequoias of California Forests," *Sunset* 3, no. 6 (October 1899), 183–88; Howard E. Davenport, *A Story of California Big Trees, Largest Living Things on Earth* (Stockton, Calif.: Calaveros Grove Association, 1949); Donald Culross Peattie, "Redwoods—America's Immortals," *Frontiers* (December 1945), 52–54; Richard A. Rasp, *Redwood: The Story Behind the Scenery* (Las Vegas, Nevada: KC Publications, 1989); Rodney Sydes Elworth, *The Giant Sequoia: An Account of the History and Characteristics of the Big Trees of California* (Oakland, Calif.: J. Berger, 1924); Ann Ensign Brown, *Monarchs of the Forest* (New York: Dodd, Mead, 1984); Stuart Nixon, *Redwood Empire* (New York: E.P. Dutton, 1966); Linda Vieira, *The Ever-Living Tree: The Life and Times of a Coast Redwood* (New York: Walker & Co., 1994).

Correspondence and details regarding the diorama and other displays from the California Museum of Science can be found in the records of the California Museum of Science and Industry, at the California Science Center, Los Angeles, California.

For the relationship between the eugenics movement and redwood preservation, see Susan R. Schrepfer, *The Fight to Save the Redwoods: A History of Environmental Reform, 1917–1978* (Madison, Wisc.: University of Wisconsin Press, 1983); Gray Brechin, "Conserving the Race: Natural Aristocracies, Eugenics, and the U.S. Conservation Movement," *Antipode* 28, no. 3 (1996), 229–45; Alexandra Minna Stern, *Eugenic Nation: Faults and Frontiers of Better Breeding in Modern America* (Berkeley, Calif.: Univ. of California Press, 2005).

For Roosevelt's visit, *Santa Cruz Sentinel*, May 12, 1903; Theodore Roosevelt, "From an address at Leland Stanford, Jr., University, Palo Alto, Cal., May 12, 1903," Willis Fletcher Johnson, ed., *Theodore Roosevelt: Addresses and Papers* (New York: Sun Dial Classics, 1908), 129–35.

For the Yurok point of view, Walter Lara, Sr., and Roland Raymond, "The Use of the Redwood (Keeth) by the Yurok People," in John LeBlanc, ed., *Proceedings of the Conference on Coast Redwood Forest Ecology and Management* (Berkeley: University of California Cooperative Extension, 1996).

For Walt Whitman's "Song of the Redwood-Tree" (1874), see various editions of Whitman, *Leaves of Grass*; see also Jerome Loving, *Walt Whitman: The Song of Himself* (Berkeley: Univ. of California Press, 1999). For the Boy Scouts and imperialism, Michael Rosenthal, *The Character Factory: Baden-Powell and the Origins of the Boy Scout Movement* (New York: Pantheon Books, 1986). On *Vertigo* (Alfred Hitchcock, Paramount Pictures, 1958), Terence Rafferty, "Mad Love," November 18, 1996, *New Yorker* 72, no. 35, 123–26.

Chapter 2: Clan of the Cave Train Ride

For representations of cave people, see Diane Gifford-Gonzales, "You Can Hide, But You Can't Run: Representations of Women's Work in Illustrations of Palaeolithic Life," *Visual Anthropology Review* 9, no. 1 (Spring 1993), 23–41; Gifford-Gonzales, "The Real Flintstones? What Are Artists' Depictions of Human Ancestors Telling Us?" *Anthro Notes: National Museum of Natural History Bulletin For Teachers* 17, no. 3 (Fall 1995), 1–7; Stephanie Moser, *Ancestral Images: The Iconography of Human Origins* (Phoenix Mill, England: Sutton Publishing; Ithaca, NY: Cornell Univ. Press, 1998); "Neanderthals On The Hunt," *Archaeology*, March/April 2007, 16. For Gary Larson, quoted in Clive Gamble's introduction to Moser, xiii, see Gary Larson, *The PreHistory of the Far Side: A 10th Anniversary Exhibit* (Kansas City, KS: Andrews and McMeel, 1989). On the cultural politics of dioramas at the American Museum of Natural History, see Donna Haraway, *Primate Visions: Gender, Race, and Nature in the World of Modern Science* (New York: Routledge, 1989).

For the Flintstones, see Megan Mullen, *"The Flintstones* Then and Now: The Long Life of American Television's First Cartoon Family Sitcom," *Mid-Atlantic Almanack* 7 (1998), 39–50; Tina Stockman, "Discrediting the Past, Rubbishing the Future: A Critical Comparison of the Flintstones and the Jetsons," *Journal of Educational Television* 20, no. 1 (1994), 27–38; George Lipsitz, "The Meaning of Memory: Family, Class, and Ethnicity in Early Network Television," in *Time Passages: Collective Memory and American Popular Culture* (Minneapolis: Univ. of Minnesota Press, 1990).

On Li'l Abner, see Edwin T. Arnold, "Al, Abner, and Appalachia," *Appalachian Journal* 17, no. 3 (1990), 262-75; Arnold, "Abner Unpinned: Al Capp's Li'l Abner, 1940–1955, *Appalachian Journal*

24, no. 4 (Summer 1997), 420–36; Arthur A. Berger, "Li'l Abner in American Satire," *New York Folklore* 23 (1967), 83–98. For Alley Oop, Vincent T. Hamlin, "The Man Who Walked With Dinosaurs," *Inks: Cartoon and Comic Art Studies* 3, no. 2 (May 1996), 20–26.

On amusement parks, dark rides, and Disneyland, start with John Kasson, *Amusing the Millions: Coney Island at the Turn of the Century* (New York, NY: Hill and Wang, 1978); Karal Ann Marling, ed., *Designing Disney's Theme Parks: The Architecture of Reassurance* (New York: Flammarion, 1997).

Chapter 3: Upstairs, Downstairs at the Cats

For C. E. S. Wood, Robert Hamburger, *Two Rooms: The Life of Charles Erskine Scott Wood* (Lincoln: Univ. of Nebraska Press, 1998); Edwin Bingham and Tim Barnes, eds., *Wood Works: The Life and Writings of Charles Erskine Scott Wood* (Corvallis: Oregon State Univ. Press, 1997); Erskine Wood, *Life of Charles Erskine Scott Wood* (Vancouver, Washington: Rose Wind Press, 1991). For Wood's own writings, see *Collected Poems of Charles Erskine Scott Wood*, collected by Sara Bard Field (New York, NY: Vanguard, 1949); Wood, *Earthly Discourse* (New York, NY: Vanguard, 1937); *Heavenly Discourse* (New York: Vanguard, 1927); *Poems From the Ranges* (San Francisco, Calif.: Lantern Press, 1929); *Too Much Government* (New York: Vanguard, 1931);

For Sara Bard Field, see Amelia R. Fry, *Sara Bard Field, Poet and Suffragist*, oral history interview conducted 1959–1963, Suffragists Oral History Project, Regional Oral History Office, Bancroft Library, University of California, Berkeley, California; "When Sara Comes, It's Always a Holiday!" *Bancroftiana* no. 76 (October 1980), 1–3; Hamburger, *Two Rooms*. For her writings, Field, *Barabbas: A Dramatic Narrative* (New York: A. & C. Boni, Inc. 1932); *The*

Beautiful Wedding (San Francisco, Calif.: Edwin & Robert Grabhorn, 1929); *Darkling Plain* (New York: Random House, 1936); *The Pale Woman and Other Poems* (New York: W. E. Rudge, 1927); *Vineyard Voices* (San Francisco, Press of Johnck and Seeger, 1930).

On Los Gatos, see George G. Bruntz, *History of Los Gatos, Gem of the Foothills* (Fresno, Calif.: Valley Publishers, 1971); Peggy Conaway, *Images of America: Los Gatos* (Charleston, S.C.: Arcadia Publishing, 2004).

Wood and Field's personal papers, including their diaries, clippings, publications, photographs, and correspondence are available at the Huntington Library, Pasadena, California. Additional papers from Wood's years in Oregon are available at the Oregon Historical Society, Portland, Oregon, as is Lisa Smith's home movie of grape harvesting at The Cats.

The Los Gatos Library's Local History Room contains clippings and photographs regarding Wood, Field, and The Cats, as well as city directories and a wealth of other materials on the history of Los Gatos. The manuscript census of the United States Census is available by interlibrary loan through any public library.

For Italians in California, begin with Dino Cinel, *From Italy to San Francisco* (Stanford, Calif.: Stanford Univ. Press, 1982); for women, see Sally M. Miller and Mary Wedegaertner, "Breadwinners and Builders: Stockton's Immigrant Women," *Californians* 4, no. 4 (July/August 1986), 8–22.

Chapter 4: I Heard It Through the Pulgas Water Temple

On the Hetch Hetchy system, consult Robert W. Righter, *The Battle over Hetch Hetchy* (New York: Oxford Univ. Press, 2005); Ted Wurm, *Hetch Hetchy and the Dam Railroad* (Berkeley, Calif.: Howell-

North, 1973); John Warfield Simpson, *Dam!* (New York: Pantheon Books, 2005); Gray Brechin, *Imperial San Francisco: Urban Power: Earthy Ruin* (Berkeley: Univ. of California Press, 1999); Warren D. Hanson, *San Francisco Water and Power: A History of the Municipal Water Department and Hetch Hetchy System* (San Francisco, Calif.: Public Utilities Commission, City and County of San Francisco, 2002); M. M. O'Shaughnessy, *The Hetch Hetchy Water Supply and Power Project of San Francisco* (San Francisco, Calif.: M. M. O'Shaughnessy, 1931).

On the temple itself, see, in addition: Brechin, "Water Rites: San Francisco's Water Temples Celebrate Classical Civilization," *Almost History*, August 1989, 14–17; Ruth Willard, *Sacred Places of San Francisco* (Novato, Calif.: Presidio Press, 1985); on Sunol's temple, see also Edward F. O'Day, "The Architecture of the Water Temple at Sunol," *Architect and Engineer* 70, no. 3 (1922), 83–85. The archives of the San Mateo County Historical Society contain a wealth of clippings and photographs regarding the Pulgas temple.

Joan Didion's "Holy Water" can be found in *The White Album* (New York: Simon & Schuster, 1979).

Regarding Abbie Hoffman and threats to put LSD in the water supply, see David Farber, *Chicago '68*, (Chicago, Ill.: Univ. of Chicago Press, 1988); Jay Stevens, *Storming Heaven: LSD and the American Dream* (New York: Atlantic Monthly Press, 1987); Marty Jezer, *Abbie Hoffman, American Rebel* (New Brunswick, NJ: Rutgers Univ. Press, 1992); Larry Sloman, *Steal This Dream: Abbie Hoffman and the Countercultural Revolution in America* (New York: Doubleday, 1998); Martin A. Lee and Bruce Shlain, *Acid Dreams: The CIA, LSD, and the Sixties Rebellion* (New York: Grove Press, 1985); Douglas Valentine, "Sex, Drugs & the CIA," *CounterPunch*, June 20, 2002.

For urban myths, Jan Harold Brunvand, *The Vanishing Hitchhiker: American Urban Legends and Their Meanings* (New York: Norton, 1981); Jean-Noel Kapferer, *Rumors: Uses, Interpretations, and*

Images (New Brunswick, NJ: Transaction Publishers, 1981); Patrick Mullen, "Modern Legend and Rumor Theory," *Journal of the Folklore Institute* 9 (1972), 95–109; Ralph L. Rosnow and Gary Alan Fine, *Rumor and Gossip: The Social Psychology of Hearsay* (New York: Elsevier, 1976) Patricia A. Turner, *I Heard It Through the Grapevine: Rumor in African-American Culture* (Berkeley, Calif.: Univ. of California Press, 1993).

Charles Robert Knight, "Neanderthal Flintmakers," by permission of the American Museum of Natural History.

Sara Bard Field and C. E. S. Wood, The Cats interior, cat sculptures, courtesy of The Huntington Library.

Marengo family pictures, courtesy of May Armann and Betty Weltzer, reproduced by Victor Schiffrin.

Pulgas Water Temple, cover photograph, interior photographs, copyright 1938, George Fanning/San Francisco Public Utilities Commission.

The Doors movie set photograph courtesy of the San Mateo County Historical Museum.

Maxfield Parrish, Daybreak, private collection. Photo courtesy the archives of Alma Gilbert-Smith. Used with permission.

DANA FRANK grew up in Los Altos, California, and graduated from Awalt High School (now Mountain View High School). She received her B.A. from the University of California, Santa Cruz, and her Ph.D. from Yale University. Since 1991 she has taught at U.C. Santa Cruz, in the American Studies and History Departments. Frank is the author of several books on U.S. labor history, women's history, trade politics, consumer activism, and banana workers in Central America. Her work has appeared in the *Nation, In These Times,* the *Washington Post, San Francisco Chronicle, San José Mercury News,* and a wide range of scholarly publications. Long active in labor solidarity work in both the United States and Central America, she is currently codirector of the U.C. Santa Cruz Center for Labor Studies.